Best wis... (handwritten)

Predicting Pearl Harbor

Billy Mitchell and the Path to War

To Ham with love Mom and Mike 2018 Happy Birthday! (handwritten)

Ronald J. Drez

(signature: Ronald J. Drez)

PELICAN PUBLISHING COMPANY
GRETNA 2017

The word "Pelican" and the depiction of a pelican are
trademarks of Pelican Publishing Company, Inc., and are
registered in the U.S. Patent and Trademark Office.

Library of Congress Cataloging-in-Publication Data

Names: Drez, Ronald J., 1940- author.
Title: Predicting Pearl Harbor : Billy Mitchell and the path to war / Ronald
    J. Drez.
Description: Gretna, Louisiana : Pelican Publishing Company, Inc., 2017. |
    Includes bibliographical references and index.
Identifiers: LCCN 2017007971| ISBN 9781455623150 (hardcover : alk. paper) |
    ISBN 9781455623167 (e-book)
Subjects: LCSH: Mitchell, William, 1879-1936. | Generals—United
    States—Biography. | Aeronautics, Military—United States—History. |
    United States. Army. Air Corps—History.
Classification: LCC UG633.M45 D74 2017 | DDC 358.40092 [B] —dc23 LC
record available at https://lccn.loc.gov/2017007971

Printed in the United States of America

Published by Pelican Publishing Company, Inc.
1000 Burmaster Street, Gretna, Louisiana 70053

Predicting Pearl Harbor

*For
Judy*

Contents

Preface

The story of William Mitchell is one of the most compelling American sagas in the short history of the United States. He was born when there was still a Western and Northwestern frontier. In his early military years in the Signal Corps, he was thrilled to be involved in affairs in Cuba and far across the Pacific in the Philippine Islands. His adventurous spirit was to be the core of his life.

My early interest in Mitchell stemmed from the film in 1955, *The Court-Martial of Billy Mitchell.* I knew nothing of the general at the time, but my favorite actor, Gary Cooper, was playing his part, so naturally I saw it. When the film was over, I remember feeling that the story should have turned out better. It, like most works about Mitchell, focused on his sensational trial. There was no hint of the intrigue that lay below the surface of his story.

My interest in pursuing research on Mitchell arose while I was writing many books and articles about World War II. In the course of those writings, I stumbled across him many times and read what had been written about him. But it wasn't until 2003, when I began leading battlefield tours following the path of the war across the Pacific, that I started to study him in earnest.

It was then that I met Syd and KT Jones. They were restoring vintage airplanes in Pensacola and took me for a ride in a B-25 Mitchell bomber. Later they became employees at the Pacific Aviation Museum at Pearl Harbor.

Their lives were always involved in adventure, and they were unique explorers. Perhaps their most notable quest was a twenty-year involvement in the expedition to recover the lost treasures of the sunken Spanish galleon, *Neustra Señora de Atocha.*

It was at the Pacific Aviation Museum where Syd first told me about the mysterious island of Niihau and the Robinson family. He was involved in another exciting expedition—this time to recover the remains of a long-forgotten Japanese Zero. After attacking Pearl Harbor, on December 7, 1941, it had crashed on Niihau. I was enthralled.

On numerous trips to Oahu, and later to Kauai, I was able to find out many details about the Niihau affair; and in 2010 and 2011, my wife, Judy, and I had the honor to meet, and interview, Keith Robinson, Niihau's owner.

For a week, he patiently sat with me for lengthy interviews and told me what he knew from his first recollections as a boy—playing in this badly wrecked and butchered aircraft that sat near his house. But it was what remained secret to him, and the rest of the world, that was

Ron and Judy Drez with Keith Robinson (at left). (Author's Collection)

most intriguing. It was the most secret connection of Aylmer Robinson, and the island of Niihau, to Billy Mitchell and World War II.

During that 2011 visit, I was also privy to an extraordinary discovery. Seventy years after the Zero had crashed on Niihau—seventy years after it had been burned, picked over, and cannibalized—a large part of a wing or tail stabilizer was discovered in the bush. Judy and I were delighted that Keith took us to see this new find, and we eagerly photographed it.

Research on Mitchell himself was more difficult. The usual sources were easy to find, but to understand the man, and his thinking, it was imperative to read all that he wrote. His most important writing was his long-suppressed inspection report of his Pacific Tour in 1923-24. That required digging in the National Archives and especially the National Air and Space Museum. To say the least, getting a copy was tedious.

The trial transcript from his court-martial was the second most important document. The unfolding of those events was better than any scriptwriter could ever concoct.

Seventy years after Pearl Harbor, a piece of a Zero fighter was discovered on Niihau. (Author's Collection)

The writings of two of his closest disciples, Gerald Brant and Hap Arnold, are necessary to delve into the after-the-Great-War fights between the Army and Navy as Mitchell pursued the establishment of an Air Force.

Hap Arnold would go on to be the commander of the United States Army Air Forces in WWII and would rise to the rank of a five-star general. Gerald Brant is a true mystery man and has mostly slipped into the recesses of history. But he was a key player in the Mitchell story, and the Niihau intrigue, and, until now, largely ignored. In this book, I have managed to shine a little light upon him.

Mitchell never lived to see the unfolding of his visions and remarkable predictions. He died in 1936. The war against Japan in the Pacific came and went, mostly following a path that he had envisioned twenty years earlier.

He was the very enigma of a man: hugely popular in an age when the nation was enthralled with the pioneering spirit of flight, but fame and drive garnered him a legion of jealous enemies. He was the common man's champion, and his select group of friends were blindly loyal. He never stopped pushing for what he knew was right for the country—even though it led to his own personal and professional demise.

Sir Hugh Trenchard, chief of the Royal Air Force in the Great War, had aptly described Mitchell's fiery personality. Trenchard said that the young American air officer would go far, "if only he can break his habit of trying to convert opponents by killing them." Mitchell never broke that habit.

Introduction

The great British military historian and theorist Sir B. H. Liddell Hart wrote, "Nothing may seem more strange to the future historian than the way that the governments of the democracies failed to anticipate the course which Hitler would pursue. For never has a man of such immense ambition so clearly disclosed beforehand, both the general process and particular methods by which he was seeking to fulfil it."[1]

Indeed, all of Adolf Hitler's writings and speeches left little doubt about his ambitions, dreams, ideologies, and anti-Semitism. His entire mind and body never strayed far from what he had revealed for everyone to read in *Mein Kampf.* Yet at every stage of his rise to power, first gradual and then sudden, his friends and enemies always seemed *stunned* when he continually pressed on toward his stated goals. When he broke treaties, nations were surprised; and when he followed a pattern of continually breaking treaties, each new rupture was also surprising. Even his conniving ally, Russia, was completely stunned when he broke their nonaggression pact and swept across its border. The self-deception of his enemies seemed to always work in Hitler's favor. Had he not declared early on that one of his goals for Germany was additional living space?

As each successive country fell before the swastika, was not the common excuse for the world's noninterventionists that now he would be satisfied? This self-induced duping was never more prominently displayed than in British prime minister Neville Chamberlain. He seemed bewildered and outraged when Hitler invaded Poland. Had Hitler not signed the "Peace-for-Our Time" accord in Munich? This was unthinkable. That piece of paper, which Chamberlain had triumphantly waved to an equally duped audience, had contained both his and Herr Hitler's signatures! To an honorable man, a signature was inviolate, and he somehow expected Hitler to be honorable. It had promised that the two countries would never go to war with each other again. And the rest of the world, like Chamberlain, wanted to believe it. All were hypnotized into self-deception.

Even as the war progressed, Hitler's actions continued to surprise those who would not see. The horror of the Holocaust found the European Jews always in a state of disbelief. The rational mind could not comprehend the predictable horror of Hitler's evil. Individuals and nations could never bring themselves to believe that he really meant to do exactly what he had promised to do. And when the Allies closed in on the collapsing Nazi regime, the revelation of that evil, displayed in the horrific specters of concentration camps and death camps, still came as a surprise.

Liddell Hart provided a possible answer. He said, "Men easily miss what is right under their eye, that concealment can often be found in the obvious, and that in some cases the most direct approach can become the least expected."[2]

Hart's premise perfectly described Adolf Hitler and the unchecked rise of the Third Reich. Hitler made no attempt to conceal anything. How could historians miss that? Not only was concealment not in his plan, he went about seizing and consolidating his enormous power completely in the open. He had announced that his violations of the Versailles Treaty following World War I were not violations; and he held massive, theatrical rallies, covered by the world news, to proclaim his goals. Murder, book-burning, destruction of synagogues, and people disappearing in the night became part of the Nazi legacy, and yet Hitler's next moves were always a surprise.

But Hart's premise could also apply to Japan, at least after 1931. And there was no shortage of suspicion and apprehension of Japanese intentions long before that. In the early years, Japan did nothing in the open and shrouded everything in secrecy and deception.

Although most of her military and diplomatic moves raised the worst of suspicions, her actions remained mostly covert. One was never sure of her inner intentions, and many turned a blind eye to reality.

The Japanese had been on the winning side in WWI against the Germans and their allies. They had done little fighting. It was almost as if they were along to pick up the pieces when and if Germany fell. Their biggest action of the war was an opportunistic move to send an expedition to conquer the far-flung, German-held Pacific islands. The Germans, outnumbered and outgunned, were easy pickings. For the rest of the war, Japan could aptly be described as an interested observer.

At war's end, they held their tongues and acquiesced to a British and American naval plan that ensured their navy would always be inferior but still guaranteed it would be the third largest in the world. And since they were on the winning side, and already held the former German Pacific islands, they were perfectly positioned to be designated, by the newly formed League of Nations, as protectors. Japan had the ability and the location to provide government and services to the people of those former German possessions. Their designation became known as the Japanese Mandate.

The mandated islands were to be administered and policed just as if they were a physical part of Japan, and the framers of the mandate obviously gave no thought or instruction to preserve local history, traditions, or culture. The only thing that the League attempted to forbid was the fortification of those various islands.[3] The mandate also demanded that Japan foster free trade, but that was wishful thinking and illusional since, within a short time, the Japanese monopolized the Micronesian trade and locked out all competitors.

The Japanese went through the motions of seeming to allow foreign trade, but their complicated rules made trade and port visits virtually impossible and ensured their monopoly. In essence, Japan's mandated islands and their people slowly disappeared behind a veil of secrecy and became exactly like the cloistered Japan in earlier ages. The mandated people soon were treated as subservient, and they were taught that their lives and efforts were all to enhance the greater glory of Japan and the empire.

The League's rules forbidding the fortifying of the islands were also useless. They were vague and unwittingly aided Japan's ability to violate both the terms and intentions of the mandate. The words *fortifications* and *military and naval bases* were simply words. They were not defined. By 1921, all economic development and construction could easily be converted to military use as *fortifications* and *bases*. Many buildings constructed for economic or civil use were also *bomb proof*. An airfield or dock for commerce was a future fighter strip or warship dock. During 1921, the Japanese had surveyed everything to be able to convert quickly to a military footing; and when that conversion became necessary, it would proceed without the prying eyes of the world looking in.[4]

Long before Germany began its land aggrandizement, or even before the world knew much about Adolf Hitler, Japan had been on the move. By 1931 she no longer needed the cloak of deception and threw it off to invade China. In 1933, when her aggression had been observed by the whole world and condemned by the feckless League of Nations, she stormed out of the League and, as a parting shot, announced that she would keep the mandated islands as her own.

The world made no move to confront her. Two years later, she again flexed her muscles and, this time, walked out of a naval arms-control conference. As if to emphasize this indignity, she simultaneously renounced all the previous naval treaties that she had signed. By 1937, having regained her much-desired secrecy, and unencumbered by inconvenient naval treaties and limits, she embarked on a massive shipbuilding program.[5]

Through all of this, what was there not to see? Sadly most did not, either because of willful blindness or self-deception similar to that of the pathetic Chamberlain. But there were a few who were not fooled by Japanese antics and perfidy, and they raised their voices in alarm. The first prophet of war was hardly an imposing figure. His grotesquely twisted spine actually made him look most insignificant. But by 1911, his pen and his voice had sounded the warning of imminent war with Japan. His book, *The Valor of Ignorance,* identified the exact mindset of those who are perpetually *surprised* by tyrants. He was Gen. Homer Lea. But an early death silenced his warnings.

The second was quite the opposite: bold, brash, and even swashbuckling. He was an adored hero of WWI named William Mitchell. His predictions of an eventual war with Japan were treated, by those who would not see, as the ramblings of a man who had lost his mind. His writings were ridiculed, ignored, or otherwise consigned to gather dust on some obscure shelf. Along the way, he built a circle of close friends who were devoted to him and a legion of enemies who were not. He minced no words, worked like a human dynamo, and tolerated no one who disagreed with him. He took no prisoners.

The common thread that bound these two military prophets was less a matter of their similar mindsets and more a matter that neither were believed. They were like the tragic figure of the mythical Cassandra, who in Roman literature was a Trojan princess with the gift of prophesy. Unfortunately she was also cursed, so despite the fact that her predictions were always right, no one ever believed her. As the victorious Trojans gleefully wheeled the gigantic horse through the gates of the walled city of Troy, she frantically warned that there were Greek soldiers inside.[6]

Predicting Pearl Harbor

Chapter 1

Unlocking Pandora's Box

In 1853, the Empire of Japan was only known to the Western world as a secretly shrouded country that had, for hundreds of years, denied any and all attempts to penetrate its closed society. Visitors, whether explorers or missionaries, were routinely confronted, ordered to leave, and often attacked and violently evicted.

In 1295, Marco Polo had given the world its only glimpse into that forbidden land when he returned from his historic, twenty-year voyage and regaled his wide-eyed, Venetian audiences with tales of "a great island to the east,"[1] off the coast of Cathay (China). Its inhabitants were a fierce and fascinating people who had hurled back the armies of Kublai Khan, the conqueror of Asia and terrorizer of all of Europe. Polo had even befriended Khan at that time and was a witness to it all; but just like Kublai and his armies, Polo had been denied entrance into the mysterious land. His writings, therefore, contained only what he had been able to learn from others or from hearsay and oft-told tales.[2]

But with the end of Marco Polo, this obscure peek into this mysterious kingdom, lying tantalizingly just off the coast of China, ended as well, and his writings and maps were eventually set aside to gather dust. In 1492, Christopher Columbus brushed off Polo's charts and notes and sailed to the west to find this Far Eastern kingdom, hoping to open it to the teachings of Christianity and to Western trade. His long and peril-filled voyage finally found land, not in China or Japan but in the Americas near Cuba. At first, Columbus thought that he had succeeded, but that secret Japanese empire was still a half-world away.

Not until 1549, more than fifty years after Columbus, did any Westerners succeed in entering Japan, and they came in the form of Jesuit missionaries, followed by Dominicans and Franciscans. They beat a path to this land of the Rising Sun to preach the word of Christianity, and the emperors and shoguns initially welcomed them.

By 1587 there were 200,000 Christians in Japan, but in that year, the ominous head of persecution reared. It came in the form of an unexpected edict from a formidable feudal lord (daimyo) who saw the increasing Christians' presence as a threat to his own power and feared European colonization, just as Spain had colonized the Philippines. He first banned the Jesuits, then set about the destruction of over a hundred churches and residences. The Christians were dispossessed of all they owned, hunted down, and forced into hiding.[3]

But ten years later, their numbers had miraculously risen to over three hundred thousand, and this prompted new and more terrible persecutions. In 1597, twenty-six Christians were crucified and many churches destroyed. By 1622, Jesuits, Dominicans, Franciscans, and Japanese laity were routinely being put to death in the grisliest of spectacles: many were burned at the stake after first being forced to witness the beheading of others.

By 1639 the all-out assault against Catholics was completed with the destruction of their last-stand stronghold. The Japanese rulers had slammed the door on openness and Japanese seclusion was again intact, as it had been in Marco Polo's time. The imperial edicts, the "Closed Country Edict of 1635," and the "Exclusion of the Portuguese, 1639," sent Japan back behind the black curtain of absolute obscurity.

The directives contained in those edicts were draconian, including: no Japanese ships could leave for foreign countries; execution awaited anyone attempting secretly to do so; any Japanese, having resided outside Japan and attempting to return, would be put to death; hidden Christians must be revealed with the promise of rewards; and arriving ships would be searched for Christians. Additionally, any Portuguese ship attempting entry would be destroyed and all occupants beheaded.[4]

These orders, imposed on a population that rendered absolute obedience to authority, kept Japan behind an impenetrable curtain for the next 200 years. All attempts to overcome that imperial will, to open Japan to trade and international intercourse, failed—all, that is, except for a small Dutch outpost that had somehow curried imperial favor and had not been evicted with the Catholics and their missionaries.

After 1640, the Calvinist Dutch ran what could best be described as a confined trading post, exclusively on the tiny island of Dezima near Nagasaki. They were the virtual gatekeepers through which a single stream of outside trade was allowed to pass. But their dubious status had been purchased, in the words of United States commodore Matthew C. Perry, "at the price of national humiliation and personal imprisonment."[5]

This "national humiliation" had come during that final persecution in 1639 when the Dutch had been requested to become shameful participants in the attack and slaughter of native Catholics at the hands of the emperor. During that final onslaught, the last baptized, faithful converts were all alone. They lived in a world of abuse, torture, and death, and their European missionaries were long since gone. But they clung to their faith, and, driven to a point of desperation, they rose in rebellion.

Eventually they barricaded themselves in an old town and conducted a spirited defense, even repulsing the emperor's forces. The frustrated emperor turned to the Protestant Dutch, and their heavy guns, to defeat the rebellious Catholics. He asked the Dutch to use those powerful weapons to batter the town and break down the Catholic defenses. If the Dutch had any qualms about taking up arms and firing against fellow Christians, maintaining the good graces of the Japanese apparently won out, and they agreed to join in on the attack. For two weeks, their heavy guns hammered the position, and when all resistance seemed at an end, the Japanese dismissed the Dutch, sent them on their way, and completed the work of final destruction and annihilation of the Catholics themselves.[6]

Over the mass grave of these murdered men, women, and children the Japanese placed an Imperial Proclamation: "So long as the sun shall warm the earth, let no Christian be so bold as to come to Japan: and let all know that . . . if he violates this command, shall pay for it with his head."[7]

Despite the Dutch cooperation with the emperor in this grisly affair, they gained no favor or thanks. In fact, the honor-driven Japanese viewed their actions as a betrayal of their fellow Christians and condemned them as despicable. A writer of the time wrote, "They both hated and despised us for what we had done."[8]

Perhaps because of this revulsion, in 1641, the Japanese evicted the Dutch from their previous comfortable factory site located at Firando and moved them to the miserable confines of Dezima. It became the only port open to European ships, and only there were Japanese allowed to buy or sell to any Westerners.[9] It also became more of a prison than a factory.[10] But the Dutch continued to embrace their questionable privilege.

One Dezima resident wrote, "So great was the covetousness of the Dutch, and so strong the alluring power of the Japanese gold, that rather than quit the prospect of a trade, they willingly underwent an almost perpetual imprisonment, for such is our residence in Dezima."[11]

The island became infested with spies, all keeping watchful eyes upon the Dutch occupants, and the Nagasaki police made frequent, annoying visits. The Japanese merchants who dealt with the Dutch were required, several times a year, to take an oath renouncing the hated Christian religion and to display that hatred by trampling upon crosses and crucifixes. Commodore Matthew Perry recorded the dismal situation at Dezima: "in short a more annoying and thorough system of imprisonment and espionage was never devised."[12]

Perry noted that the feudal system of Japanese government was enhanced by a devious practical practice: everyone spied on everyone else. There was "a system of checks and balances founded in an all-pervading secret espionage, ramifying through all classes of society, from the highest to the lowest."[13]

In 1831, almost two hundred years after the destruction of Japanese Catholics, a Japanese vessel, plying the waters of the eastern Pacific Ocean, encountered a storm and was blown about, finally making landfall on the West Coast of the United States near the Columbia River. The American and British residents of the area assisted the stricken Japanese seamen and after six years made it possible to transport them back to their homeland. An 1837 voyage took them first to Macao, a Portuguese-held island off the coast of China, before their return to Japan.

To make that final run, an American shipping merchant outfitted a vessel named *Morrison;* and to make sure that the Japanese would not misinterpret her voyage as hostile, he had all of *Morrison's* guns removed. When the ship reached and entered Tokyo Bay (Bay of Yedo), the Japanese soon discovered that she was unarmed and promptly fired upon her. The American vessel quickly moved to another anchorage off the island of Kyushu, but there too the Japanese opened fire. *Morrison* promptly weighed anchor and returned to Macao with the long-missing Japanese seamen still aboard.[14]

Nine years later, in 1846, there was a second American attempt to enter Japan. This time, it was an expedition from the U.S. government authorized by Pres. James Polk. Commodore James Biddle led a two-ship force to attempt to open U.S. trade with Japan. The 90-gun *Columbus* and the corvette *Vincennes* were to enter Tokyo Bay in a show of American power and the hope to pry open Japan's closed door.

But things went badly from the start. Upon entering the bay, the ships were immediately surrounded by an estimated four hundred boats, and *Vincennes* was boarded by Japanese sailors who placed two carved sticks on the bow and stern. The bewildered American crew, seeing this as some sort of attempt to lay claim to the vessels, voiced enough objection that the sticks were reluctantly removed. All requests to go ashore and present the emperor or his representative with the president's letter were denied, and after ten days of frustration, the Americans left. The answer from the emperor had been more of the same: "No trade can be allowed with any foreign nation except Holland."[15]

But there was more than just frustration that rankled the Americans. In later years, *Harper's New Monthly Magazine* published a report of humiliating treatment of Commodore Biddle at the hands of bullying Japanese seamen:

To the polite letter of President Polk, an answer of impudent defiance was returned, and Commodore Biddle was insulted. While in full uniform, stepping from a junk, a common Japanese sailor gave the American chief a push which landed him unceremoniously in the bottom of his own boat. Japanese officers promised to punish the man, but nothing was done, and the American ships went away.[16]

In February 1849, Capt. James Glynn was sent with his 16-gun sloop of war, USS *Preble,* on an expedition to rescue sixteen American sailors who had been imprisoned by the Japanese since June of 1848 when their whaling ship, *Lagoda,* presumably sank in waters off of a Japanese island. A later investigation revealed that *Lagoda* had not foundered, but the fifteen whalers had apparently jumped ship and deserted when they had come within sight of land and found an opportunity to escape their captain's "cruelty."[17]

Whatever the reason, they eventually became prisoners of the Japanese, who forced them to desecrate the cross of their religion, accused them of spying, and kept them in a state of close confinement. Numerous attempts to escape made by this rough and tumble crew did not endear them to their captors, and their several confinements became more and more stringent.

As Captain Glynn approached the coast of Japan, the ever-watchful lookouts fired their cannons to signal his intrusion. But Glynn, undaunted, pressed in to the confined waters of Nagasaki. *Preble* was then surrounded by the usual swarm of hostile Japanese boats filled with soldiers and demonstrators all shouting and gesturing for the American vessel to turn back. But Glynn, with a full wind billowing his sails, pushed through the cordon and navigated to a favorable anchoring position. In short order, the Japanese flotilla caught up to him and landed men on the shores, who mounted sixty cannons on the high ground and trained them upon his ship.[18]

Ignoring this show of force, Glynn got to the business at hand and demanded the release of the sixteen captive men. Those nearby who heard his demands mocked him with indignation. The story of the previous humiliation of Commodore Biddle, unceremoniously knocked to the bottom of his boat, had spread far and wide. The American prisoners would later report that during their captivity, one of them had warned a Japanese guard that his rough treatment of them would be avenged by his country. The guard scoffed:

> If any officers from your country come here, we'll serve them as we did the American commodore . . . , who was knocked down at Yedo by a soldier. If the Americans took no notice of that, why should they look after you, who are only poor sailors? You are here now and can't help yourselves. If their ships come here, our priests will blow them to pieces.[19]

But Captain Glynn was not Commodore Biddle and turned the Japanese shouting tactics against them, using his own booming voice and descriptive sailor's language to hurl invectives down upon them. The irate captain further promised that his American government had both the power and will to protect its citizens.

The Japanese were taken aback and hushed and, in a sudden change of heart, pledged to send emissaries within two days. In exactly that time those emissaries approached USS *Preble,* with the American prisoners, and released them. Glynn weighed anchor and sailed triumphantly out to sea to rejoin the American squadron off the coast of China.[20]

Because of Glynn's success, the United States, at the urging of both Glynn and Commodore Matthew Perry, set into motion a plan to open Japan to Western trade.[21] Pres. Millard Fillmore enthusiastically ordered the mission, and his letter to the emperor was friendly and to the point.

At least, he asked, "abrogate the ancient laws . . . for five to ten years so as to try the experiment." And Fillmore also requested that the emperor "treat with kindness" any unfortunate seamen whose "ship is wrecked on your imperial majesty's shores." And finally he asked to establish coaling stations for the growing presence of United States commercial and military vessels in the Pacific. But his concluding paragraph contained some thought-provoking words, including that he was sending a *powerful squadron:* "These are the only objects for which I have sent Commodore Perry, with a powerful squadron, to pay a visit to your imperial majesty's renowned city of Yedo [Tokyo]: friendship, commerce, a supply of coal and provisions, and protection for our shipwrecked people."[22]

The *powerful squadron* to which the president referred was just that. The initial flagship was the steamer *Mississippi;* along with the steamers *Powhatan* and *Allegheny*; the 74-gun *Vermont;* and the sloops-of-war *Saratoga, Vandalia,* and *Macedonian.* Three other ships, including *Susquehanna,* the final flagship, were already at the East India station and would join the squadron.[23]

On July 7, 1853, after an eight-month voyage from the United States' East Coast, Commodore Perry's squadron called the "Black Ships" were poised to enter the forbidden waters of Tokyo. He planned to enter with only four of his twelve ships, having left the rest behind and confident that his mission could be easily accomplished with those at hand. The following morning, *Susquehanna* bore in, with the steamer *Mississippi* and the sloops-of-war *Saratoga* and *Plymouth*.

The astonished Japanese watched the big steamer enter at nine knots into the wind, with all sails furled, and some of the boats that routinely swarmed any entering ship took to their oars to give a wide berth to the smoke-belching behemoth.

Perry ordered all decks cleared for action, and the guns were loaded and prepared. Marines and armed sentinels stood to their posts and observed the Japanese, who, "when they fancied themselves at a sufficiently safe distance, rested upon their oars and gazed with anxious looks at the intruding strangers."[24]

Perry's four ships pushed deep into the bay and anchored at 5:00 P.M. in its western reaches, and now the Japanese, feeling somewhat emboldened, dispatched a huge number of their guard boats to surround the Americans. They made several attempts to board *Saratoga*, but each time they cast lines onto the American ship, the crew cast them off. Some tried to climb up the anchor chains but were unceremoniously greeted by pike-wielding defenders also armed with cutlasses and pistols, and they soon gave up their efforts.[25]

One boat came alongside the flagship, *Susquehanna,* and passed up a scrolled note demanding that the ship's ladder be lowered so that a functionary could come aboard. Perry refused and declared that he would receive no one but the person with the highest rank in the town of Uraga.

Matthew Perry's Black Ships reached the forbidden waters of Tokyo in 1853, aiming to open the trade door to Japan. (Illustrated London News, 1865)

He did receive one lower functionary but refused to communicate with him face to face, only speaking through his own aide, Lt. John Contee. The Japanese emissary gave a predictable speech announcing that, by law, Nagasaki was the only place to negotiate foreign business, and they should go there. The Americans were not moved and Perry instructed his aide to convey his displeasure to the demanding Japanese official: "The Commodore had come purposely to Uraga because it was near Yedo, and he *should not go to Nagasaki;* that he expected the [president's] letter to be duly and properly received where he was; that his intentions were perfectly friendly, but that he would allow no indignity; and would not permit the guard-boats which were collecting around his ships to remain where they were, and if they were not immediately removed, the Commodore would disperse them by force."[26]

With that, the startled Japanese representative went to the gangway and signaled the gathered boats away. Most of them left, but a few remained where they were, clustering in groups, with no intention of moving. However, they soon changed their minds when suddenly an armed, American small boat, bristling with armed Marines and sailors, confronted them and waved them away. None ever returned.

Perry wrote, "It was well to let them know that other people had dignity also, which they knew how to protect, and that they did not acknowledge the Japanese to be their superiors."[27]

But on July 9, the Japanese will had hardly been broken when the governor of Uraga, outfitted in his elaborately embroidered silk robe, boarded Perry's flagship and delivered to Lieutenant Contee the same message as before; Japanese law forbade receiving President Fillmore's letter at Uraga, and even if it was somehow received there, it would only be forwarded to Nagasaki, so it was best for all concerned for the Americans to leave here and go there. Again Contee's answer conveyed the commodore's extreme displeasure: that he would never consent to such an agreement and would deliver his president's letter to the emperor here in Uraga. Contee further advised that "if the Japanese government did not see fit to appoint a suitable person to receive the documents in his possession addressed to the Emperor that he, the Commodore, whose duty it was to deliver them, would go on shore with sufficient force and deliver them in person, be the consequences what they might."[28]

When the governor told Contee that he would get instructions and give an answer in four days, Perry gave him only three. As he departed, the governor was further chagrined when he observed a number of the American ships' small boats spreading out in the bay. When he asked what they were doing, he was told they were making soundings of the bay and surveying the harbor. He responded that that also was not allowed by Japanese law, to which he was told that American laws commanded them.

So as the governor departed, Matthew Perry had won each and every confrontation. He had entered the forbidden Japanese sanctuary; he had cleared the swarming guard boats from around his squadron; he had prevailed in his demand for a meeting with a person of the highest rank—the governor; he had refused to go to Nagasaki; and he had begun to survey Yedo Bay while steadfastly maintaining his "peaceful" presence there awaiting a Japanese answer.[29]

That came on July 12, but it was a day spent in frustrating diplomatic thrusting and parrying. In the end, it was not until late on July 13 that the governor returned carrying a sandalwood box with documents from the emperor, wrapped in velvet, that named two imperial princes to receive President Fillmore's letter.[30]

The next day, in an elaborately costumed ceremony on the Japanese shore, the fateful documents were delivered and the princes presented what amounted to an official receipt to the commodore—it too sumptuously encased and trimmed in silver and gold. Their short message, once again reminding Perry that this was not the place designated for foreign conferences, concluded: "The letter being received, you will leave here."[31]

But that is exactly what Commodore Perry chose not to do—at least not immediately. Although he rose and departed the building with his entire American cohort, he had his aides inform the Japanese that he would leave in "two or three days."[32] When asked when he might return for the emperor's answer, he indicated in April or May of the following year (1854); and when the Japanese asked if he would be returning with all four of his vessels, he said, "All of them, and probably more as these are only a portion of the squadron."[33]

The governor and his party returned with Perry to *Susquehanna* and were treated to the friendliest hospitality and a tour of the ship and its machinery. But when they departed and headed toward the shore, they were alarmed to see Perry's squadron not re-anchoring in its old position but moving twenty miles farther to the west and approaching Yedo (Tokyo). The following day, Perry brazenly continued his nautical and hydrographic surveying, with his small boats probing the waters but remaining within range of the steamer's large guns. Finally, on Sunday, July 17, Perry transferred his flag to *Mississippi*, and the squadron departed Yedo Bay and set a course to China.[34]

Perry's report stated: "The survey of the bay of Yedo in spite of the protests of the authorities and under the very guns of their batteries was an important advantage. It not only taught the Japanese the folly of attempting to sway the Americans by bravado and sham exhibitions of force, but proved to the world for the first time the practicability of sailing even [to] the capital of Japan."[35]

* * *

Commodore Perry returned to Japan on February 12, 1854, and his Black Ships stood in Yedo Bay. The distinctive Mount Fusi-Yami (Fuji) was in full view in the distance with its conical peak covered in snow. The seven ships anchored, twenty miles from Yedo, in what had been dubbed during the previous visit the "American anchorage."[36]

When the Japanese emissaries arrived, the first few days were consumed with diplomatic wrangling and posturing over where Perry should anchor to receive the emperor's answers to the American proposals. The Japanese demanded anchoring at three sites, each of which the Americans found unacceptable, and when the Americans suggested that the Japanese should come aboard the ships at their present position or at least meet ashore, the Japanese refused. With that, Perry informed them that "the Commodore should go to Yedo."[37]

Still the Japanese insisted the anchorage should be at Uraga, and from February 15 to 24, the diplomatic impasse continued among the aides. It consisted of one frustrating meeting after another, with no solution on the horizon. Finally, Commodore Perry, abandoning all hope of a timely and favorable solution, weighed anchor and moved his ships to within sight of the city of Yedo. When he redropped his anchors, the frantic Japanese suddenly abandoned their obstinate positions and ultimatums, and the impasse of the previous ten days melted away.

An emissary quickly boarded Perry's flagship, now in its advanced position, and said that a satisfactory site to receive the emperor's answer had suddenly been found. It would be in a village that just happened to be just opposite Perry's fleet! Again, Perry had prevailed.

"I was convinced," he said, "that if I receded in the least from the position first assumed by me, it would be considered by the Japanese an advantage gained; and finding that I could be induced to change a predetermined intention in one instance they might rely on prevailing on me . . . to waver in most other cases."[38]

Perry had been unmoved by all the pomp and ceremony demonstrated by Japanese officials, for he knew that when it came to substance, pomp and ceremony was just window dressing. Commodore Biddle and Captain Glynn had witnessed Japanese stubbornness, and Perry called them "very sagacious and deceitful people."[39]

His unyielding stance on selection of the anchorage had, in essence, forced the Japanese to back down, and in that backing down, four Japanese princes had to abandon their heretofore unyielding positions and follow after the ships of Perry's squadron to within sight of their capital. And it necessitated the humiliating construction of yet another building for diplomatic intercourse after Perry deemed Uraga to be unacceptable.

One month had passed since the squadron's arrival in the bay, and now Perry anchored his ships in an unmistakable battle line with their guns covering the entire shoreline. He went ashore in his barge, having been preceded by Marines, sailors, and officers who stood in tight formation in full regalia, awaiting his arrival. That arrival was signaled by *Macedonian* unleashing an intimidating seventeen-gun salute.[40]

Inside the great hall that the Americans called "the treaty house," both sides took their positions, and the commodore was presented the long-awaited answer from the emperor. It was announced that the old emperor from last year was dead and the new emperor "cannot bring about any alteration in the ancient laws." But they would furnish "coal, wood, water, provisions, and the saving of ships and their crews in distress."

That was as far as the Japanese seemed willing to go, and although Perry and his officers pressed for an agreement on opening trade, the emperor was intransigent. On March 16, the Japanese commissioners informed Commodore Perry that the previous concessions concerning coal and provisions, and helping storm-tossed sailors, were reasonable, and they were willing to meet the American requests. "But as to opening a trade such as is now carried on with China by your country, we certainly cannot yet bring it about."[41]

Two weeks later, the undaunted Commodore Perry signed a treaty with the Japanese concerning those agreed-to matters, but it also contained articles dealing with what the Japanese had proclaimed they "could not bring about." They had somehow further consented to open some limited trade at *two* designated ports for use by the United States! Article VII declared: "It is agreed that ships of the United States resorting to the ports open to them shall be permitted to exchange gold and silver coin and articles of goods for other articles of goods under such regulations as shall be temporarily established by the Japanese government."[42]

Beyond all expectations, Commodore Perry had suddenly pulled off the unthinkable. He had, through persistence and determination and using all the tools of effective negotiations, unlocked Japan's 200-year-old, double-bolted door. He had paved the way for other trading nations to attempt to negotiate a similar treaty and had forcefully stipulated that such treaties could not grant greater trade terms without granting those to the United States. He had, most importantly, eliminated the subservient Dutch at Nagasaki as the middlemen through which Western nations must pass.

In all negotiations he assured the Japanese of his friendly intent. He entertained them onboard his flagship, wining and dining them and conducting tours of the inner workings of his great ship that no Japanese had ever seen or even imagined. The inquisitive commissioners were enthralled, eagerly poring over the machinery and drinking in all they were shown. Awestruck, they held American knowhow in the highest esteem. Perhaps in showcasing the inventiveness of his great ships, Commodore Perry unlocked Pandora's box.

The Japanese needed just forty years to avenge Perry's humiliating intrusion and develop their own world-class fighting navy. They burst upon the international power scene late in the nineteenth century, when they trounced the Chinese Fleet in the 1894 Battle of the Yellow Sea. In 1905, they crushed the vaunted Russian Fleet in the Battle of Tsushima. Historians would label that battle as decisive as Nelson at Trafalgar.

Between those two shocking Japanese victories, the United States pushed its borders westward and entered the Pacific Ocean area as the result of its victory in the Spanish-American War. With their new possessions of Guam and the Philippines, the Americans moved into Japan's backyard.

Brilliant tactician Homer Lea predicted war with Japan. (The Homer Lea Research Center)

Chapter 2

The First Cassandra:
Gen. Homer Lea

"How soon are we to have war with Japan?" On July 6, 1911, this unexpected and shocking question caused the casually seated luncheon audience to sit more upright in their chairs. A New York City men's club had invited a very popular author to be the guest speaker at their lunch gathering, and he had gotten their attention with his opening line.

But this speaker was more than simply an author. He was a general—not a general in the United States Army but a lieutenant general in the Chinese army. This thirty-four-year-old, bespectacled American was also not an imposing figure. Standing just over five feet, he was barely visible behind the speaker's stand. And his diminutive five feet seemed even further reduced by the debilitating scoliosis that bent his spine.

He was Gen. Homer Lea, and his book, *The Valor of Ignorance,* had captured the imagination of military tacticians and strategists the world over. In it he had exposed the fragility of the American defenses, especially in the Pacific, and he predicted a most certain war with the rising power of Japan.

He had shockingly written, "Japan could land an army in California in less time than a force could march from Los Angeles to San Francisco. The entire merchant marine of . . . Japan can be converted into transports immediately upon the declaration of war and land, within a month, more than a quarter of a million men."[1] He had scoffed at the popular notion that the United States was protected by its isolated position between two great oceans and said, "The isolation of America is a false idea."

And he attacked the romantic idea that an untrained, hastily gathered militia would rise up, grab their weapons from over the fireplace, and defeat a trained, invading army. "That the American people can arise and repel a foreign invader is a false idea," he said. "Never was there a single instance in the history of the world when a people untrained in the art of war arose and destroyed an invader."[2]

Had not George Washington himself warned against the reliance upon an untrained militia? He had emphatically denounced the idea.

> Regular troops alone are equal to the exigencies of modern war . . . and when a substitute is attempted, it must prove illusory and ruinous. No Militia will ever acquire the habits necessary to resist a regular force. . . . I have never yet been a witness to a single instance that can justify a different opinion.[3]

Lea, echoing Washington's stern warnings, had scoffed at the idea that a militia and regular army were interchangeable. "In civil life a butcher is not called upon to exercise the skill of an oculist, nor to remove a cataract from the dulled eye; barbers do not perform the operation of laparotomy; nor farmers navigate sea-going vessels, nor sailors determine the value of mines, nor clerks perform the functions of civil engineers."[4]

How then should anyone expect untrained soldiers to function as military experts? And if a militia soldier could not rival a trained soldier, untrained officers were worse. Lea asserted, "The most promiscuous murderer in the world is an ignorant military officer. He slaughters his men by bullets, by disease, by neglect; he starves them, he makes cowards of them and deserters and criminals. The dead are hecatombs of his ignorance; the survivors, melancholy specters of his incompetence."[5]

With the same fiery eloquence displayed in his writings, the general now addressed his captivated luncheon audience. "War," he said, "is determined by the angle of convergence of two nations toward a common objective. . . . Before the Revolutionary War there was a convergence of the interests of the colonies with the interests of England."

Those opposing interests, and their movements to war, were never even. Sometimes it was a headlong rush, and at other times a slow drift, but it was always in motion. Friction between the colonies and the Crown sometimes boiled and sometimes cooled, until, Lea noted in dramatic fashion, "a single incident . . . the destruction of the tea in Boston Harbor," accelerated events to a flashpoint. "War," he said, "was almost simultaneous with this increased rate of speed."[6]

His words seemed to be those of a physicist explaining the forces of nature or the flashpoint of an explosion, and he compared these physical forces to those that led nations to wage war. To him, contesting nations were like two trains on separate tracks, but those tracks eventually converged on a single track where the trains were destined to collide. And to Homer Lea, that collision was most predictable. The only unknown was when. If the trains stopped, or occasionally reversed, the wreck was temporarily avoided; but when both moved forward, as was their instinct and tendency, the disaster was a certainty.

* * *

Homer Lea was the essence of an enigma. He was born in 1876 in Denver, Colorado, and at age four had developed the spine-bending disease that afflicted him for the rest of his life. But he never let it dampen his spirit of adventure, and although he did not excel in academics, mostly because of his noninterest, he excelled in the study of military history, concluding that "the only real great careers in history were those made of the sword."[7]

He mastered the strategy and tactics of the great military leaders including Alexander the Great, Julius Caesar, Robert E. Lee, Ulysses Grant, and Napoleon Bonaparte. He virtually committed to memory every detail of every Napoleonic action.[8] He sought to enhance his zeal for the military by dropping out of Stanford University after one year and devoting his energies to the support of an unlikely reform movement whose purpose was to restore the deposed Chinese emperor to his rightful place on the throne of the Manchu dynasty.

As quirky as all this sounded to his friends and classmates, Lea embarked upon his mission described by biographer Lawrence Kaplan as "stranger than many stories found in romantic fiction."[9] But the members of that Chinese reform movement didn't find him strange and had, early on, taken note of Lea, mostly because he was Caucasian and embraced their movement. And they certainly did not shun the attention of any American who might be sympathetic to their cause, since most Americans were totally indifferent if not hostile to Chinese affairs. The Chinese exclusion laws passed in the late nineteenth century, and extended by Congress, had rendered most of the Asian races persona non grata. They were seen as encroaching on jobs, culture, and space.

And, as Homer Lea sought to develop his Chinese contacts, it had not been beneath him to embellish upon his own acumen and talents: to even claim that he was a relative of the famous Robert E. Lee—which he was not! This special relationship, he suggested to his Chinese listeners, was the reason for his great military insight. Whether that mattered to his Chinese counterparts or not, those reformers thought Lea could be helpful to their cause, perhaps by raising money or recruiting other Americans to join in the revolution. And recruiting should be enhanced by the allure of the spoils of war. "If our cause succeeds," promised one of the leading Chinese reformers in Los Angeles, "they will be rewarded with rights in China, such as mines and railroads."[10]

Many who knew Homer Lea shook their heads. To them, his quest appeared to be more about chasing rainbows and pots of gold, but through it all, he remained steadfast. To all who advised him to abandon this seeming folly, he blithely answered, "A man never dies until his work is done." And when others even suggested that the Chinese would cut his head off, he mocked his own spine deformity, saying, "They'll have a hard time finding my neck."[11]

But Lea truly believed in his China mission and felt it was a matter of his own destiny, and he pursued it with undaunted vigor. In 1900 he embarked to China, where he was made a lieutenant general in the yet-to-be-formed revolutionary army,[12] and undertook to train its future soldiers. Despite his zeal and faith in the China mission, his efforts ultimately came to nothing and the revolution failed to restore the emperor to the throne.

But the forever-optimistic Lea did not accept defeat and returned to the United States. A second effort was obviously necessary and he was determined to make it a successful one. His mind was filled with ideas that would lend a new impetus to the revolutionary quest. Four years later, in 1904, he had managed to establish a string of military schools in more than twenty cities, where they clandestinely trained the soldiers to bring about victory. He paid former U.S. soldiers as instructors, but, in the end, this endeavor also came to naught. In 1908, the deposed emperor died, and the reason for revolt died with him.[13]

Two years later, Gen. Homer Lea was again in the spotlight. This time he was aligned with another revolutionary. Dr. Sun Yat-sen championed an attempt not to restore a deposed emperor to the throne but to actually topple the throne of the Manchu dynasty and bring about a Chinese Republic. Through contacts and personal meetings, Homer Lea became Sun's most trusted military advisor. Lea was "perhaps the most brilliant military genius alive," one of Sun's aides noted. "He is the perfect master of modern warfare."[14]

And when the overthrow of the Manchu dynasty finally succeeded in 1911, Homer Lea received his fair share of fame and acclaim. Even representatives of the U.S. State Department sang his praises and were quoted as saying, "Sun Yat-sen . . . did not make a move without first consulting Lea."[15]

That Lea had become a most recognizable figure within many military and strategic circles is undeniable. In 1909 he had published his military thoughts in *The Valor of Ignorance*, and many proclaimed him to be a strategic and tactical genius. His book predicted war with Japan and actually detailed how it would be fought. He assailed the unpreparedness of the military of the United States. While the book was not widely read in the U.S., selling only a few thousand copies, and was scorned by isolationists and peace-at-any-price disciples, European and Asian leaders seemed to have read and digested every word, and they begged for more.

Like the prophet rejected in his own land, Lea spread his gospel to the rest of the world. In Japan his book sold 84,000 copies and became required reading for every Japanese cadet.[16] German Kaiser Wilhelm II held *The Valor of Ignorance* in high regard. In Great Britain, Field

Marshal Sir Frederick Roberts, the former commander-in-chief of the British Army, was so impressed that he bought every available copy in London to give to his friends and associates. He contacted Lea imploring him to consider writing a similar book warning of British unpreparedness, especially for a future war with Germany, and Lea obliged by publishing *The Day of the Saxon*.[17]

Not to be outdone by the British, the Germans invited Homer Lea to witness some of their military maneuvers, and Lea was certainly the center of attention, sporting his baton and decked out in his ornate Chinese general's uniform. Lea had presented his case that, like the U.S. and Japan, Great Britain and Germany were on a collision course to war. He predicted the expansion of a great Reich. After World War I, some thought that his prediction was off base. But Lea was only one war off in his prediction, and World War II unfolded as he had foretold.

The Valor of Ignorance had not only sounded an alarm to a future U.S. war with Japan but even included detailed maps and attack scenarios against the U.S. in the Philippines and along the American West Coast. Two prestigious former U.S. Army officers were so impressed with his work that they wrote enthusiastic introductions to the book. Lt. Gen. Adna Chaffee, the former army chief of staff, exclaimed: *"Hail—the Valor of Ignorance!!* The popular belief that the United States is free of opportunities for invasion is all 'tommy rot.'"[18]

And Maj. Gen. J. P. Story, former army chief of artillery, said, "Lea sees clearly the menace of the 'Yellow Peril,' yet it is less than sixty years since the United States went to the uncharted shores of Japan with an olive branch in one hand and in the other a naked sword."[19]

* * *

So now, on this hot, July day in 1911, just two years after the release of *The Valor of Ignorance*, this diminutive figure stood before his audience like a giant in the field of military strategy and tactics. His reputation had preceded his appearance at this luncheon lecture. Newspapers such as the *San Diego Union* had earlier heralded his military genius: "Everywhere among all nations General Homer Lea . . . is recognized as an authority on military attack and defense."[20]

His lunch audience was equally enthralled, and all eyes were fixed upon him. Of Lea's countless presentations given to numerous audiences, this was one of only three to have ever been published and recorded for history.[21] His theme that day was his oft-repeated warning that Japan would attack in the Pacific against the United States.

"The sources of war," he said, "once determined are as a great rock on the brink of a precipice, and as a child may push over this rock, so a nation in a fit of passion may in no greater length of time hurl down the great rock of empire."[22]

To Homer Lea, the source of war with Japan had already been determined. Two incidents had cast the die for war, and the two nations, like the two trains, were on a collision course. The first incident had been the American occupation of the Hawaiian Islands. When the U.S. annexed the islands, Japan had been the lone voice of protest among the world's leading nations. She said that she would not then nor at any time agree to U.S. possession of that critical territory. Japan had never withdrawn that protest.[23]

The second incident had been the perceived insult to Japanese national pride when, in 1906, following the devastating earthquake, the San Francisco School Board suddenly created segregated schools for Japanese students after a tremendous influx of Japanese immigrants to California. That action had become a "single incident," much like the throwing of the tea into Boston Harbor that had accelerated the colonists' rush toward war against the Crown.

As the school board crisis unfolded, it had crossed no one's mind that a tiny portion of the American population could actually agitate Japan to hostilities, but that's exactly what happened, and it brought about a diplomatic fracture. For quite some time, along the Pacific Coast of the United States, anti-Asian sentiment had been brewing. Big Labor was hostile to the cheap labor performed by these immigrants to the detriment of its rank and file, and their seeming non-assimilation rankled much of the population.

The charges of Japanese clannishness and non-American loyalty were detailed in 1908 in a hotly worded petition to Congress by an association calling itself the Asiatic Exclusion League. This group claimed a membership of a quarter of a million people and purported to speak for the vast majority of the West Coast population when it said, "The presence in our midst of a large body of Asiatics, the greater number of whom are armed, loyal to their governments, entertaining feelings of distrust, if not of hostility, toward our people; owning no allegiance to our Government or our institutions; not sustaining American life in time of peace, and ever ready to respond to the cause of their own race in time of war—render these Asiatics an appalling menace to the American Republic."[24]

The wording of the San Francisco School Board's exclusion decree was equally insulting. The board wanted to protect the district's schoolchildren from the negative influences brought about "by association with pupils of the Mongolian race."[25] That led to the formation of the Oriental Public School for the education of Chinese, Japanese, and Koreans.

The Japanese press fanned the flames of insult into a raging inferno of indignation and shock. This incident had become the "fit of passion" described by Lea. The Theodore Roosevelt administration scrambled to defuse the issue both with the Japanese government and the city of San Francisco. So severe was this crisis that Roosevelt feared war. He prepared a special memorandum for his labor secretary, Victor Metcalf, who was rushing to do damage control in San Francisco. In that frantically drafted memo was the shocking admission that if this crisis indeed led to war, the U.S. would be helpless to stop a Japanese attack against the Philippines, Hawaii, and even the West Coast.[26]

While the U.S. naval brain trust had not anticipated any likelihood of war with Japan in 1906, Adm. George Dewey assured Roosevelt that the navy could control the Pacific Ocean against Japan "within ninety days of the departure of the battle fleet from the Atlantic coast."[27]

And the U.S. had an impressive array of fifteen battleships compared to Japan's five, but none was available for immediate combat. Fourteen of the great ships were in the Atlantic Ocean and faced a long voyage before they could even enter the Pacific battle area. The Japanese by then would have seized whatever they wanted long before the "ninety-day" arrival of the American fleet.

Whether or not Admiral Dewey's words soothed Roosevelt's nerves, the president chose to embark on a conciliatory path. To the Japanese he promised fairness and to the Californians he promised an end to the influx of cheap Japanese labor if the school board would only rescind the order for the segregated schools. This proposal brought about what became known as the "Gentlemen's Agreement." The Japanese agreed to curtail immigration, the school board rescinded the segregation order, and the genie was back in the bottle.[28]

But this brush with disaster had raised many eyebrows. While in 1906, war with Japan had seemed remote, by 1907 that was not the case. War seemed almost at the doorstep. The American naval attaché to Germany was very concerned and offered a sobering analysis. He thought that war between the U.S. and Japan was now a foregone conclusion and that when the two countries actually came to blows, the Germans would most likely be sympathetic to the Americans. But he noted that both British and German intelligence had concluded that Japan would win.[29]

The temporary blunting of the 1906 crisis had brought President Roosevelt to a new understanding of the volatile state of Japanese-American relations. There had been harsh words, akin to saber rattling; and there had been a fear of war and frantic diplomatic maneuvering; and despite Admiral Dewey's assurances that war was remote, Roosevelt was not convinced.

It was time to take matters into his own hands, and rather than be guided by the promises and speculations of admirals and advisors, he ordered a spectacular movement of the American fleet from the Atlantic to the waters of the Pacific and continuing on to the Atlantic again. He had been troubled by reports that neither the British nor the Germans believed it was possible to take a fleet of battleships around the world.

"I determined on the move without consulting the Cabinet," boasted Roosevelt, "precisely as I took Panama without consulting the Cabinet. A council of war never fights, and in a crisis the duty of a leader is to lead and not to take refuge behind the generally timid wisdom of a multitude of councilors.

"I made up my mind that it was time to have a showdown in the matter; because if it was really true that our fleet could not get from the Atlantic to the Pacific, it was much better to know it and be able to shape our policy."[30]

This "practice cruise" became known as the voyage of "The Great White Fleet," taking its name from the peacefully painted white ships contrasted with the usual black wartime painting. On December 16, 1907, Roosevelt embarked on his yacht *Mayflower* and led the impressive battleship line out of the anchorage at Hampton Roads. Many proclaimed this was a show of force and would lead to war as soon as the fleet approached the Japanese fleet, but they were wrong, as Roosevelt had predicted.

The Great White Fleet sailed to enthusiastic receptions at a multitude of ports in the next 433 days as it circumnavigated the globe. Perhaps the most enthusiastic was in Japan itself, where the reception was the most elaborate.[31] On February 22, 1909, George Washington's birthday, the fleet finally reentered the waters of Hampton Roads.

So what did this round-the-world, dazzling show of American might and determination mean? Had it assuaged the Japanese to appreciate a new, warmer relationship with the United States? Had it defused tensions and convinced the Japanese that the increased American presence in the far reaches of the Pacific Ocean was nonthreatening and peaceful? Did the warm, elaborate Japanese reception modify Japanese war plans?

Whatever it meant to the Japanese, Gen. Homer Lea argued that the anti-Japanese feelings among Americans had only increased. Between 1908 and 1909, the legislatures of California, Oregon, Washington, Nevada, Arizona, Colorado, Wyoming, Idaho, and the Hawaiian Islands had taken up Japanese exclusion bills.[32] And the immigration of Japanese labor had not ceased nor even slowed down as Japan had promised.[33] The Gentlemen's Agreement was an agreement in name only.

To General Lea, the whole San Francisco school-segregation affair, followed by the round-the-world battleship cruise, was not a dispute followed by an American effort to defuse the crisis. The seemingly happy ending, with a spirit of good feelings described by Roosevelt, was illusory. Those two events were, in fact, actual signposts to war.

The San Francisco action and the Great White Fleet's reaction were proof of war's inevitability.

"War is not the result of disputes per se," Lea wrote. "Disputes or disagreements between nations, instead of being the source or cause of war, are nothing more nor less than the first manifestations of approaching combat. . . . To remove them by arbitration, or any other means, is at best but procrastination."[34]

Recognizing this inevitability, Lea had constantly railed against ignoring the vulnerability of the Pacific and Hawaiian Islands and questioned why the United States had not fortified them against possible attack. "While the establishment of American naval and military power in the Pacific or Hawaii has not been attempted yet," he said, "Japan has prepared for this eventuality . . . these islands can be seized from within and converted into a Japanese naval and military base so quickly that they will be impregnable."

How could all this have been stopped? was a commonly asked question. "If this republic had created at any time a great naval and military base in Hawaii," Lea told his lunch audience, "Japan's opportunity of seizing the islands would have been lessened if not prohibited."[35]

Seven months after his inspiring address in New York, Gen. Homer Lea contracted influenza while in China and was left blind and partially paralyzed. He returned to the United States but died on November 1, 1912, just shy of his thirty-sixth birthday. His clarion voice was silent, and his acclaim and warnings of war slowly drifted into obscurity. His predicted drift to war would continue, and it would be eleven years before another prophet emerged to warn a sleeping nation of the impending peril. This new prophet was Gen. William Mitchell.

Chapter 3
Mitchell

Billy Mitchell was the outspoken herald of the invincibility of the newest weapon of war: air power. His devotion to military tactics had not been honed at West Point or any other military school. He had graduated from Racine College in Wisconsin and enlisted as a private in the 1st Wisconsin Infantry during the Spanish-American War. He quickly gained a commission as a second lieutenant because of his father's great political influence.

He served in Cuba and, in 1899, was under Douglas MacArthur in the Philippines. Assigned to the Signal Corps, he was a 1903 pioneer who completed the telegraph lines in Alaska. A year later he became a twenty-four-year-old instructor at the prestigious Staff College at Leavenworth. His rise was meteoric, and he became a distinguished graduate of the Army School of the Line.[1]

His combat skills, however, were more than successfully tested in the Great War, and to him, air power had demonstrated itself as the decisive weapon. Its impact made the tactics of massed armies now obsolete. So too were the long-revered battleships of the large navies. "With the advent of air power, all these things changed," he said. "The air covers the sea and land in equal measure, there is no restriction."[2]

No one knew air power better or expressed its advantages more vociferously than Mitchell. And he spoke not from the position of a theorist but as an air warrior. He had been in the war from the very beginning, as an American observer. He actually joined French

General Petain at the front just a few days after the United States declared war on April 1917. Two weeks later he was on a French battlefield for ten days.[3] He became the first American to join the French in an attack;[4] and he remained on the battlefields or flying over them for the entire war—to the very end: November 11, 1918, the "eleventh hour of the eleventh day of the eleventh month."

In the beginning of WWI, the American Air Service of the American Army was called the Aviation Service of the Signal Corps and had a paltry sixty-five officers and 1,100 men. There were 200 training planes in the Service, but none was suited for combat in an actual war. There were no plans, tactical doctrine, deployment, or even a chain of command other than it was part of the Army Signal Corps. But all that dramatically changed during seventeen months of war. At the end, it was called the Air Service, American Expeditionary Forces, and counted over 7,700 officers and almost 71,000 men in its ranks.[5]

In the early summer of 1918, the American Army, with its fledgling Air Service, would be called upon to earn its spurs. The British and French armies had mostly fought the war, when, in late May, a massive German offensive, with 4,500 guns and seventeen divisions, targeted the French Army and drove it back to the river Marne. When the onslaught, called the Third Battle of the Aisne, was finally halted, the American 2nd Division was moved in to replace a battered French corps.

The lines between the two opposing armies were anything but straight. They naturally bent following the contours of the river, but at one point, there was a large bulge in the line left over from fighting in 1914 around Verdun. It was called the Saint-Mihiel salient, and this giant arrowhead thrust into the Allied line. Its fifteen-mile-wide point was on the Marne River near Chateau-Thierry, and its fifteen-mile-distant base was thirty-five miles wide.[6]

At the insistence of Gen. John "Black Jack" Pershing, the American Army was tasked with fighting the next battle against the Germans—as a unit, and not as supplemental forces to flesh out the British and French armies. The air arm for this proposed massive counterattack would be under the tactical command of the feisty Col. Billy Mitchell, who now found himself in control of all Allied air assets assigned to this operation.

Mitchell was a true zealot—all air, all the time—and no one, not even his superiors, were spared the lashes of his razor-sharp tongue. He had no use for the General Staff, which he felt was not qualified to make policy decisions. He scoffed that none of them had ever flown or even knew the first thing about aviation.

He once called a group of newly arrived officers, green to the front, "a shipload of aviation officers . . . almost none of whom had ever seen an airplane." And anyone arriving to replace or augment battle-tested officers were "carpetbaggers."[7]

But his bombast was enabled because his arguments were mostly on solid ground. No high-ranking officer had ever flown over the front lines. Mitchell had. The French, who had borne the brunt of the war, thought he was an aviation genius, and he further endeared himself to them with flashes of pomp and ceremony as he moved within the circles of the rich, famous, and influential. Those included the leaders of the war-making and aviation industry. This one-man dynamo maneuvered and operated like a practiced politician, and all was in advance of the arrival of General Pershing and his staff.[8]

Mitchell toured every aspect of the front, just as if he had been appointed an inspector-general. He popped in on senior commanders without appointment or invitation and made himself at home prying into anything dealing with aviation.

Such was the case when he brashly approached British air chief Sir Hugh Trenchard. When asked if he had an appointment and Mitchell said no, one would think that Sir Hugh would have recoiled at this lack of respect, but Mitchell simply pressed on. "I still want to see as much of your organization as you can show me."[9]

Onlookers would certainly expect the senior British general to put this brash, uninvited Yank lieutenant colonel in his proper place. But Sir Hugh did not and, quite to the opposite, said, "Come along young man, I can see you're the sort who usually gets what he wants in the end."[10]

And Trenchard held nothing back. He allowed Mitchell to see all aspects of what the British were doing, including airfields, shops, and modern tactics of combat aviation. The use of massed bombers particularly enthralled Mitchell, and he began to envision future air offensives that would use *thousands* of planes. This thought, certainly unreasonable in 1918, was almost as remote as the idea of space travel. This lofty goal shrouded the reality that, in 1918, America had exactly one plane in France.[11]

Despite that, Mitchell continued his nonstop activities and did not diminish his penchant for blurting out whatever crossed his mind. But Sir Hugh Trenchard found this young American compelling and noted, "Mitchell is a man after my own heart. If only he can break his habit of trying to convert opponents by killing them, he'll go far."[12]

That would never be Mitchell's style. He targeted the General Staff, labeled them as pariahs, and mocked their inherent ignorance of air matters. He said that "an organization of this kind" distracted from the efforts at the front. The Staff was an obstacle to what he really wanted: a single air commander, not a bureaucracy of "Tom, Dick and Harry . . . who were neither pilots nor had ever seen an armed German."[13]

Mitchell and Pershing: the brash aviator (left) and the General of the Armies. (National Archives)

By August 10, 1918, Pershing had his sixteen American divisions formed into the new U.S. First Army and promised that his force would eliminate the troublesome Saint-Mihiel salient and smash the German line. Mitchell immersed himself deeply into the planning and could regularly be found in a school building, huddled together with his most trusted companions. They were like schoolchildren themselves, excitedly examining a twelve-by-twelve-foot relief map that had been furnished compliments of a French balloon company. On that map were the details of the entire Saint-Mihiel area.[14]

There, displayed before them, was each and every land contour, defensive position, and avenue of approach. There were barricades and destroyed buildings and all the killing fields, and no detail escaped their prying eyes. An officer, present in that cramped room, described the scene of Mitchell and his cohorts, all bent over the map or crawling around on the floor. "It was fascinating," he said; it was "like toy-soldier stuff, but in deadly earnest."[15]

Mitchell felt that this final map study had set him far above any officer on the General Staff, or any Tom, Dick, or Harry, to lead the air arm of this American attack. He had studied all this for many years, and, "now from flying over it with both French and American observers . . . it made me feel that I knew this part of the world as well as any man living."[16]

Mitchell formulated his plan into the American air mission. His huge force, an incredible 1,481 aircraft of all types, was the largest air armada ever assembled.[17] His eye was on the complete destruction of the German air capabilities and on wreaking havoc on the German rear-area supply, support, and communications. And without their own air, the German army on the ground would be doomed.

He envisioned his force to be "a central mass, hurled at the enemy's aviation, no matter where he might be found, until complete ascendancy had been obtained over him in the air."[18] Once started, Mitchell wanted an incessant, unrelenting attack. It would be round the clock, "to force him either to arise and accept combat, or to lose his airplanes in the hangars themselves on his own fields."[19]

On September 12, the massive air-ground attack began. Mitchell's plan was daring and deadly. He had formed his force into two air brigades, 500 planes each, on the two flanks of the German-held salient. Depending on German maneuvering, these brigades would alternately destroy or drive off enemy aircraft, strike surface targets within the salient, or hammer German ground forces that would be devoid of their own air cover.[20]

His plan and tactics went off like clockwork, and four days later, on September 16, the battle was over. The Saint-Mihiel salient was no more. The front was now a straight line, and Mitchell's 1,481 aircraft had also demolished the German 500-plane air force. He became an instant hero and Pershing promoted him to the rank of brigadier general. The Germans would never recover from this attack, and two month later, the war was over.

But it was more than the strategic planning and execution of the Saint-Mihiel operations, and the following Meuse-Argonne offensive, that exhilarated Mitchell and spurred him on to his never-ending promotion of air power. In his mind all this was just the embryo of a long-range concept of air power and its decisive ability to win wars. That concept was to attack a warring nation's industrial and civilian population. Before the November 1918 armistice, the American air forces had actually begun to venture out to attack cities along the Rhine. If the war had gone on, Mitchell had envisioned targeting Berlin.[21]

Mitchell was not alone in his vision of the massive use of air power to devastate an enemy force—although proponents of his tactics were few and far between. One of his disciples wrote that the way to stop an enemy army was to stop its supplies and communications from ever reaching the front. A campaign like that would require round-the-clock bombing, offering no respite and obliterating everything in its path, so that the enemy's war-making industry would be overwhelmed. "Manufacturing works would be wrecked and the morale of the workmen would be shattered,"[22] prophesied Col. E. S. Gorrell in 1919.

Mitchell and his war prophets faced formidable opposition to their concept of *total* war. Speaking in opposition was none other than Secretary of War Newton Baker, who invoked the *civilized* principles of a traditional war. Despite the recent lost generations of four countries, pulverized on the killing fields of France, including the 1,000,000 casualties at Verdun alone, Baker chose sentimental reasoning to champion this "civilized" approach to traditional warfare. It was an easy sell to most listeners.

It was natural to recoil from the specter of shattered cities and dead, innocent women and children. To Baker, to carry on an offensive that included the enemy's factories and workers "constituted an abandonment of the time-honored practice among civilized peoples of restricting bombardment to fortified places, or to places from which the civilian population had an opportunity to be removed."[23]

But what about a civilian population that would not be removed from the extended battlefield? Secretary Baker never addressed that possibility, nor did he address an enemy force that purposely operated within a civilian population or the fact that factories producing armaments and munitions were most likely to be in civilian areas. His high-minded thoughts seemed to ignore the reality of France's shattered cities and enormous numbers of civilian deaths.

These realities seemed to indicate that Baker was either totally unaware of the German air assault against London or willfully chose to ignore it. The German action of attacking *civilian targets* flew in the face of his proclamations concerning his "time-honored practice among civilized peoples."

The German Zeppelin raids against London killed 522 Londoners and wounded or maimed another 1,500 who were helpless against the aerial assault. They dropped over eight hundred bombs on London during the course of the war and, on one occasion, created what amounted to an early firestorm that caused $8,000,000 damage—in 1918 dollars.[24]

Baker thought like many others who never fought and who viewed war as some sort of special athletic event, pitting opposing armies to fight in splendid isolation. To them it was a contest on some remote battlefield—a *field of honor*, so to speak. The winning side was then deemed the winner of the war.

To Baker and his ilk, war was to be sanitary, fought without the slightest thought of breaking or crushing the enemy's will to fight. If war was indeed an ugly thing, then Baker chose to turn his eyes away.

Gen. Lucian Truscott would famously say, "Polo games and wars are not won by gentlemen."[25]

To Mitchell and his fellow air-power prophets, this squeamishness and pontificating was all nonsense. Sentimentality should have nothing to do with war. "The entire nation is, or should be, considered a combatant force,"[26] said the feisty general. Was it not logical to assume that women, children, and others, although not capable of bearing arms on the battlefield, were more than capable of turning out the tools of war? Was not their participation in the production of the war machine of a nation even more valuable than a soldier on the front line staring across no man's land?

Stripping sentimentality from the argument, could a reasonable person then argue against Mitchell's coldblooded logic? Despite the stigma of *total* war, was it not better, strategically and tactically, to kill a soldier's wife working in a munitions factory, turning out

British women in WWI work to turn out thousands of artillery rounds. (© Imperial War Museum)

hundreds of artillery rounds a day, than to kill her isolated husband in a trench at the front?

Mitchell's view of the war and its terrible battlefields was made from his observations at the front. The war "was a slaughterhouse from beginning to end on the ground," he confided to his diary. "Maybe one side makes a few yards, or maybe a mile, and thousands of men are killed. It is not war, it is simply slaughter."[27]

That slaughter would continue until one steeled himself to the task of attacking the vital centers and preventing these terrible weapons of war from ever reaching the front.

"War is decided by getting at the vitals of the enemy, that is, to *shoot him in the heart,*" Mitchell wrote. "This type of war is like clipping off one finger, then a toe, then an ear, then his nose and gradually eating into his vitals."[28]

These arguments were all to be grappled with in the future. For now, Mitchell was a bigger-than-life hero. Allied aviators and generals alike wanted to see him. That included Sir Hugh Trenchard, who told him that his air offensives were "the most terrific exhibition I have ever seen."[29]

And Mitchell, ever the showman, ate it all up as shutters clicked and cameras rolled; and he held forth with eager crowds that followed his every move. One airman said, "He didn't walk like other men . . . there was pride in every movement. If he had only eight or ten feet to walk, he went at it as though he was marching a mile, *and was late.*"[30]

Armistice Day in Paris is best described as riotous. It was "the most spectacular outburst of feeling that I have ever seen," said Mitchell. Throngs filled the Paris streets, especially the Champs-Elysees. Singing and dancing were the order of the day, and when the French national colors and army flags came into view, veterans rushed to embrace them and reverently kiss the sacred cloth.

Mitchell departed Paris and continued to advance with the American Army into the Ruhr section of Germany but was soon thereafter ordered home. But before his triumphal return to the States, he could not resist first stopping in London, where he had a "delightful chat" with King George V. He then boarded the ship *Aquitania,* which carried him home to his hero's welcome.[31]

Despite reveling in the worldwide jubilation marking the end of the "war to end all wars," Billy Mitchell had little hope for a lasting peace. He had already perceived Japan to be a future threat, but it wasn't only Japan that worried him. "Germany gave in too quickly and the Allies have been too eager to agree to Armistice . . . ," he said. "Germany would rebuild, and, in time, the United States would have to return to finish the job."[32]

In 1919, no one had room for these depressing predictions. It was time to celebrate. Washington was "in a giddy mood," historian Burke Davis noted. "There was an exhilarating air of triumph . . . the Army was hastily being disbanded as if it were an obstacle to progress and an embarrassing burden to a magnanimous conqueror."[33] No one was interested in disparaging words or dire predictions that clouded an otherwise sunny glimpse of a future peaceful world.

So when Mitchell returned to the *giddy* Washington environment, he was horrified that most of the 20,000 Air Service officers that had been recruited and trained, and had shown the world what air power could do, were being dismissed from service; only a paltry 1,300 would remain.[34] Even his own title, Director of Military Aeronautics, was on the chopping block. His office, including all of his furniture, had already disappeared; and he had not been named the new Air Service chief. That title and position went to a ground officer, a man who had never flown an airplane: Gen. Charles Menoher.[35]

In this world of reckless disarmament, there appeared a small ray of hope. During his first week on his new job as Menoher's operations officer, Mitchell received an encouraging phone call from none other than Franklin Delano Roosevelt, the acting secretary of the Navy. Roosevelt invited him to address the Navy General Board as they explored the future of naval air. Here was his chance to have his ideas included in the conversations of the Navy's top brass.

He broached the sticky subject of battleships and their vulnerability to air attack and urged the Navy to develop defensive measures. That type of conversation had always been brushed aside before, and Mitchell anticipated a similar dug-in stance. But he was pleasantly surprised to find the Navy's spokesman, Adm. Albert Winterhalter, most agreeable and willing to exchange ideas.

Billy Mitchell, aviation genius of WWI. (National Archives)

"My opinion is that you can make a direct attack on ships from the air in the future,"[36] Mitchell began. Although bombs to do the job of ship-sinking did not exist in the 1919 arsenal, he envisioned development of ship-busting bombs as large as two tons.

Again, the Navy was most pleasant, not balking at any of Mitchell's revolutionary thoughts; and the admiral even suggested working hand in hand with Mitchell to learn his attack methods so an effective ship defense could be designed. Encouraged by the friendliness, Mitchell pressed on and proposed maneuvers in and around Chesapeake Bay, where planes would conduct mock attacks on ships. Again, Admiral Winterhalter agreed and deemed such exercises to be most important.

When the three-hour meeting ended, a sense of cooperation seemed to prevail, in contrast to the previous atmosphere of rancor. But this cordiality was all illusory, and it would prove to be the only civil and friendly meeting between Mitchell and the Navy. All his thoughts would be rejected outright, and any mention of his ideas was to be shunned and deemed, by the Navy's high command, to be blasphemous. That initial, conciliatory tone disappeared, along with Admiral Winterhalter, who was never to be heard from again.[37]

It was not just the Navy that spurned Mitchell's ideas, visions, and suggestions. His own Army colleagues rejected most of what he had to say, and he had said a lot. So copious were Mitchell's submissions concerning a dizzying array of inventions and armament improvements that the secretary of war as well as the General Staff were convinced "that the war had deranged Mitchell." And it was rumored that "the War Department had a special place for discarded Mitchell proposals. It was called the Flying Trash Pile."[38]

In April 1919, General Pershing had appointed various boards to study the usefulness of air independence, and his top panel concluded that such independence was justified only if the Air Service could *prove* that it was as decisive a weapon as the Army and Navy.[39] Obviously Mitchell's successful 1,500-plane attack at Saint-Mihiel, and its destruction of the German air force, didn't count with Pershing's top board, and it proclaimed that the last war had offered no such proof of air decisiveness.

But Mitchell's nonstop speeches, rallying, and presentations, aided by the press, found favor in Europe. His rejection in the United States did not translate into European rejection. When the secretary of war sent commissioners to study overseas aviation, they stepped into Mitchell's world. Europe loved him, and his old comrades, including his superior, Sir Hugh Trenchard, sang his praises. So too did most of the senior aviators who had served and flown with him. They had watched him plan and bring about the stunning air success in the Saint-Mihiel offensive.

So when those American commissioners returned to the States, to Secretary Newton Baker's chagrin, they reported on Mitchell in glowing terms and said, "Immediate action is necessary to safeguard the air interests of the United States."[40] This was exactly what Baker did not want to hear, because he hated Mitchell and was repulsed by his theory on bombing "vital centers" of the enemy that included towns and populations.

To him, any favorable reporting would bring attention to this abhorrent idea. As such, Baker acted like a spoiled child and refused to endorse the commission's report, and he buried it from public circulation. But while it was hidden from the general public, it was exposed to the full glare of light and inspection throughout military circles. Many read it with enthusiasm.

The report particularly infuriated the Navy and forced the chief of naval operations, Adm. William Benson, to indignantly proclaim, "You're wasting your time. I cannot conceive of any use that the fleet will ever have for aircraft. . . . The Navy doesn't need airplanes. Aviation is just a lot of noise."[41]

But Mitchell's energy and popularity led him to boldly tweak the Navy's nose at every turn. His twenty-seven appearances before various congressional bodies gave him the perfect platform to expound on his ideas and the backwardness of the Navy's. He missed few opportunities.

In September 1919, while addressing the House Military Affairs Committee, he said that a developed air force would "almost make navies useless on the surface of the water." To the Navy this was a shot across their bow; and Mitchell doubled down, publically proclaiming, "There can no longer be any doubt that complete control of the air by any nation means military control of the world."[42] The newspapers hung on every word.

Mitchell also had a flair for embellishing his stories and proclamations, and he did just that before that Military Affairs Committee. No one cared, least of all the newspapers. He had claimed in that meeting that "the Navy General Board agrees with me." When the newspapers flashed his words for all to read, they sold copies. When the Navy howled that the statement was not true, and that they in no way agreed, the papers dutifully printed a correction and retraction somewhere on an obscure interior page.

Mitchell's daily life in 1920 was one of constant exposure to an adoring public. He was photographed on horseback, talking with officials at Goodyear about lighter-than-air flight and dirigibles, and at West Point he was the equivalent of a movie star. Following a speech before a gathering of the enthralled Corps of Cadets, the old walls rocked with a thunderous applause that echoed across the Great Plains.[43]

But this Hatfield and McCoy feud between Mitchell and the Navy mostly played out behind bureaucratic closed doors. That obscurity was not advancing Mitchell's agenda. To move his crusade into the limelight, he needed to involve the public; and that public was eager to be enthralled with the exploits of aviators, air races, and barnstorming.

It was not uncommon to see these enchanted citizens at state fairs and far-flung airfields, lining up for the ride of their lives. For a small fee, many, never having been in a car, could experience the exhilaration of flight, and soar to the clouds far above their gawking friends below. Years later, poet John Gillespie Magee captured that feeling in his famous sonnet, "High Flight": "I have slipped the surly bonds of Earth . . . and touched the face of God."

And in the 1920s, there was a lot about aviation for the public to be excited. America was not far removed from its recent pioneering past. A very young George Gay, whose future included the Battle of Midway, had visited the State Fair of Texas in Dallas with visions of flight dancing in his head, but his parents said no. When his grandmother saw the boy's slumped shoulders and obvious disappointment, she stepped forward, took him by the hand, and remarked, "Come on, son; I came here in a covered wagon, and I'm not afraid of that thing."[44]

And despite the Navy's bluster and denial about the importance of air power, it was their own aircraft that first grabbed the national headlines. Three of their seaplanes had attempted the first transatlantic crossing, and although two of them failed, one made the 1,380-mile leap from Newfoundland to the Azores. It then went on to Portugal and England, and the unthinkable had been done—the ocean was no longer an effective barricade.

At home, commercial flight became a possibility when a cross-country race of seventy planes suddenly brought tiny communities and their mule-tended farm fields into the presence of the airplane. Despite five crashes and three deaths on the first day of the race, the air pioneers were undaunted. Just ten of the planes finished the race, and the crashes, which some attributed to too much booze among the daredevil pilots, only added to their legendary tales, driving the public's pioneer interests higher.

As pioneers, they always expected setbacks, and resulting difficulties and crashes left the fawning public undaunted. They were charmed and thrilled to find out that the eventual winner had even flown with his dog! Any political questioning and second guessing, usually coming from cautious politicians and breast-beating obstructionists, was drowned out by Americans clamoring for more adventure from these dashing young men.[45] It was no time for the squeamish or faint of heart.

It was in the electricity of that euphoric atmosphere that Billy Mitchell broadsided the Navy. The nation was not safe! The *New York Times* had plastered those words, in bold type, on the front page: *"America was not safe!"* To the old guard, this was the shriek of fingernails on a blackboard.

Sensing his long-sought upper hand, Mitchell further pressed his advantage and wrote that tests were necessary to determine if the Navy could protect the homeland as it claimed it could. "We must at all costs obtain the battleship to attack and the necessary bombs, planes and so on to make the test a thorough and complete one."[46]

Obviously sensing that they were playing the losing hand, the Navy sought to preempt the fast-moving Mitchell and planned their own secret bombing of the old battleship *Indiana*. Perhaps they saw the necessity to determine what could be done by an air attack and at the same time what they could expect from Mitchell. But lest they create their own panic among the population, they moved to hide their test from public view.

In November 1920, the old battleship was attacked by air, with the Navy planes dropping inert bombs. On deck, explosive charges were set off where the dummy bombs struck *Indiana*, which was already partially sunken in the shallow waters of Chesapeake Bay.[47]

Amazingly, the official Navy report seemed to perpetuate their state of denial. Despite the simulated and actual damage that their own eyes had witnessed, the Navy concluded, "The entire experiment pointed to the improbability of a modern battleship being either destroyed or completely put out of action by aerial bombs."[48]

Nor did their plan of secrecy work out, despite their best efforts. Shocking pictures, not meant for the public eye, were published in the *Illustrated London News*, showing *Indiana* sitting on the bottom in the shallows of Chesapeake Bay; and her deck and superstructure were shattered and twisted.[49]

That hardly jibed with the Navy's official report, and the fact that she had been sunk before the test, so as to be a stable target, made no difference to the observing public. The photos showed her *sitting on the bottom*, and that was grasped by everyone. Wide-eyed readers saw what they saw—case closed.

What was really sitting on the bottom was the Navy's credibility; and Mitchell's warnings, about American vulnerability to enemy attack, flew high above the Navy's debacle.

Public outcry translated into swift congressional action. In January 1921, Mitchell presented his case to yet another congressional panel. He was the very picture of a nonstop dynamo. He alternately laid out drawings, or pointed to photographs of the destroyed *Indiana*, or traced his finger along the lines of charts; and for three hours he unrolled even more charts and drawings, all in front of the mesmerized congressmen.

While they tried to follow his seemingly endless supply of facts and figures, he often paused to conclude that he could "destroy or sink any ship in existence!" Was not the Navy's shameful denial of the fate of *Indiana* proof enough? Had they not sunk a ship themselves, something they had sworn the Army could not do? All the damning photographs were in the members' hands.

Mitchell presented everything—armament, armor, costs of planes and battleships—in dizzying numbers and details. When it was over, the congressmen pummeled him with questions. Why was he right and others wrong? Why couldn't he convince his superiors, and why did he think air was superior to the Army in the aftermath of the Great War? What was the value of air compared to submarines, and what about aircraft carriers?

Each of his answers generated new questions until one representative said, "It seems to me that the principal problem is to demonstrate the certainty of your conclusions." The hours of wrangling had come down to the perfect challenge: the one that Mitchell had hoped for, and he was ready with the perfect answer. "Give us the warships, and come watch it."[50]

Within two days, Congress pressured the Navy to come up with the necessary target ships. Mitchell now had the Navy, and all of his critics, in his crosshairs. "We are going to smoke these people out . . . ," he wrote triumphantly, "and either make them fish or cut bait!"[51]

The *New York Tribune,* obviously miffed by the Navy's attempt to deceive, took the admirals to task. Flashing even more pictures of the sunken *Indiana*, they branded the admirals as adolescent schoolchildren caught in a lie and proclaimed that the photos said everything that needed to be said. Was it not obvious to all that the battleship would have been put out of action and its crew destroyed?

Mitchell girded for the upcoming contest pitting him against the Navy. He wrote to his chief in charge of men and equipment and alerted him to be ready with the aircraft and crews necessary to pull off this great challenge. It would affect the entire future of air.

There was only one problem. His materiel chief, Col. Thurmond Bane, quickly separated his highflying euphoria from the cold facts of reality: "Of course you know we have no crews assigned to [air] ships. In fact we have not a single officer who ever dropped a bomb with a bombsight; or ever was instructed to drop bombs with the idea of hitting a target."[52]

Chapter 4

"Make the Navy Eat Bombs"

Through it all, the American people began to understand that their safety was not only in peril from an enemy air attack that could explode ripping bombs into their cities and population areas; but there was also the horror of terror weapons. Mitchell had warned about the assortment of gases available in the enemy's arsenal that could be used to attack our own "vital centers" and easily break America's morale and will to resist.

If military and political leaders were squeamish about the thought of the destruction of an enemy's populated areas, including women and children, then what about Mitchell's predictions of a "bolt from the blue" that would devastate America's homeland, including their own women and children?[1]

The much-anticipated bombing tests were scheduled for the summer of 1921, and in the run-up to the date, a blackout of news miffed the press. Everything was shrouded. Having been burned by their deception and secrecy about the *Indiana* tests, one could argue that the Navy had learned nothing.

Mitchell's headquarters was at Langley Field at the mouth of the Chesapeake Bay, and when eager newsmen arrived, anticipating the excitement of the upcoming events, everything they saw was labeled off-limits, and there were mysterious black buildings. When they tried to interview anyone, all were tight-lipped.

People came and went, aircraft taxied and parked, and the reporters had never seen so many planes in one spot. Fully aware of Mitchell's one-man war against both the Army and Navy, one reporter wrote mockingly of the numerous planes, "The Army thinks these are not Army at all, just fancy playthings used by reckless young men. The Navy agrees."[2]

Mitchell's men, however, after months of hard training were no longer men who "had never dropped a bomb"; and they were not reticent to tell the eager newsmen of their proficiency. Bravado was not in short supply. Maj. Davenport Johnson boasted, "Our men think bombs, talk bombs, and expect to make the Navy eat bombs."[3]

This latest stage of development for Mitchell's team was a wonder unto itself. There had been months of frustration and bureaucratic haggling, and little money, and fierce bickering as to how the test was to be conducted, and ridiculous rules. Even the removal of a few trees that threatened the takeoff of heavily loaded Army bombers was a matter of red tape. After months of requesting the tree cutting, two cadets were killed when their plane grazed the obstructing treetops, burst into flames, and exploded a bomb. The Army, still not moved to action, simply reported that the request for tree removal had been kicked to the proper authority.[4]

And the Navy persisted in their own opposition. The Fleet Air commander announced in all seriousness that "the mere sinking of ships was not the purpose of the tests." If he remotely realized that his words *"mere sinking"* were an admission by the Navy that it recognized Mitchell's long-shouted claims concerning sinking, he did not show it and prattled on.

"By careful inspection of decks, hulls, turrets, communications systems and fire stations," he recited, "the effects of bombs on warships could be measured. A boarding party must make an inspection after each hit, targets must not be destroyed before evidence could be examined."[5] It was all mind-numbing, and many recognized the ploy as an attempt to minimize the dreaded anticipation that Mitchell would actually sink a battleship.

To Mitchell it was simple: could an airplane sink a ship, especially a battleship? All the rest was fluff and boiled down to a silly exercise in nitpicking and parsing of words. The further interjection of restrictive rules seemed to be the action of terrified Navy leaders who saw disaster looming as the result of these tests. Alarm had moved in with the Navy's scoffing, and their pretest chatter was designed to distract. Historian Alfred Hurley correctly identified Mitchell's straightforward goal. There was no parsing of words. He wanted to sink "each target [ship] in as vivid a manner as possible."[6]

And so it began. Encumbered with a complete news blackout that could not help but call into question the honesty and integrity of Mitchell's adversaries, Navy, Marine, and Army aircraft readied for the test. They would each participate in attacks against a variety of floating targets: a submarine, destroyers, a cruiser, and two battleships. The services would participate in the tests on alternate days and the Navy went first.[7]

Mitchell's team had overcome the most daunting obstacles. When he first pushed for the bombing tests, he had neither a bomb that could sink a capital ship nor a bomber capable of lifting, and delivering, such a nonexistent bomb. Who in his right mind approaches a test to prove a theory without having the necessary tools? It is even more intriguing to try to understand how Mitchell came to champion his ship-sinking theories.

His wartime experiences had nothing to do with sinking ships. His great wartime achievement had to do with aerial warfare and his massive 1,500-plane raid to eliminate the German air force and shatter German supply and communications. His every act had been on the offensive, not defensive; and it had been to support the Army's ground attack against the Saint-Mihiel salient.

It was the rapid disarmament of the American military after the war that had brought him to action to save the air forces, and it was with the defense of the homeland in mind that he began his air crusade. He envisioned a sea and air force, not an army, as the deadly threat to the United States. But that crusade to convince the political and military powers that air was the salvation had taken him out on a very slippery slope. His perceived destruction of such an attacking naval and air force by U.S. air power was only a theory. He had no tools to prove anything. He might as well have been arguing for a test to prove space travel without having a space vehicle.

Longtime vaudeville and movie star Groucho Marx famously described the kind of impossible situation Mitchell was in. "If we had some eggs we could have eggs and ham, if we had some ham." And when Congress finally demanded that the Navy provide the ships for him to prove his bombing theories, he still had nothing, other than a target. His first question to his ordnance chief was: "Do we have a bomb that will sink a battleship?" His ordnance chief emphatically answered, "No!"

But, although it was a tall order, that same officer, Capt. C. M. H. Roberts, seemed confident that he could design and build one.[8] And within three months, he made good on his word. Roberts and his team rolled out a massive 2,000-pound bomb and then a 4,000-pound behemoth. When a 2,000-pounder was finally test-dropped, the pilot described the detonation as "like a volcanic eruption."[9]

The question of the necessary aircraft was another problem. The new Martin bombers, the plane capable of lifting the massive bombs, were only in the early stages of testing; and gloomy reports confirmed that the plane could not lift such a load. But when it all looked darkest, a daring pilot offered a glimmer of hope. His plane managed to lift a 1,700-pound load.

Still, Mitchell was very worried. It was only a single success among many failures. "It's going to be possible to take off . . . carrying a 1,600-pound bomb . . . if there is very little wind [and] it is going to require the entire length of the field."[10] He made no mention of lifting a 2,000-pound bomb.

And Mitchell's own words about the untested heavy bombers could not have instilled great confidence in the men who were to fly them. In the Great War, they could have been accurately described as "widow makers."

Mitchell said, "Our experience in flying large bombers from Italy to the western front in Europe had been quite disastrous, as nearly all crashed in transit across the Alps, and great fears were entertained that many accidents would happen to these great ships on their long journey."[11]

But then came some better news. A pilot had managed to get a big Martin bomber airborne with a 2,512-pound payload. He ventured to say that the plane was capable of lifting an additional 500 pounds, but he quickly added that could only happen "under more favorable conditions."[12]

Mitchell knew it would take the 2,000-pound bomb, or larger, to successfully attack the battleship, but it wasn't just the size of the bomb that mattered. It had to be dropped in an unconventional fashion. He said, "It had always been held as a principle that the vessel had to be hit directly by a thrown missile in order to affect it. In studying the battleship, we found that its bottom was pipe connecting with the condenser system. The use of the water hammer, or water impelled with great force by an explosion under the bottom of the vessel would certainly cave in the bottom, spring the seams, and cause the vessel to sink."[13]

An explosion that damaged the condenser system would also bend props, shafts, and rudders. "So," wrote Mitchell, "we determined the best depths in the water at which bombs should explode to get these effects and made our fuses accordingly."[14]

Mitchell left nothing to chance. He would fuse his bombs to be effective if they hit the ship and more effective if they were near-misses. "The fuses of these great bombs were also arranged so that if they actually hit a vessel on its deck, they would cause an explosion which would dish or crack the deck, smash up the superstructure, tear down the masts, kill all exposed personnel by the detonation and others by the concussion, put out of commission the telephones, electric light systems, and speaking tubes, and would probably blow up the magazines and the boilers."[15]

* * *

So now that the long-awaited bombing tests were at hand, there was no room for error. The first target, by luck of the draw, belonged to the Navy. It was an old German submarine, *U-117*, and it proved to be no match against the Navy's smallest, 180-pound bombs. It broke up and went to the bottom so rapidly that Mitchell beamed. "These bombs tore her all to pieces. . . . Some of these skeptics began to be convinced that there was something to air bombing."[16] Others minimized the spectacular results and said that it was just an *unarmored* submarine, hardly comparable to a capital ship!

But their nervousness was easy to spot. General Menoher, head of the Army's Air Service, and no friend of Mitchell, required every officer to acknowledge receipt of his orders on "Avoidance of Publicity in Connection with Bombing Experiments."[17] This was especially aimed at Mitchell and his disciples, whose quotes and opinions were a delight to every newsman.

The next phase was to find a ship at sea and attack it. The Navy could not, but an Army dirigible did, but when the informed Navy then attacked the ship with *eighty* dummy bombs, they scored only two hits. Their inefficiency served to raise the Navy brass's confidence that when the Army's turn came, their bombers would do no better.

Up next was a destroyer, and it was the Army's turn to bomb. Mitchell led the attack off with light bombers carrying 100-pounders and followed with heavies toting 600-pounders. The Navy's hopes for a lack of marksmanship by the Army bombers went up in geysers of flame, water, and smoke, as the Army bombardiers did not miss. Mitchell was ecstatic. "In less time that it takes to tell, bombs began churning the water around the destroyer . . . in front of it, behind it, opposite its side, and directly in its center. Columns of water rose hundreds of feet into the air . . . the vessel looked as if it were on fire. Smoke came out of its funnels. . . . Then it broke completely in two . . . and sank out of sight."[18]

Then the cruiser, *Frankfurt,* was the target. Her heavy side-armor and multiple steel-door compartments presented a formidable defense against air attack. Light bombers did nothing to her but kill the test animals representing humans on deck. After their examination, the inspectors proclaimed, almost with an air of satisfaction, that *Frankfurt* was just too stout to sink, and they ordered scuttling charges prepared to send this gallant ship to the bottom. She had successfully shrugged off the 100-pounders as if they were simply an annoyance. But Mitchell would have none of that. He brought in his heavies from Langley airfield—six of them, each hauling a 600-pound bomb—and *Frankfurt* was doomed.

"The bombs fell so fast that the attack could not be stopped [for inspection] before mortal damage had been done to the ship. . . . Tremendous columns of water shot up, some falling in tons on the deck, sweeping it clear."[19]

Mitchell's bombers crushed the Navy's ships during the bombing tests. (© Imperial War Museum)

It was the first test for the 600-pound bombs, and they worked to perfection. Mitchell swept down from the sky in his small plane, and flew just yards over the doomed ship for one last look before the cruiser slipped beneath the waves. And Mitchell had ensured that the public would see the dramatic results of the tests being hidden from their eyes. Despite the orders to avoid publicity, his photographing planes were working, so that all would be seen in movie theaters.

"We had photographic planes equipped with both still and motion picture cameras so as to make a complete record of every shot."[20]

Still the naysayers clung to their grasped straws. If a light cruiser could resist such a furious attack, Mitchell would have no chance against a mighty battleship. The *furious* attack had actually been delivered by only six planes, each carrying one, 600-pound bomb.

So now, the mighty *Ostfriesland* would be the last and most formidable test of the plane against a battleship. The winner would most likely be anointed to be an invincible weapon: a title always claimed by the Navy. The future of the Air Service certainly hung in the balance. Was it a decisive weapon or merely a supporting arm to be used as the Army and Navy saw fit? The senior Army and Navy leaders had seen little reason to grant the airplane the title of "decisive weapon."

To many, Mitchell was a flash in the pan, flitting around, and acting like a child enthralled with a new toy. Neither his tactics nor those of his disciples were a substitute for longstanding traditions, of smashing victories at sea with massive ships pounding their adversaries into submission with thundering broadsides. On land, it was massed artillery and rolling barrages in front of charging infantry that would prevail, not flying to the enemy's rear and eliminating planes, "vital centers," and women and children.

On July 19, as the sunset cast long shadows over the sea, Mitchell flew his small observation plane over the target area for a calm look at the anchored battleship, *Ostfriesland*. She rode silently at anchor, highlighted by red, white, and blue bullseyes painted on her hull. Mitchell stared in awe as he circled the great ship. In his mind she was noble, "a grim old bulldog with the vicious scars of Jutland still on her."[21] At Jutland, *Ostfriesland* had blazed away and taken a terrific pounding: she had absorbed eighteen naval-gunfire hits that smashed into her body and even had struck two mines; but her thick skin, numerous watertight compartments, and excellent crew had left her unsinkable. She was a formidable adversary.

On the morning of July 20, the test flights against the battleship were postponed, first for one hour, and then another. As noon approached, the Navy test administrators had still not called for Mitchell's planes, loaded and ready at far-off Langley Field. At 1:00 P.M., Mitchell had enough of waiting and flew his small plane out to the test site. To his surprise, he saw the test and observation ships, as well as ships of the fleet assembled to witness the test, departing the area, as if everything had been called off. Mitchell was furious. He hotly radioed that he and his crews were ready; just what was the holdup?

"We found out," he later said, "that since there was a 20-knot wind blowing, they [the Navy] had determined an airplane could not act." In no uncertain terms Mitchell informed all that he and his bombers were ready, and nothing was going to be canceled.

The bombers, with their 600-pound bombs—so ordered by the Navy—immediately took off and were on station off the Virginia coast at 3:30. They shifted into attack formation, began their runs, and dropped five bombs, one behind the other. All five either hit the battleship or very near, delivering underwater hammer blows against its deeper, less-protected hull. But the follow-up damage inspection was not possible in the face of an approaching violent storm that drove the attacking aircraft back to base; and the ships with their observers, newsmen, and officials beat a hasty retreat to the sheltered waters of Norfolk. Along the way back, the Secretary of the Navy, Edwin Denby, was heard to boast to several of the Navy brass that the bombs had simply been pinpricks against the mighty ship. The relieved naval officers "sniggered cheerfully," reported one newspaper, and others reported that the *Ostfriesland* was "absolutely intact and undamaged . . . riding snugly at anchor on the high seas."[22]

The next morning, July 21, 1921, Mitchell's bombers were again rigged for combat, this time with 1,100-pound bombs. The first one was dropped by young Capt. Clayton Bissell, who was a disciple of bombing a ship by laying the bomb directly upon her. True to form, his bomb struck *Ostfriesland's* forecastle, producing a spectacular explosion. But to ordnance chief Captain Roberts, this was not the optimum method of attack.

"I remember Bissell was especially hard to win over," said Roberts. "He had been trained to hit what he aimed at." He had *"the pickle-barrel mentality."* The water-hammer effect was the way to sink ships. It required a *near-miss* mentality.

"I talked until I was blue in the face," Roberts exclaimed, "to all those bombardiers . . . that when they hit a ship, all they did was knock off the bric-a-brac and tear up their bomb, but when they hit within fifty feet, the explosions and contractions of gas from underwater explosions would tear those hulls apart."[23]

Mitchell had explained the physics.

> If, for instance, we were to explode five hundred pounds of TNT in a city street, we would create a certain amount of havoc. Increasing the charge . . . would not produce a very great difference in the amount of destruction. On the other hand, if we were to explode TNT in water,

a medium that is practically incompressible, we obtain altogether different results.

If we double our charge of explosive under water, we get not two but perhaps four times the effect. It is terrific. When water is impelled by these great charges it has practically the striking force of steel. If it hits the sides of a ship it smashes all the way through.[24]

Seeming to have forgotten these instructions, Captain Bissell's other bombers now roared onto the scene and received a frantic wave-off from the control vessel that wanted to inspect the damage caused by Bissell's bomb. But it was too late, and four more bombs plummeted down. Two more found their mark on the hull. The wave-off was finally recognized, and the seven other bomber crews aborted and were forced to turn back with their 1,100-pound bombs still nestled firmly under their bellies. Mitchell reported them "mad as hornets."

The umpires ventured below the battleship's deck but could not go below the third deck because of the damage caused by Bissell's bomb. Even without being able to see or inspect, they promptly concluded that the ship "was still in action," and obviously believing their own hype, they joyously proclaimed, "By Jove, we're not going to sink this ship!"[25]

To make sure that their proclamation would be correct, the Navy resorted to more skullduggery. The officer in charge radioed Mitchell that although the Navy had originally agreed, in writing, to certain terms in the Army bombing attack that included the use of the massive 2,000-pound bombs, it was now reneging on the deal. The Army was to have flown and attacked until they had gotten two hits on the ship; but now the Navy ordered Mitchell to bring out only three aircraft, each with one of the big bombs. If the bombers didn't get two hits with those three bombs, then the test was over!

Mitchell screamed bloody murder and called the Navy's reneging *"the last straw."* He promptly waved off the Navy's instructions and sent his eight bombers rumbling down the runway. The big biplanes struggled to lift off the ground, each straining with the enormous weight under their bellies. Like before, they barely missed the tops of the still-standing pine trees. Once aloft, Mitchell radioed his own verbal backhand to the Navy: "the attack will be made until we have secured the two hits."[26] On the other end, the Navy radio was silent.

The eight bombers pressed on to the target area. But along the way, as if the gods of fate had suddenly decided to choose sides, Captain Roberts' bomber spiraled down toward the sea. The bomb's inventor frantically worked to jettison the monster before impact, and managed to set it free at the last second and avoid a catastrophe. Observing from above, the others saw the fallen aircraft, floating with its nose down and tail up, and the crew paddled around in their life vests. The brush with disaster was over, and off they went for their rendezvous with *Ostfriesland.*

The roar of their engines announced to the onlookers that they were approaching the target. "Captain Lawson circled his target once to take a look at her and make sure of his wind and altitude," said Mitchell. "He then broke his airplanes from their 'V' formation into a single column and attacked. Seven planes followed one another."[27]

The skyward-gazing guests and observers saw the first massive bomb released. Its long sleek shape fell from beneath the first aircraft and glinted in the sunlight. It gathered speed with every passing second and seemed to be a giant arrow, streaking toward the ship. These pilots, after months of training, seemed more aware of the optimum bombing techniques. It would be near-misses, not direct hits, that would deliver the killing shots to the battleship.

That first bomb slightly missed the huge outline of the ship and sent up a small splash where it entered the water. To the observers, it was a miss, but a split second later, it detonated, delivering the water-hammer blow that struck the lower half of *Ostfriesland's* hull like a wrecking ball. 30,000 tons of erupting water soared into the sky as if gravity had suddenly lost its grip, and the observers saw a volcanic geyser like no other.

Even before the gasping observers could react, the second bomb hit; but this one struck directly on the ship with an earsplitting explosion. Then the third was a perfect near-miss delivering a second water-hammer blow. The fifth bomb streaked into the water just off the ship's stern and that hammer stroke lifted *Ostfriesland's* bow skyward. The great ship rose like a giant whale from the deep, broaching high into the air, and then toppled over on her port side.

"We could see her rise eight to ten feet between the terrific blows from under water," said Mitchell from his observation plane. "On the fourth shot, Captain Streett, sitting in the back seat of my plane, stood up and waving both arms shouted: 'She is gone!'"[28]

The doomed ship began her death spiral, sinking by the stern. All watching from the deck of the observer ship stared in disbelief as the battleship disappeared in a final plunge.

Mitchell described it.

> When a death blow has been dealt by a bomb to a vessel, there is no mistaking it. Water can be seen to come up under both sides of the ship, she trembles all over, as if her nerve center had been shattered, and she usually rises in the water, sometimes clear, with her bow or stern. In a minute the *Ostfriesland* was on her side; in two minutes she was sliding down by the stern and turning over at the same time; in three minutes she was bottom-side up, looking like a gigantic whale, the water oozing out of her seams as she prepared to go down to the bottom, then gradually she went down stern first.[29]

Mitchell's 2,000-pounders doomed the ship. (© Imperial War Museum)

A reporter on board the observation ship wrote, "The chins of Navy officers . . . dropped. Their eyes seemed to be coming out of the ends of their marine glasses . . . they seemed to be watching the end of an era."[30]

Some of Mitchell's enemies could only set their jaws and try to put on brave faces. Among them was Mitchell's adversarial boss, General Menoher. He was guarded as he delivered his reluctant remarks to excited reporters. "I don't think this shows that the battleships are doomed," he said, "but I fail to see how anyone can doubt that the aerial bomb does constitute a real menace."

The celebrations at Langley Field went on through the night. Euphoria reigned supreme. Mitchell was the man. His sister wrote of the joyous night: "Now at last, everyone, even the stupidest, must understand." She concluded, "And there would be no second world war."[31]

Mitchell had won. There was no question about that. The hard-losing Navy trotted out its parsings: "if the ship had been armed . . . if it had been under way . . . if it had been maneuvering . . . " But the American people knew what they saw, and all who crowded into movie theaters saw the dramatic, flickering film. They may not have remembered the movie, but they would never forget Mitchell's bombers crushing unsinkable battleships. It had been pulse-pounding. They had watched, mesmerized, as *Ostfriesland* rose on her long axis, as if for a last goodbye, before plunging to the bottom to join the *unsinkable Titanic*.

America hailed him as a hero among heroes. Newspapers all across the country flashed headlines lauding what Mitchell and his airmen accomplished. It was "Epoch Making"; it was the greatest breakthrough in naval warfare since *Monitor* and *Merrimac*; its significance was "far reaching"; the age of forts was gone, and no nation would ever *"lay the keel of another battleship."*[32]

The editor of *National Geographic*, who was a witness to the bombing tests, seemed to delight in skewering the Navy brass. "I saw a lot of admirals and captains . . . who used to parade around like a lot of big red bulls, sitting quiet-like and blue."[33]

Billy Mitchell was never loath to enhance his positions and

arguments, and he lost little time exploiting his spectacular win. To him it had always been easy to destroy a navy ship. It was straightforward, and he had written about and preached on the subject at every opportunity.

First, as an enemy fleet or air force approached its objective, reconnaissance would locate it. Second, superior American air would destroy the enemy air force protecting it, and third, the now vulnerable enemy fleet would be destroyed by coordinated air, submarine, and torpedo bomber attacks.[34]

The hard part of advancing Mitchell's tactical theories had been advancing the subject of "total war" and the necessary attacks launched against what he called the "vital centers." Secretary of War Baker had emphatically ruled out all attacks against civilians. Military men often understood the concept of attacking vital centers, but it was abhorrent to public military thought, many politicians, and most of the general public. It required destruction of every facet of the enemy's ability to make war, wherever that may be found.

"To gain a lasting victory in war," said Mitchell, "the hostile nation's power to make war must be destroyed—this means the manufactories, the means of communications, the food products, even the farms, the fuel, the oil, and the places where people live and carry on their daily lives." And, "Not only must these things be rendered incapable of supplying the armed forces, but the people's desire to renew the combat at a later date must be discouraged."[35]

To make his point he decided to conduct a mock attack on the cities of the United States. Since the military leaders had been horrified to talk about destruction of an enemy's homeland, he would demonstrate how just such an attack on the vital centers of America would bring about a desire to capitulate. He would show that horror of total war to the unprotected American citizenry, much as Homer Lea had terrified West Coasters with his published, 1909 theoretical attack on San Francisco.

On July 29, Mitchell led his heavy bombers on a simulated bombing run down Broadway. His planes dropped 21-tons of theoretical bombs. When he landed on Long Island, he gave eager reporters details of the targets he had hit and the bombing.

The next day, the headlines of the *New York Herald* blared: CITY IN THEORETICAL RUIN FROM AIR RAID.[36] The newspapers flew off the newsstands, and everywhere readers waited to cross streets, sat on busses, or absentmindedly drank their morning coffee with their noses buried in the newsprint. The picture Mitchell had painted was grim:

> The sun saw, when its light penetrated the ruins, hordes of people on foot, working their way very slowly and painfully up the island. A few started with automobiles but the masses of stone buildings barricading the avenues soon halted their vehicles. Rich and poor alike, welded together in a real democracy of misery, headed northward. They carried babies, jewel cases, bits of furniture, bags, joints of meat and canned goods made into rough packs . . . bodies lay like revelers overcome in grotesque attitudes . . . the majority had died swiftly of poison gas.[37]

Mitchell was not through. His virtual bombing attacks continued on Philadelphia, Wilmington, Baltimore, and the Naval Academy at Annapolis. At every stop, the reporters were there to create the horrific headlines and stories for the next day.

Later that summer, a second bombing test was conducted. "We were given another battleship to practice on," said Mitchell. "It was the *Alabama*. She was towed into about thirty-five feet of water near Tangier Sound in the Chesapeake Bay. This time we went in to sink her as quickly as possible. . . . The first two thousand pound bomb did its work, she sank to the bottom in thirty seconds."[38]

There was a lot of breast-beating, excuse-making, and alibis from the Navy. But to Mitchell, he had proven that the battleship was a dinosaur, and a very expensive dinosaur. Over four thousand planes could be had for the cost of one of these great ships.[39] But to the unconvinced Navy, the battleship was, and would remain, the backbone of the fleet. To Mitchell, that backbone should be another vessel—one that did not look formidable at all, and not nearly as expensive: the submarine.

Mitchell wrote that in the last war, despite their grandness, surface ships had little impact. They were mostly used for transportation and patrol. Did anyone realize that during the entire course of the war, "no battleship sank another battleship," or that of the 134 ships sunk or destroyed during WWI, submarines sank 70 of them? Why was the submarine being ignored as the deadly weapon that it had proven to be? It far eclipsed the prowess of battleships.

"They sank the British battleship *Audacious*," he continued, "the British cruiser *Hampshire* with Lord Kitchener on board, the American cruiser *San Diego* off Fire Island near New York, and nearly sank the American battleship *Minnesota* off the mouth of the Delaware River.[40]

"Aircraft have great difficulty in attacking and destroying submarines at sea," Mitchell said. "They are very hard to detect, dive with great rapidity and are very difficult to see under water. The effect of air power on submarines is probably less than on any other target."[41]

To Mitchell, the Navy had, in worshiping its history and traditions, blinded itself to reality and to what was necessary to now defend the nation. He adamantly proclaimed that battleship power was gone. "Only a few nations still maintain it," he said. "If an attempt is made to use it in future, it will be so menaced by aircraft from above and submarines from underneath that it will be much more of a military liability than an asset."[42]

The explosions that had crushed the lineup of target ships, especially the *unsinkable Ostfriesland,* had also broken the backs of the previous theories championed by hardnosed military and political mindsets. During the backslapping among the Mitchell supporters and the opposite excuse-making among the Navy's brass, reality set in and there was a seismic shift in attitudes. Few verbally credited Mitchell with changing hardened hearts, but actions spoke very much louder than words.

No better example could be presented than that of Utah's Sen. William King—an avid pacifist, backed by religious and other groups that favored what amounted to unilateral disarmament. On the floor of the Senate, King had previously railed against Navy appropriations that included expenditures to develop a naval base on Guam, and he vociferously opposed the building of two aircraft carriers. His side had demanded an arms conference between the big three (Britain, U.S., and Japan) to move toward a disarmament agreement and, if necessary, unilateral disarmament. Despite tremendous Republican opposition, King and the Democrats, for the most part, had carried the day in Congress. In a final House vote, the pacifists managed to strip the two carriers from the bill and eliminated funds necessary to develop the base on Guam.

That political victory, however, was short-lived. Mitchell's bombings changed it all. Recognizing an impending defeat, the left-leaning *New York Times* suddenly lamented, "Who will now defend the actions of the House in striking from the Senate bill the appropriation for two carriers?"[43] The newspaper realized that Mitchell's successes had converted the House's recent political victory into a very large albatross firmly hung around the Democrats' necks.

And Senator King, ever the politician, became anxious to at least partially distance himself from his previous, nonsensical disarmament mindset. Recognizing the impact of Mitchell's spectacular results, he moved quickly to soften the shift in public opinion and introduce a bill that would "convert" two battle cruisers into carriers. But he made sure that there was face-saving incorporated in his bill: he also proposed to scrap the construction of three battle cruisers and six battleships that had previously been approved.

And Navy Secretary Denby suddenly found his voice and left-handedly recognized Mitchell's air success. He said, "The fleet must at all times be accompanied by airplanes for offensive and defensive purposes." Later on, the General Board itself let it be known that it wanted to start construction of three carriers, which it labeled as "absolutely essential."[44]

But Mitchell's victory over the naysayers was significantly tainted when the Joint Army and Navy Board issued its formal findings the following month. It stated that nothing conclusive concerning air power had been proven. Acknowledging that airplanes were a valuable auxiliary, the Board's conclusion came down on the side of tradition. The battleship was "still the backbone of the fleet and the bulwark of the nation's sea defense."

Several members of the Army and Navy were the authors of the report and had prepared its final form, but curiously none of the authors' names appeared on it. There was but one signature: Gen. John J. "Black Jack" Pershing.

Maj. Hap Arnold said, "The press and members of Congress snorted at this verdict."[45]

* * *

Mitchell's zeal did not end with the ship-sinking tests. He continually sought to find uses for air power; it didn't have to be war. He took on every subject that the airplane could possibly influence. Nothing escaped his keen eye, and he even suggested waging aerial warfare to benefit America's farmers. "Some of our fruit trees have been attacked by various parasites," he said, "and we have successfully sprayed the trees from the air and eliminated the insect and parasitic pests. Locusts and boll weevils can be destroyed."[46]

The airplane, he predicted, could influence life in general. Take for instance, the matter of rain. "Many interesting experiments have been conducted along that line to show that fogs can be eliminated and that the clouds can be made to deposit their moisture in the form of rain."[47]

These, like many of his other ideas and predictions, would find residence in the "Flying Trash Pile."

Chapter 5

Crying in the Wilderness

Billy Mitchell was not new to the art of predicting. After the air tests in 1921, he had become a household word. But long before then, he had developed a penchant and dexterity for seeing into the future and predicting the course of events. In 1911, as an unknown Capt. Billy Mitchell, he had embarked on a two-year inspection tour of Japan, China, and Manchuria to find what might be hidden from American eyes in those far-flung places. One could correctly label it a "spy" mission, and he photographed what he could and took notes on everything else.

So when he returned in 1913, he dutifully filed a thorough report with the War College Division of the General Staff. It included a stern warning that "increasing friction between Japan and the United States will take place in the future . . . and that this will lead to war sooner or later." He added that in such a war, America's recently acquired possessions, Guam and the Philippine Islands would be in great peril.[1]

Presumably this important report was read. It later became part of the War College papers deposited in the National Archives. But read by whom? It seems to have been more shunned than read. It was never used as part of a War Department study, nor was there a call for papers to either support or refute Mitchell's conclusions. There was no symposium convened to discuss its content. There is simply nothing official or unofficial to be found referencing his 1913 report—except one. A tiny word has been preserved that could conceivably be labeled an *unofficial* comment. Crudely scribbled in the margin of a page, next to Mitchell's dire Japanese predictions and warnings, is the single word "Arse."[2] That solitary word perhaps perfectly described the absolute naivety of all who dismissed Mitchell and his warnings of a Far Eastern threat.

But what about this Far Eastern threat? Just what had Japan done during the war? Had she not been allied with the winning side? Had she not been a comrade in arms with the United States? There is no doubt that her entry into the war was due to her alliance with Great Britain; but since the war was not fought at sea, which was Japan's great strength, she was virtually free to be part of the winning team without any sacrifice. There were no Japanese troops in the trenches in France or charging across deadly fields in no man's land. There was no mobilization of the Japanese nation or economy.

In fact, Japan *volunteered* to enter the war against Germany with the proviso that she was allowed to seize German-held territory in the Pacific. The British, totally focused on the conflict in Europe, readily accepted the offer to clear German ships that were operating in the waters near China. Historian Edwin Hoyt wrote: "The Japanese were delighted to do so because it gave them new opportunity to seize territory. It took only two months . . . to seize the German colony of Kiaochio in China's Shantung Province . . . then [they] moved into the German Pacific colonies. They took the Marianas Islands and the Marshalls without much trouble . . . and moved into the Caroline Islands."[3]

That was virtually the end of Japan's participation and they cruised the waters of their ever-expanding empire. But Japan was not done with seizing opportunities. They struck again while the iron was hot, and with the world's attention fixed on the trenches in the fields of France, they moved to colonize the biggest prize of all: China.

In 1915, they presented their "Twenty-One Demands" to China. Their attempt to take over China was not concealed or even thinly veiled. It was an outright power move. They demanded, among other things, a ninety-nine-year lease on southern Manchurian railroads and economic control of Manchuria and all former German rights in Shanghai; and China would have to give them economic control of certain mines and employ *Japanese advisors* to the Chinese government.[4] The overwhelmed Chinese, seeing the enemy at their doorstep, surrendered; and the seemingly impossible Japanese vision of total Asian-Pacific empire became possible.

* * *

In 1924, six years after WWI and nine years after Japan's Pacific power grab, the troop ship *Thomas* plowed through those Pacific waters from Nagasaki toward the United States. General Mitchell bent to his new task—yet another report. He carefully composed this one, detailing his new findings from his latest "spy" mission to the Far East. The depth and breadth of his travels was staggering and included inspections of all U.S. possessions in the Pacific as well as lengthy stops in Java, Singapore, India, Siam (present-day Thailand), China, and, most importantly, Japan.

The War Department had specifically ordered him to not visit Japan in any official capacity lest it aggravate "strained relations" over immigration policies. Not to be stymied by official orders, Mitchell made it his business to visit Japan *unofficially:* as a "tourist" with his new wife.[5] Japan's wounded pride over immigration exclusion was never far from the Japanese diplomatic front, but to most Americans, including Mitchell, this was a straw-man argument: one designed to foster a concocted and feigned indignation.

How could the world's most closed and abusive society claim, with a straight face, that their national pride had been wounded and offended? They barred any non-Japanese entry into their own country. And if a foreigner somehow managed to gain entry, that offending party could expect nothing short of enslavement, imprisonment, humiliation, and even death. Innocent shipwrecked sailors that washed up on Japanese shores, were promised that same terrible fate. Even their own citizens who might have unwittingly wandered from Japan's shores, or found themselves marooned in a foreign country because of a shipwrecking storm, were shunned, banished, and threatened with death should they ever dare to return. Although Commodore Perry had pried open that closed Japanese door in the middle of the nineteenth century, the Japanese *exclusive* mentality was still as strong as ever in the twentieth century.

Among the vast majority of Americans who scoffed at Japan's "wounded pride" mantra, Mitchell was most critical and blamed the whole contrivance on a willingly perpetuating Japanese press.

"The Japanese are now boiling over in the anti-American agitation," he fumed. "Its object is to see if America will be 'scared.'"[6] To him it was a massive deception. "The average Japanese knows no more about America than the farmer behind the Kansas plow knows about Manchuria. He has been told by his superiors that the national pride has been hurt."[7]

Mitchell noted that all the Japanese whining and posturing had been recognized as phony, not only by the average American but also by other Asian nations—especially China, who secretly reveled in Japanese missteps and stumbling. "The Chinese knew . . . that when Mr. Hanihara, the Japanese ambassador to Washington, announced to our State Department that 'GRAVE CONSEQUENCES' would follow an exclusion act, . . . the Japs had 'cooked their goose' with America."

That ill-advised Japanese diplomatic statement concerning *consequences* had indeed hurt their image; and their pride, for once, had legitimately been "mortally offended." They lost credibility and friends throughout the world. They had certainly not been able to stand and deliver on the bravado of their "grave consequences" threat, and the world recognized the hollowness of their claim. Billy Mitchell gloated, "The 'pride business' had a bad case of the 'jumps' on all occasions."[8]

But while the Japanese still practiced their own virtual exclusivity, Mitchell pointed out that it was exactly the opposite in the United States. "There are many more Japanese in American possessions than there are Americans in Japanese possessions." Those 250,000 Japanese were "protected by vested rights and free to circulate as they desire."[9]

This great perpetuation of the myth of American insults to Japan had been advanced not only by the Japanese but had been aided by America itself and by the reckless words of some of her duped diplomats. They seemed eager to apologize for any feigned Japanese offense.

"Unfortunately," said Mitchell, "our diplomatic representative in Japan handled our case very badly. When the matter of the exclusion laws came up, instead of maintaining a dignified attitude as the representative of the great American republic in Japan, he gave utterance to all sorts of puerile statements and complaints with the greatest publicity."[10]

This childish diplomatic pandering, breast-beating, and acquiescence to Japanese complaints had emboldened the Japanese to further press their case. They then claimed that congressional exclusion acts, and immigration laws, were actually contrary to the wishes of the majority of the citizens in the United States. That was certainly not the case since most Americans favored exclusion to protect tradition, culture, and jobs. But it all played well in the Japanese press, and their "pride business" remained their central military and political theme.

Mitchell thought that an opposite tactic should have been in order. Instead of diplomatic pandering and bowing to the cult of Japanese victimology, he favored a much tougher line, as if dealing with a posturing bully. "Japan needed stepping on badly and needs more of it. A little now will do a great deal of good in the future."[11]

He saw Japan not as a victim but as a very dangerous enemy and prominently wrote in his report, "She knows that war is coming some day with the United States, and it will be a contest of her very existence."[12] War with Japan would not be like war with a European enemy. Japan's centuries-old, closed societal mindset would make it virtually impossible for an adversary to penetrate her veil of secrecy with spies. There would be no double agents embedded in her ranks, while there would be many in America. And a war without intelligence on Japanese movements and intentions would be a war that the U.S. would fight in the dark.

Even during the Revolutionary War, George Washington continually sent agents behind enemy lines and saw to it that random travelers were questioned for useful details. During the Civil War, the Union Army was greatly assisted by what was called "Black Dispatches": intelligence furnished by runaway slaves or by other slaves when Southern lands came under Union control.

And the ancients knew very well the value of intelligence. In the sixth century B.C., the Chinese general and military strategist Sun Tzu wrote that if you are "ignorant both of your enemy and of yourself, you are certain in every battle to be in peril"; but "if you know the enemy and know yourself; in a hundred battles you will never be in peril."[13]

A more recent historian offered a fitting paraphrase: "A state that wages war without good intelligence is like a dim-sighted boxer who, even if he avoids losing, will suffer unseen blows a fighter with sure vision would likely have parried."[14]

Billy Mitchell knew all these intelligence maxims; but he also knew that the obvious intelligence-gathering tools that had been used in the past would hardly be useful, or even available, in a war with Japan. There would be no Japanese turncoats, nor shadowy Japanese citizens, crossing over in sympathy to the American side to compromise Japanese security. Their collective mindset was virtually homogeneous, and their long tradition of patriotic devotion precluded such actions.

In Japan's previous wars in which they crushed the Chinese in 1895 and the Russians in 1905, they always had the superior intelligence, and nothing ever leaked from their side to the enemy. In a future war with Japan, the United States would be very much at an intelligence disadvantage and could very well find itself as the dim-sighted boxer.

Conversely, there would be no need for the Japanese to infiltrate American society. They were already there, ingrained in all aspects of American living. They would be able to have an unobstructed view of life and activities in the United States and its territories. Mitchell noted: "When I inspected the defenses of the Hawaiian Islands in November and December, 1923, this could have been done with ease by Japan."[15]

But there was much more. The very nature, mystique, and intransigence of the Japanese, first encountered by Commodore Matthew Perry in 1853, made them a formidable adversary to the art of gathering intelligence. Mitchell wrote:

All of their people are instructed from their earliest childhood not to divulge anything of a military nature to foreigners. This is carried absolutely to extremes and results in the attitude of the Japanese . . . of avoiding issues, equivocating, and downright misrepresentation. On the other hand, the greatest stress is laid on the gaining of information from the other person. . . . The Japanese that will come into your office, will note every picture on the wall, will note all the buttons on your clothes, and will report on the most trivial things. This gaining of information of all foreign matters and concealing their own activities is a long established practice with them.[16]

Mitchell reasoned that there were "two schools of thought in Japan" regarding how to take military action against the United States.[17] But despite their differences, both schools agreed that America should be exterminated commercially, diplomatically, and militarily in the Far East. The Japanese reasoned that, by default, if the Americans got stronger, Japan would get weaker; and sooner or later, the Americans would conclude that any great Asian military force would be a threat to American interests, especially to, "Anglo Saxon" destiny in the Pacific. "Therefore," Mitchell predicted, "sooner or later, they must fight. The only question is how, when, and where?"[18]

Both opposing factions of Japanese military thought agreed on one other thing: when war came, it must be fought close to Japanese shores, where an invading American armada would surely be destroyed. But one faction wanted that war immediately. They were for using some concocted provocations that were sure to annoy the Americans. They envisioned the U.S. countering such provocations and moving to strengthen its possessions in the Philippines. Japan would then counter that move as if reacting to an American *threat*. That would become "a pretext . . . to declare that the United States had violated existing treaties."[19]

Their next card to play would be to dramatically declare to the world that Japan needed to take appropriate actions for self-defense. Hopefully all this would escalate into the war they really wanted, and their best chance for a sudden decisive clash—and victory—while America was still downsizing her armed forces after World War I.

The other side was not as confident and calculated that while Japan might gain some initial successes, "a prolonged war with America would mean her ultimate doom."[20] The time was not yet right. Mitchell had observed, during his visit to Japan, that aviation, submarines, and light cruisers were at the top of the Japanese preparedness list. Their navy was one of the most powerful in the world—certainly the most powerful in the Pacific Ocean. While Japan was on a footing consistent with preparing for war, the U.S. was not. The United States was more concerned with turning away from the horrors of the last war and scaling down her armed forces. There was no thought to prepare for a future war.

"The [Japanese] air development is clothed with more secrecy . . . ," said Mitchell, and "has many more men, more machines, and more factories working in her air force . . . than has the United States."[21] In fact, the Japanese had a threefold advantage in those fields as compared to the U.S.

If Mitchell's strategic and tactical predictions that air power would dominate the battlefield in future wars were right, then America's *air inferiority* placed her at an extreme disadvantage. "The United States must not render herself completely defenseless by thinking that a war with Japan is an impossibility," cautioned Mitchell, "and . . . by sticking to methods and means . . . as obsolete as the bow and arrow is to the military rifle."[22] Not recognizing the supremacy of air power was akin to fighting with ancient weapons.

Also to be considered were the U.S. territories in the Pacific acquired after the Spanish-American War in 1898: Guam and the Philippines. When it came to protecting those far-flung possessions, the penchant to embrace backward military thinking would be most dangerous. It was more than a simple comparison of bows and arrows and rifles. A war there would be a matter of survival. Noting that the Japanese airways came menacingly, in a straight line, directly from Japan to Guam, Mitchell warned, "The only military element that could hold this island would be an air force at least one half as strong as the total air of Japan."[23] No such American force existed or was even in any stage of planning, and Guam's peril extended to the entire Philippines area.

To strategists, tacticians, and politicians who scoffed at the possibility of war with Japan, Mitchell offered sobering Japanese statistics. A quarter-million soldiers were already under arms, and another two million had been trained and were ready. Japan had the second-largest air force in the world, with upward of eight hundred planes "and the industry to maintain them."[24] But his voice was truly like the biblical voice crying in the wilderness.

Once in a while a likeminded voice could be heard. British aviation authority C. G. Grey said, "Japan is preparing for war on a grand scale." It mystified him that there was an American mindset of "pacifists, copperheads, pussyfoots, and the rest,"[25] determined to diminish U.S. air power.

A new war with Japan or any other first-class military power would be like no previous war—including the recently concluded Great War. There the world paraded through the trenches to launch human wave assaults across a no man's land in a four-year effort to break the opposing army. Flesh and bone had proven to be no match for quick-fire machine guns and massed artillery; and an entire generation had disappeared from the future populations of France, Germany, and Great Britain.

In Mitchell's future war, there would be no trenches. "The world will be the theatre of operations," he said. The fields of fighting and devastation "will extend to all parts of the country that is forced to take the defensive."[26]

So how was this inevitable war with Japan to begin, and where was the United States most vulnerable to enemy attack? Of all the stops on his Pacific tour to inspect aviation capabilities, Mitchell said, "the air forces in Hawaii were by far the poorest that I inspected in any country."[27]

The scheme of defense of the Hawaiian Islands had been for the garrison at Oahu to hold on until reinforcement could arrive from the mainland. That in itself was a tall order, but that defense applied exclusively to protecting the island of Oahu. The rest of the vast island chain was unguarded. Should an enemy seize any of the other islands and establish a base with air assets, the Oahu station "would be destroyed in three or four days."[28]

These other inhabited islands in the Hawaiian group extended to the northeast for 300 miles, a long trip for ships but a short flying distance for aircraft. Mitchell especially noted the tiny island of Niihau, almost unnoticed as the most northern of the islands, just to the west of Kauai. He saw it as the first steppingstone of a series of small islands and reefs that formed the path directly to Midway, 1,100 miles to the west. All along the way, these seemingly insignificant islands were perfectly suited for observation and radio stations but, most importantly, for use as landing fields and airdromes.[29]

In any operation where Japan would have determined to reduce Oahu's defenses or seize the Hawaiian Islands, Mitchell envisioned her to embark ten submarines, each loaded with six pursuit or fighter aircraft in deck crates. Once loaded, this submarine force would head for Niihau. Additionally, two sea transports, modified with flattop decks, each carrying fifty bombers, would head for Midway. Both flotillas would arrive at their destinations on the same day.[30]

The submarines, landing at Niihau, would be virtually undetected, since the island had less than 150 inhabitants and no means of communication other than by a messenger in a boat. It would be reasonable to expect that the first indication of the Japanese presence at Niihau, and the danger to Honolulu, would be the actual attack when the planes arrived over Oahu. If any help was needed it was reasonable to expect assistance from the numerous Japanese sampans that routinely plied the waters around the Hawaiian Islands.

The 100 bombers delivered to Midway would have been configured with extra fuel tanks for the eleven-hour flight to Niihau—easily within their sixteen-hour cruising range. Once there, and joined with the sixty fighters, the combined air fleet could attack and destroy American defenses at Oahu. Simultaneously, far across the Pacific, Japanese forces would seize Guam; and now deprived of support and supply, the neighboring Philippines would die on the vine in short order.

The attack force from Niihau would make the short 150-mile flight to Oahu to deliver a forty-minute attack. It would all be over in less than four hours, well within the four-and-a-half-hour fuel range of the fighters and the six-hour range of the bombers. The first target would be Ford Island, in the middle of Pearl Harbor, with all of its airdromes, hangars, and ammo dumps. Next would be the Navy's fuel tanks, and water supplies at Honolulu and Schofield Barracks, followed by polishing off the submarine station. All the bombs would be large: 300 pounds. That translated into seventy-five tons of bombs per attack delivered against the surprised and panicked Americans. The bombs would not be solely high explosive; there would be a combination, including mustard and phosgene gas bombs.

When the initial attack was over, the strike force would rendezvous over Barbers Point for the return flight to Niihau to prepare for a second strike. It would be possible to stage three strikes a day, every day, until Oahu would collapse from the air siege that would also prevent its relief. It was all very obvious to Billy Mitchell. How the American political and military leaders could not recognize the peril was beyond him. The Oahu defense was only designed to prevent a hostile seaborne landing across the beaches.[31]

"If it is considered that a hostile force can land on the island of Oahu," said Mitchell, "think how very easy it is to land on the island of Niihau, how easy it is to make it an operating point for aircraft, and how easy it is to prepare it for defense against water or land attack. Actually nothing can stop it except air power."[32] Mitchell even envisioned when such an attack would be made: *"[It is] to be made on Ford's Island at 7:30 A.M."*[33]

To Mitchell, there would be an almost simultaneous attack on the Philippines, similar to the attack on Oahu. Clark Field would be bombed, as well as Manila, Cavite Navy Yard, and Manila water supply. Munitions would consist of a combination of high explosive, phosgene, and mustard gas bombs. The time? *"Clark Field bombed at 10:40 A.M."*[34]

Chapter 6

Niihau: The Forbidden Island

The history of the tiny island of Niihau closely paralleled that of the other five islands in the Hawaiian chain. In 1778, it was visited by Capt. John Cook, quite by accident, after he had first sighted Oahu. An unfavorable wind blew him to the northwest and to the shores of Kauai and Niihau. Like on the other islands, its society was influenced by ruling families, feudal lords, white missionaries, and royal unification efforts—particularly by King Kamehameha. The people who worked the island lands were illiterate and had no ownership.

That all began to change in 1830, when the Great Mahele was proposed by Kamehameha III in an attempt at land reform. By 1850 it was a reality and commoners who worked the land could petition for title to that land—much like the American homesteading laws. But the bureaucracy requirements, fees, and literacy necessary to navigate through the legal maze left most Hawaiian lands unclaimed by those working them; and that void opened the door for foreign investment and foreign land ownership. The promise of capitalism soon found great plantations, especially sugar, and other ventures springing up on the islands. The occupants of Niihau longed for their lands to be surveyed and bought. But the desert-like terrain did not attract buyers, who saw no venture worthy of their investment capital.

Unlike her five sister islands, Niihau was not the lush, green paradise where everything grew in profusion. Just twenty miles to the east, Niihau's neighboring island, Kauai, was the wettest place on the face of the earth and was constantly verdant and brilliant

97

with colorful flowers. Dramatic waterfalls cascaded down its sheer mountain drop-offs and highlighted the abundance of water.

But those high, cloud-piercing mountains on Kauai were the very curse to Niihau. Those lofty peaks acted as a giant sponge and grabbed all the moisture from the dark rainy clouds that rode in on the trade winds. The result was that Niihau was parched and often drought-ridden. Its landscape was deceiving. From Kauai, Niihau looked to also be mountainous, but it was a misleading image. While the sheer cliff on its eastern shore jutted up to a substantial height, it was merely a false front. It was as if the island gods had draped an impenetrable curtain to conceal Niihau's true arid flatness from view from the lush paradise of Kauai. So the Niihauans continued to live as before—almost isolated, working the king's land with no means to pay the king's rent. Niihau was a burden to everyone.[1]

A Hawaiian historian once wrote, "Just across the channel on Kauai, rain, trapped in high mountains, was superabundant, but the same mountains cast a rain shadow over Niihau, and natives there had to depend on small catchments and wells that yielded only brackish water."[2]

So the Great Mahele that brought a degree of prosperity to the rest of the Hawaiian Islands bypassed Niihau, and its unwanted lands remained unwanted through the 1850s. Its small population remained ignorant and lived in relative poverty and obscurity. Even the most romantic optimist could not have imagined the sequence of events, already unfolding, that would bring Niihau not only out of obscurity, but directly into the path of WWII.

* * *

In August 1840, a forty-two-year-old Scotsman, Francis Sinclair, with his wife and six children, embarked with a larger party of other Scottish emigrants bound for a new life in New Zealand. He had bought a £100 entitlement for 100 country acres and one town acre whenever it would become available, and he was setting off to obtain it. The four-month ocean crossing was not in luxury, but their steerage accommodations were included in the entitlement price.[3] Their ship landed on December 27 in Wellington, where the enterprising Francis immediately bought a boat and went to work "till we get our place. So we shall not starve in the interim."[4]

While waiting for his land entitlement to be settled among never-ending paperwork and claims and counterclaims, Sinclair became impatient and took matters into his own hands. He sailed his family to Banks Peninsula on South Island and took up residence on the shore of an enticing inlet named Pidgeon Bay. Francis described his new home as "perhaps the sweetest spot in this favoured country"[5] and renamed the bay Sinclair Bay.

But Francis Sinclair was not long for this beautiful country. In 1846, while plying his cargo trade to Wellington, he and his son George, along with two other ship's hands, were lost at sea when his vessel foundered in the rough waters. In her grief, his wife, Elizabeth, took the rest of the family to live in Wellington but returned in 1849 to build a large home, which she named Craigforth. For the next fourteen years, the clan lived there with Elizabeth as the matriarch.[6]

In 1863, Elizabeth determined that her expanding family needed new horizons, and an opportunity to pick up stakes again presented itself when she was able to sell all of her land for timber holdings. In March, with almost £9,000 from the land sale, she and twelve family members, with some animals, furniture, and farming tools and equipment, boarded their three-masted ship, *Bessie*, and set sail for distant British Columbia.[7]

The three-month voyage found the family anchoring in Victoria, British Columbia (Vancouver Island)—a land most primitive compared to their previous home in New Zealand and best described as a fur-trading post. Elizabeth's inspection of possible farmland was most disappointing. Available land was heavily forested and before that land could be made ready for farming, the family would face the enormous task of forest removal. There was also the worrisome presence of a hostile Indian population.[8]

So the family reluctantly packed up again, certainly disappointed that their long sailing odyssey had led to nothing, and considered returning to New Zealand. But Elizabeth was intrigued by information of possible land dealings available in Hawaii and decided to visit the islands on the return voyage. On September 17, 1863, six months after having left New Zealand for greener pastures, the family ark sailed into the waters of Honolulu, on the island of Oahu. Their arrival at the port's primitive wharf created a surprising sight for the locals, and the wandering Sinclair clan was equally enamored by the vista of this lush tropical scene.

The port's chaplain "was surprised to find the trim barque with its large party on board, with a beautiful old lady at its head, books, pictures, work, even a piano, and all that could add refinement to a floating home, with cattle and sheep of valuable breeds in pens on the deck."[9]

The Honolulu society welcomed the sixty-three-year-old matriarch and her family as immigrants who could add much to Hawaiian life, and they were deemed by all to be worthy landholders. But the Great Mahele had sold many small parcels of land on Oahu, so putting together a large tract suitable for the Sinclairs was difficult.[10] However, this was not the case on the northwestern island of Niihau, where no one seemed able or willing to purchase the land. Two of Elizabeth's sons visited the island and were obviously impressed because, according to historian Syd Jones, "Niihau was in a rare rainy cycle, the dry lakes were full of water and the island was verdant in freshly grown grasses."[11]

So the Sinclairs offered $6,000 in gold for the whole island. King Kamehameha IV, not pleased with the offer, countered with $10,000. The family accepted, and the deal was sealed on January 23, 1864. But what the Sinclairs had actually bought was not quite the lush tropical paradise that it seemed to be. The island was in full bloom because of an extremely rare rainy season. In reality, "for just under twenty-two cents an acre, they got seventy-two square miles of land, mostly low-lying, hot and dry, sparsely wooded, and uncertainly watered,"[12] wrote Gavan Daws and Timothy Head.

The present-day owner of Niihau, Keith Robinson, lamented, "The clan could have had forests, and streams and salmon fishing, and a gold mine or two and endless lumber supplies in Vancouver. Instead, they came back and settled on a smoking piece of Kalahari Desert surrounded by salt water."[13]

So began the Sinclair story on Niihau. One of Elizabeth's daughters, Helen, arriving on the family ship, *Bessie,* in 1864, had been divorced from her husband, Charles Robinson. But she traveled with ten-year-old son Aubrey, who would grow up on Niihau, earn a law degree in Boston, and travel the world extensively. He would become the heir apparent, and by the time his grandmother Elizabeth died in 1893, he indeed took control of the family's estate and business.[14]

His resourcefulness seemed boundless. His mind was filled with ideas and inventions. He directed massive irrigation projects and tree renewal on Kauai, and on Niihau he introduced and endless variety of plants and animals: "the first Arabian horses ever seen in Hawaii, game birds, coffee, tea, honey bees, cotton, and several new varieties of trees."[15] By 1924, Aubrey went into semiretirement and passed control of the island to his equally talented and forward-looking son, Aylmer.

* * *

It was just such an imaginative and resourceful person as Aylmer Robinson that Gen. Billy Mitchell would have approached during his 1923 inspection of the Hawaiian Islands. We know from his writings that he detailed the tactical usefulness of each and every one of them. That there was a meeting with Aylmer Robinson is beyond doubt, but that meeting has been shrouded in mystery for over ninety years.

Aylmer Robinson was not a recluse. His island of Niihau might have been restricted to outsiders, but he was not. His family had vast landholdings on Kauai, and he would have been most accessible to Mitchell as the general fleshed out his report on islands that would be useful to the Japanese in a future attack on Oahu. Mitchell's accuracy in his report on the terrain on Niihau suggests the sort of detailed input that Robinson could have offered. Mitchell was certainly a well-known military authority that Aylmer Robinson would have met with if Mitchell had sought a meeting. Mitchell's background proved that he left no stone unturned when seeking details. But any record of this meeting is lost behind an impenetrable veil of secrecy.

"If you want to talk about forward-looking men," said Keith Robinson,

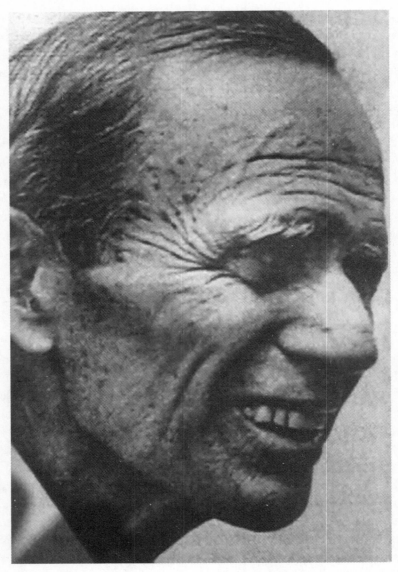

Aylmer Robinson, the owner and lord of the island of Niihau.
(Keith Robinson Collection)

"my father and Uncle Aylmer were the men that teamed up with the Mitchell faction to anticipate the attack on Pearl Harbor. My father once made an unguarded comment to me, not realizing the significance, that as soon as the Japanese occupied Midway, they were coming to Niihau. That was the original prediction; then he clammed up for several more decades."[16] The secret was back in the box.

Other events of World War II, such as the breaking of the German enigma code, the invasion of Normandy, and the development of the atomic bomb, have long since revealed their secrets with the passage of time and declassification of documents. But not so Niihau. The events that took place there from 1923 to 1941 remain grudgingly shrouded; and the participants involved with Gen. Billy Mitchell, and his daring predictions concerning Niihau and the beginning of the war with Japan, are all now dead—and they mostly went to their graves with their lips tightly sealed. Small glimmers of light occasionally seep out from under the shroud, and when they do, they add to a most remarkable story.

* * *

Mitchell's inspection of the Hawaiian Islands was the most detailed of all of his inspection stops. His rank and fame certainly opened doors to him, but the thoroughness of his inspection was nothing short of brilliant, as if he were a besieged military commander preparing for an attack from an enemy already camped on his doorstep. His analysis that the Japanese attack would originate from Midway and use an island-hopping path to gain control of a forward operating base was the result of painstaking inspections. If he were the enemy commander, he would have used Niihau from which to launch his devastating attack against Pearl Harbor. It was not theoretical to him; it was a matter of fact, having eliminated all other military possibilities to achieve that goal.

Mitchell had written in his report that from Midway, the Japanese would only be 1,100 miles from Niihau. The first steppingstone from Midway to Niihau was the tiny island of Lisianski, as obscure as its name would suggest. To the casual observer, this one-mile long by three-quarter-mile wide, flat sand and coral island was worthless. In 1805, its discoverer, Urey Lisiansky, wholeheartedly agreed, having literally *stumbled* upon the island and run aground. "This island promises nothing . . . but certain danger,"[17] he lamented in his journal.

It was hard for Billy Mitchell to disagree. "The entire island is a waste of loose sand, undermined by bird burrows." But his keen eye saw more, much more. "There is a level stretch, one half by three-quarter miles that is highly suitable for aeronautical use."[18]

He made similar observations on the next steppingstone, Laysan, 115 miles to the southeast. It was another tiny, useless, abandoned island—of some commercial interest; but that was long ago, and only in an age when men hunted for bird droppings to use as fertilizer. "The vegetation had been denuded by rabbits," Mitchell acknowledged, "but there remains a dock, a guano car tramway, freshwater well, and ample level space for an airdrome."[19]

Three hundred ten miles farther to the southeast was the large atoll of French Frigate Shoals. Its protected waters were perfect for an anchorage and refueling operations; and its largest island, Tern Island, was ideal for an airdrome made possible by its flat, 1,200-foot length.[20]

The final leap would be to Niihau, only 380 miles away. And to Mitchell, Niihau was the prize. It was nothing more than a "large sheep ranch with close cropped pastures," he wrote, but "plenty of airdrome space."[21] The fact that he either personally explored the island or had a trusted confidant do the exploring and surveying can be found in his report. He wrote: "Details of reconnaissance of islands: Niihau, Kaali Bay. Entire island forms on large sheep ranch. Airdrome sites are available in sheep pastures."[22] At no time, however, did he mention in his 1924 "confidential" report any meeting with Robinson, although he uses the word *reconnaissance*. Was it a map recon, or an aerial recon, or a physical walking of the grounds? He certainly knew the size of Niihau's population and even minute details about the island. Keith Robinson did not think that Mitchell ever came to Niihau to meet the Robinsons because "he was such a famous, well-known figure at that time, I think it would have been recorded."[23]

But secrecy had been the trademark of the Robinsons and would continue even unto death, and Mitchell obviously flew at his own discretion wherever he wanted. He had been directed by his orders to "inspect the Air Units and investigate the air activities in our Pacific possessions."[24] To think that Mitchell would have done less would not fit into his persona. In fact, his report recorded miniscule details that would not appear from just a casual inspection.

He noted that the five largest islands in the Hawaiian chain (Oahu, Hawaii, Kauai, Maui, and Molokai) had all recently established landing fields. A flyover, or casual observation, could discover those facts, but such a general inspection would not reveal that on Molokai, Mr. George Cooke had voluntarily run a water pipe to the field and voluntarily took care of storing the oil and gas. Nor would a casual inspection reveal that on Maui, Mr. William Clark had voluntarily cleared a large tract of land for the landing field; or that on Hawaii, civilian assistance was rendered in building the field.[25]

These details all indicate personal contact. Of the remaining islands in the chain, Niihau and Lanai, Mitchell noted that there were no airfields but also that these islands were of "strategic importance."[26] As such, he prepared detailed maps and charts, which he included as attachments to his inspection report.

The first chart, labeled "Airways" (Chart No. 14), copiously noted all the possible air locations and corresponding air assets to be placed on all the islands in the Hawaiian chain in preparation for a meaningful defense. Niihau was included in these notes: "Niihau field has no facilities, Ranch House, Weekly Boat Service."

The second, labeled "Diagram of Plan of Reconnaissance" (Chart No. 15), depicted a scheme of four interlocking circles of aircraft reconnaissance to cover the entire, 300-mile-long Hawaiian chain. No part of the islands or approaches to them would be shrouded from observation. Again, Niihau was included on that chart and designated as an "emergency landing field."

The third chart (Chart No. 11—Air Force Radio Net and Wire System), again included Niihau. It was designated as a "line of radio communications."[27]

It is logical to conclude that details on Niihau's importance could only have been noted after a close inspection. And since Niihau was a private island and could only be entered with permission from the owner, Mitchell without a doubt visited Aylmer Robinson, on Niihau or at his home on neighboring Kauai. It is improbable to conclude otherwise.

The arid island of Niihau was virtually isolated from the rest of the chain and the world in general. It bore the name "Forbidden Island," not only because of its private ownership that restricted travel and protected its pure Hawaiian population but because of its extreme isolated position and secrecy. It had instantly caught Mitchell's eye as a perfect staging area, and forward operating base, for a Japanese aerial strike against Pearl Harbor—a tantalizing 150 miles to the southeast.

The island "offered the most favorable position for an airdrome . . . Niihau had a population of one hundred and forty-eight," Mitchell wrote. "Submarine bombardment and sorties by landing parties" would easily secure Niihau. Then, "aircraft would be set up on level pastures near the beach," he continued. "Working parties would be covered by gunfire from the submarines. Any remaining hostile portion of the population would be subdued by air attacks and by garrisons landed for protection of the airdromes."[28]

Then with any luck, the occupying Japanese forces could pull off their invasion of Oahu undetected. Niihau was often shrouded in fog, and even when it was not, its high eastern cliff concealed the rest of the island from all observation from neighboring Kauai. Mitchell had laid out in detail just how the Japanese might approach, and once they were in striking distance, how they would attack. And their supply and communications lines, instead of being vulnerable, would be secure—all the way up the island chain to Midway. From there they were in contact with Tokyo by direct cable communications.

"The possession of Midway and Guam," warned Mitchell, "would give uninterrupted cable communication from Midway to Japan; and the whole Japanese base by way of both Guam and Yap. At the same time, the attack would sever communication over our own cables from Honolulu west to Guam and then to the Philippines."[29]

And every mile of those communications, after nullifying the U.S. fleet, would be easily protected by the powerful Japanese Navy. Could any commander ask for more? In the vastness of the Pacific Ocean, the Japanese would be impregnable. To Mitchell it was all so obvious.

The attack itself was to be the very model of simplicity. There would be no necessity for long-range patrolling to first find the enemy before he found you, and no far-flung targets to engage or multiple targets to overcome at scattered sites. Having to eliminate such targets required difficult coordination and communications. This was simple. The Japanese air forces would face a military operation no more complicated than attacking the concentrated buildings on New York's Manhattan Island.[30]

"The Island of Oahu," said Mitchell, "with its military depots, both naval and land, its airdromes, water supplies, the city of Honolulu with its wharves and supply points, forms an easy, compact and convenient object for air attack."[31] And without an opposing air force to contest the Japanese entrenched forces on and around Niihau, Oahu could be pounded into submission with continued attacks, as long as necessary, up to three times a day.

And what about a rescuing American force? Once Oahu capitulated, any American seaborne force, sailing to the rescue, would soon find it to be a futile effort. That force, no matter how strong, would be out on a limb and a lucrative target, subject to aerial interception and bombardment and underwater attack while still far out at sea.[32]

* * *

War Plan Orange evolved as the tactical and strategic plan to confront any Japanese attack against the United States, but it was especially designed to react to an attack against the Philippines and Guam. Many disparaged it using the words of William Shakespeare: *"full of sound and fury, signifying nothing."*[33]

But while many based their criticism on the fact that the plan would fail to prevent a surprise attack at Pearl Harbor, and the loss of Guam and the Philippines, it should be remembered that Orange was never a plan about defense. Orange was all about offense and the *offensive* tactics and strategy to crush Japan in the event of war.

Even at the outbreak of such a conflict, including a surprise attack, the stated goal of War Plan Orange was to inflict as much damage as possible during Japan's first strike—to make it so costly to the enemy that America's counteroffensive would be easier.

"The entire war against Japan might hinge on losses inflicted on the Japanese during their initial assault on the Philippines,"[34] said the Joint Planning Committee. Even from the opening shot of a future war, Orange was all about absorbing the first blow to enhance a counterattack. The order of importance to defend against such a first strike was: Hawaii, Manila, and Panama. Even if the Philippines were to fall in the early stages, "the Orange Plan provided for an advance by the fleet westward from Hawaii to Guam and Formosa without reference to the fate of the Philippines."[35]

Orange had been born in 1906, just seven years after the United States had moved into Japan's back yard by acquiring Guam and the Philippines from Spain after the war with Spain. War planners gamed multiple situations for future conflict with both allies and adversaries, and they color-coded the various nations: Blue was the U.S., Red was Great Britain, Black was Germany, Green was Mexico, and Orange was Japan.

Dozens of scenarios were considered over the years, but in the end it was always Blue against Orange, the United States and Japan, fighting in splendid isolation to a final showdown for domination in the Western Pacific. There would be no allies, nor would there be great land engagements pitting armies against armies. It would be a naval struggle across the 5,000 miles of ocean from Hawaii to the Asian mainland. Later, as air power materialized, it would be a naval/air contest. And why was this war so inevitable?

Historian Edward S. Miller said, "The root cause would be Japan's quest for national greatness by attempting to dominate the land, people, and resources of the Far East [while] America regarded itself as the guardian of Western influence in the orient."[36]

Eventually Japan would not be able to resist the urge to throw the invaders off their doorstep and would, in typical Japanese fashion, suddenly attack with all the force and vitality she could muster. She would easily sweep up the American possessions and then settle down to await the predicted American counterattack. She had no capabilities to sortie out across the thousands of Pacific miles to engage the American main battle fleet in the classic showdown she desired, so she would wait for the American fleet to come to her.

But to Japan, that was the ideal situation since she could marshal all her forces in her home waters and snipe at the American fleet with her submarines as it plowed across the ocean. Japan would be able to determine the battleground and the time, and when the American fleet finally arrived, it would step onto the battlefield like the boxer who had sustained many jabs to the face and was noticeably weakened. Japan would then finish off the opposing fleet in the grand style of the *big battle,* just as she had quickly disposed of the Chinese fleet in 1895 and the Russians ten years later.

And if for some reason Japan was not able to finish off the American fleet, she would engage it in a grueling, protracted struggle with the Americans dangling at the end of a very long supply line. An impatient American public would quickly tire of this far-flung venture and demand an end to it, and the ensuing peace terms would all be in Japan's favor.

For the Americans, the Blue team, it was all very straightforward and remarkably similar. After the original attack by Japan, Phase I, it was a matter of Blue superior naval and air power steaming out to that final showdown. Along the way, in Phase II, Blue would establish bases and supply lines, crush any harassment by Japanese raiders and snipers, and sweep aside Japanese island strongholds or bypass them. In a couple of years, Blue would reestablish its base in the Philippines. There they would begin the strangling blockade that would be the end of Orange. If the Japanese, in a last act of desperation, sortied out for the heroic showdown, Blue's superior battleships would decisively prevail.[37]

That would bring about Phase III: Blue advances toward the Japanese homeland and, from new bases, begins the air offensive that would systematically smash and destroy Orange's industries and cities until it sued for peace. It was this tactic that Billy Mitchell had called "total war." The big difference was that Mitchell had vocally called for it, thereby creating an uproar, while War Plan Orange simply penned it in the classified pages of its strategy to be used at a later date.

The damning problem with Phase III was that it glossed over the consequences of Phase II, and that was the obvious sacrifice and abandonment of Guam and the Philippines. Despite an original supposition and declaration that Manila defenders could hold out for sixty days awaiting relief, no one seemed to want to mention the fact that the *rescuing* fleet would not arrive on station for *one thousand days!* That all added up to the assumption of an initial, humiliating U.S. defeat. And who was going to tell the defenders of Guam and the Philippines that they had been written off?

In 1922, the governor general of the Philippines, Leonard Wood, got wind that War Plan Orange would sacrifice the Philippines. The former Army chief of staff and Roosevelt Rough Rider was outraged, and bitterly protested. "Such a policy of abandonment spells . . . national dishonor and the beginning of a retrogression which God alone can see the end of. Abandonment will be highly injurious to us abroad and far-reaching in its disintegrating and demoralizing effect upon our people."[38]

In 1924, Gen. Billy Mitchell painted a gloomy picture for the Philippines. "The mission of United States forces in the Philippines would be to prevent their capture until the arrival of military forces. This would require some four months, if it were not entirely stopped by the Japanese."[39]

During that same year, War Plan Orange had thrown off defensive considerations that some planners had attempted to tag it with and returned to its original offensive posture, which was "seek the initiative in all operations."[40]

This led to a 1925 strategy to sail the entire fleet by the fourteenth day of hostilities (Z+14) in a mad dash across the Pacific, straight to Manila. It was called "The Through Ticket to Manila." It anticipated the 554 vessels of the fleet with its 300 aircraft and 72,000 troops racing nonstop across the 5,000 miles of ocean, refueling at sea, on a path that took it south of Midway and then north of Marcus Island.

That track would have avoided all Japanese-held islands until it became necessary to steam close to Iwo Jima. As the mighty fleet passed that danger area, it would put out flank security as a protective screen. Once clear of Iwo Jima, the only other danger area would be on the final leg between Formosa and the Philippines, where flank security would again be deployed. Then it would be a simple matter of a safe arrival into Manila Bay.

All this was anything but simple. In fact, it was all absurd and dangerously ambitious. It was the stuff of fantasy and wishful thinking, more suited to the movements of pieces on a children's board game where a sweep of the hand moved toy ships thousands of miles in an instant. It was, as historian Edward Miller labeled it, "a preposterous cavalry charge across the Pacific."[41]

Mitchell certainly was aware of each iteration of War Plan Orange, even though he never called it by name. Presumably he had spread the charts out on a table, just as he had studied the model of Saint-Mihiel in the French school building during the Great War. It would not have taken him long to conclude that the plans of the Blue Fleet to counter the strategy of the Orange Fleet were possible only if there indeed was a Blue Fleet.

But what if there was no Blue Fleet at Pearl Harbor? What if the Blue Fleet had been severely damaged or destroyed in a first strike by the enemy? Mitchell had preached the consequences of a first-strike tactic to all who would listen and, in 1924 he had written his prophetic words, "Attack to be made on Ford's Island at 7:30 A.M." He had imagined the unimaginable: a crushed Blue Fleet at the beginning of war.

Mitchell had seen what only one other man had dared to see: an attack on Pearl Harbor itself. Rear Adm. William Fletcher had carried his own message to the Navy in 1919. He warned, "Sea planes brought by swift carriers . . . could rise from the lee of the nearest reefs to the northwestward and westward, on the neighboring islands or from the sea itself, sweep down on Pearl Harbor and destroy the plant unless adequate defense is provided."[42]

Those *nearest reefs* to which Fletcher referred included the island of Niihau, as well as the entire line of islands, which Mitchell later pinpointed, running from Midway southeasterly to Hawaii. All the other planners routinely ignored this possible invasion route and specifically eliminated a cross-ocean, Japanese attack except in the unlikely event that Japan would be aligned with Great Britain.

That mythical alliance was labeled War Plan Red/Orange.[43] In the dozens of iterations and progressions of War Plan Orange, such a cross-ocean attack was never once envisioned where Japan would be the single adversary. It was axiomatic among all the planners that the Japanese fleet would never dare exit its home waters. When the Blue Fleet moved to Pearl Harbor in mid-1940, those planners became more convinced than ever that Orange would keep its ships at home.[44]

War Plan Orange would remain the cornerstone of American strategy until the specter of Hitler could no longer be ignored. Then Orange was replaced by a series of vague war contingency plans labeled Rainbow—the final modification entitled War Plan Rainbow 5.

It assumed the first priority in any war would be to conduct limited action to safeguard the homeland and the "Monroe Doctrine" territory. Once that was accomplished, then the U.S. would commit to Europe and Africa, in conjunction with military allies, to confront the fascist threats. A close examination of its wordy assumptions reveals that Rainbow 5 was more a laundry list of possibilities and assumptions relating to friendly and enemy alignments. It was hardly a definitive plan.

> That the Associated Powers, comprising initially the United States, the British Commonwealth (less Eire), the Netherlands East Indies, Greece, Yugoslavia, the Governments in Exile, China, and the "Free French" are at war against the Axis Powers, comprising either:
> a. Germany, Italy, Romania, Hungary, Bulgaria, or
> b. Germany, Italy, Japan, Romania, Hungary, Bulgaria, and Thailand.[45]

Rainbow 5 further stated, "If Japan does enter the war, the Military strategy in the Far East will be defensive . . . but will employ the United States Pacific Fleet offensively in the manner best calculated to weaken Japanese economic power."[46]

Rainbow 5 was hardly the specific plan that Orange had been, which had focused on the immediate offensive. Orange had called for *confrontation*, followed by *attacking*, and a final *vanquishing* of the Orange forces. It was very specific.

During all the stages of military planning, in the shifting from Orange to Rainbow 5, the one thing that remained constant was that no one, other than Mitchell and his cohorts, acknowledged the possibility of the cross-ocean attack by Japan alone. War Plan Orange went into hibernation.

Chapter 7

The Flying Trash Pile

General Mitchell and his wife landed in San Francisco after their nine-month Pacific sojourn during the first week of July 1924. The world to which they returned was not quite the same world they had left in 1923. One of Mitchell's many warnings about conflict with Japan had already come true. The Japanese penchant to continually foment unrest and anti-American propaganda was again in the news. Once again it was over "insults" that tended to whip up emotional demonstrations among the people back in the homeland.

The West Coast Asian immigration problem that had existed since 1907 had resurrected to a new level of unrest. Back then the "Gentlemen's Agreement" had sidestepped San Francisco's school exclusion of Japanese and saved the day for the U.S. Open Door policy. For the most part, both sides kept their word—the Japanese limited their flood of immigrants, and the U.S. kept the door open.

But now the American Congress decided to close that door. Predictably the Japanese were outraged. Somehow the Chinese were not, and they remained stoic on the issue. That Japanese indignation had always irked Billy Mitchell, and knowing the hypocrisy and history of their own closed-door policies, he had written, "Japan needed stepping on badly, and needs more of it."[1]

In 1924, the U.S. Senate seemingly had similar thoughts and voted to pass the Immigration Act of 1924, which was incorrectly labeled the Japanese Exclusion Act. The Asian exclusion provisions of that law had been attached to the bill as an amendment. Eventually,

Pres. Calvin Coolidge signed it into law in May 1924, with the Asian exclusion amendment.

During the senatorial debates on the bill, Japanese ambassador Hanihara Masanao had frantically lobbied against it. He emotionally appealed to Secretary of State Charles Evans Hughes, who personally opposed the act, but to no avail. Americans reacted to what they saw as an odious spread of the Red Scare in Europe after the Bolshevik Revolution had toppled the Royal House in Russia. Atheistic Communism became the new totalitarian evil seeking world domination. It was the perfect opportunity for Americans, also perceiving the danger of an Asian invasion along the West Coast, to rise up in protest.

The clear aim of this immigration law had been to restrict an East Coast invasion of immigrants from Southern and Eastern Europe. The news of the times that was being flashed all across the length and breadth of America was frightening. Had not Americans just spent their treasure and blood on the fields of France to end the Great War, and was that not all about the penchant of Europeans to never get along? Had not George Washington warned to avoid entangling foreign alliances? Now they were at it again, and this time it seemed to be heading in an even worse direction. The murderous Russian Communists were on the march, and a new dangerous political party was on the rise in Germany, led by a radical named Adolf Hitler. In 1922, Benito Mussolini's Fascists had marched on Rome; the Greeks were fighting the Turks; and the German economy was in total collapse, opening the door to an anticipated totalitarian takeover. In 1914, four German marks had equaled an American dollar; in 1923, that same dollar was worth four trillion German marks.[2]

America's longed-for *tranquility* was slipping away and hardly to be found anywhere; and most Americans perceived that all this stemmed from the ill-advised, open-door welcoming of undesirables from nations who knew nothing about freedom or who contrived to take it away from those who did. If Europeans wanted to forever fight one another, then let them. To the average American, they all richly deserved each other. Isolationism was the popular mindset.

The Asian exclusion, attached to that 1924 Immigration Act, had also restricted anyone who was *ineligible* for citizenship, and that included the Japanese.[3] Only six senators voted against the bill as it passed with overwhelming support. But in Ambassador Hanihara's frustration, he issued an ill-advised warning to the United States that there would be "grave consequences." After that verbal faux pas, many attributed the final overwhelming support for the bill to senatorial outrage over Hanihara's remarks.[4]

There is little evidence to support such a conclusion, but true or not, it definitely set the stage for a spirited rebuttal. Democratic senator Ellison DuRant Smith of South Carolina, nicknamed "Cotton Ed," took to the Senate floor to express his extreme displeasure with Hanihara and his thinly veiled threat. Smith was the perfect example of the isolationist mindset of the day.

To him, enough was enough. Why should Americans be threatened by the representative of a nation that had routinely practiced the art of excluding everyone from its own territory while routinely invading others?

In 1922, Japan's practices were well known by all. Isaac Marcosson, a contributing writer to the *Saturday Evening Post*, said, "Japan's open-door policy meant open to her and closed to all others."[5] That Japanese notoriety had generally been known to the whole world for centuries and was revealed in detail in the reports of Commodore Matthew Perry after his 1853 Japanese expedition.

Japan's problem was land. She had the problem of "a growing population upon a restricted area . . . and a stationary food supply."[6] She could allow no one in and needed to export goods and people out. A famous Japanese quotation used to condone her use of force to occupy neighboring lands was: "We must starve in saintly righteousness, or move into our neighbor's back yard."[7]

As a staunch advocate of her own closed doors, Japan again demanded an American opened door. When she didn't get her way, her ambassador dared to threaten American policy. Well, Sen. Ellison DuRant "Cotton Ed" Smith was having none of that and, with practiced bombast, bellowed out from the Senate floor:

> The time has arrived when we should shut the door. We have been called the melting pot of the world. We had an experience just a few years ago, during the great World War, when it looked as though we

had allowed influences to enter our borders that were about to melt the pot in place of us being the melting pot.[8]

There was no mincing of words. Smith thought that immigration should not include those from the lesser nations that had mostly been under ruling masters and accustomed to political servitude. And he recognized that not all nations were equal, nor were their people the same as all others.

"There is a dangerous lack of distinction between people of a certain nationality and the breed of the dog," he said.[9]

In Cotton Ed's estimation, a modern-day immigrant seeking the American dream should be more like those who came before him, "who cleared the forests, conquered the savage, stood at arms and won their liberty from their mother country, England.

"Let us keep what we have, protect what we have, make what we have the realization of the dream of those who wrote the Constitution," he said. "I think we now have sufficient population in our country for us to shut the door and to breed up a pure, unadulterated American citizenship."[10]

The rest of the senators agreed, all but six, and the majority added its own words of disdain for Hanihara and his bad manners: "no foreign nation has the right to influence the legislative action of the United States by a veiled threat."[11]

The damage was done. Hanihara resigned in disgrace, never to hold a public office again. But his disgrace had not been in vain, since his message was picked up by the agitating Japanese press. Ever sensitive to "insult," they created headlines that were nothing short of sensational. "SURGING ANTI-JAPANESE SENTIMENT MAKES REPUDIATION OF ACT HOPELESS."[12] Tokyo movie theaters suspended showing American films. War scare books rolled off the presses, to be eagerly consumed by the offended Japanese. They went so far as to declare July 1 as a "Day of National Humiliation."[13]

Through all these sensational Japanese theatrics, Billy Mitchell was amused. "The Chinese knew that when Mr. Hanihara announced that 'GRAVE CONSEQUENCES' would follow . . . the Japs 'had cooked their goose.'"[14] Mitchell wrote that Hanihara's actions had not elicited sympathy from other Asian nations but had brought down stinging ridicule on himself and all of Japan, while the more patient, stoic Chinese rose to the level of statesmanship by listening to and accepting the reasons for the U.S. action.

Hanihara's emotional outburst was emblematic of the Japanese proclivity to control freedom of thought and speech with the threat of punishment. Future Japanese laws enforced that control of thought with the threat of death. In its final totalitarian form, this hideous control over people's thought and expression was embodied in a law entitled: "Law for Protection Against and Surveillance of the Holders of Dangerous Thoughts."[15]

If anything was un-American, this was it. Americans who balked at being told how to lead their lives in any fashion were now being lectured to and threatened by Hanihara. He represented the country that would bring "dangerous thoughts" in American to heel, and all offenders would be summarily executed.

Despite obvious embarrassment, Japanese apologists still attempted to excuse Hanihara's words. He was only guilty of a verbal gaffe, they said. But an examination of the total Japanese mindset reveals that his threat was much more than a verbal gaffe. He had blurted out what he truly felt, and what the Japanese all felt and simply regarded as normal behavior. Any perceived insult to Japan was an insult to the emperor, and was to be dealt with in the sternest of fashions. Hanihara resigned not because he had misspoken, or was sorry for what he had said, but because he had failed in his mission to avenge the perceived insult to the emperor brought about by U.S. resistance to his wishes.

The *Japan Times and Mail* was quick to deflect blame from Hanihara and pointed the finger at the Americans for the whole crisis. The editors called the American senators "the exclusion Senators," and the newspaper went on to exonerate the ambassador and castigate the Americans: "The Senators were looking for some excuse to get angry, and insinuations and falsifications were so engineered as to entrap Ambassador Hanihara into committing himself with words such as could be turned into a most effective weapon by them."[16]

Notice that the Japanese editors did not condemn the ambassador for using the *wrong* words; it was all a matter brought about by *conniving* senators who had somehow *forced* Hanihara to use the *wrong* words. They had *forced* Hanihara "into committing himself with words" that were used as "weapons." None of this report was about reality. It was all about Japanese saving face, a trait long present in their very makeup.

The problem was that Hanihara had been caught in the practice of applying these Japanese principles of threats of retaliation not against a neighboring country that they could dominate and intimidate but against the United States Senate—and the likes of Sen. Ellison DuRant Smith and his cohorts.

Mitchell had correctly described Hanihara as a *cooked goose*, after uttering his inflammatory words. The resulting, sidestepping flurry of Japanese outrage in Tokyo was not unexpected. It was a long-practiced routine to make rebuff more palatable.

Hanihara's action was, in fact, a figurative form of *seppuku:* the ritual suicide by disemboweling as part of the bushido code. Historian Stephen Turnbull wrote, "In the world of the warrior, seppuku was a deed of bravery that was admirable in a samurai who knew he was defeated, disgraced, or mortally wounded. It meant that he could end his days with his transgressions wiped away and with his reputation, not merely intact, but actually enhanced."[17]

In Hanihara's case there was no bloody ritual of ripping open his abdomen and slicing the knife back. There was no excruciating minute of utter agony finally relieved by decapitation with the samurai's sword. But politically speaking, that is exactly what Hanihara did. He committed political seppuku, exited public life, and vanished into obscurity, as if he had never existed. His noble act of resignation, like ritual suicide, atoned for his failure to bring about the emperor's will.

* * *

This entire renewed immigration fight was very much emblematic of a new isolationism embraced by American citizens, and perhaps that isolationism blunted any military fervor to delve deeply into Mitchell's Pacific inspection report and its conclusions. Although he had completed it in October, there is evidence that by the spring of 1925, few had read or even seen it. One of his disciples, his ardent supporter Maj. Gerald Brant, had a copy of it, and that was only because Mitchell had given it to him.[18]

His own boss, Gen. Mason Patrick, had sidestepped the entire issue and did not note or comment on the report; and when asked why that was so, he offered the lamest of excuses. First he was sick; then he was considering other matters. "A reply will be delayed,"[19] was his only comment.

Despite numerous requests from the War Department that he review and comment, Patrick ignored it all. Finally after fifteen months, during April 1926, he acquiesced to the task. By any stretch of the imagination, his tardiness was inexcusable and smacked of deliberate foot-dragging, especially since it was he who had sent Mitchell on the inspection tour. So why had he shied away from the demands of the War Department and his own responsibility to report on Mitchell's "clandestine" tour?

Mitchell was a firebrand, and it was obvious that Patrick did not want him in the public eye. He had ensured that Mitchell would be muzzled, and out of touch, when he sent him on the nine-month inspection tour; but now he was back, with his detailed report in hand, and God only knew what was in that. Historian Burke Davis described the report as being received "with the enthusiasm of a green demolition team approaching an unexploded bomb."[20]

Patrick's actions were disgraceful. His reputation of being measured and fair is severely strained by his planned procrastination and shunning of his own subordinate who had followed Army orders to the letter.

And following closely in Patrick's steps were the various divisions of the War Department, including Intelligence, Operations, and War Plans. They also chose to ignore Mitchell's report. It was not until the five months between December 1925 and May 1926 that comments from those departments trickled in.[21]

In the end, Mitchell's work was consigned to the shelf—that same place that had been described early on as the repository for all his revolutionary ideas: the "Flying Trash Pile."

Mason Patrick, a flawed leader of the Air Service and no friend of Mitchell (National Archives)

When the tardy staffs' comments arrived, they each began with a rehearsed, perfunctory statement that the report was "worthy of consideration." But after that, the divisions of the Army General Staff embarked upon a pattern of derision. War Plans proclaimed that "many of the opinions expressed . . . are based on the author's exaggerated ideas of the power and importance of airpower, and are therefore unsound."[22]

That division even questioned whether Mitchell's comments and conclusions were based on anything he had actually seen on his Pacific inspection. But while raising this provocative question, it did not present any evidence as to why it might have thought that Mitchell concocted his report, or had not seen what he had seen. It concluded with the shortsighted proclamation that would follow these petty detractors to their graves.

"Since he so notoriously overestimates what could be done with air power by the United States," said one report, "it is not improbable that he has likewise grossly overestimated what Japan could do and would be able to accomplish with air power."[23]

Presumably this jab at Mitchell's "overestimating" was in response to Mitchell's assertions that air power alone had the ability to be decisive in war, especially in war with Japan, where the Army and Navy did not.

Mitchell had written that three things were necessary to win such a war. First, destruction of the enemy's own forces; second, the destruction of the enemy's ability to wage war; and third, the destruction of the morale of the hostile population.[24]

"An air offensive against Japan itself would be decisive because all Japanese cities, centers of population, and agricultural areas, lie along the valleys and streams, are congested, and easily located. . . . Their structure is of paper and wood or other inflammable substances."[25]

Brig. Gen. Harry A. Smith triumphantly signed War Plans' inflammatory report of denial and added his own derogatory comment: "The document has been used . . . as a vehicle for propaganda."[26]

The Intelligence Division's report was hardly better. It said that General Mitchell's claim that Japan had 600 planes was "a grossly exaggerated conclusion." Its own studies had indicated that he was in error. (A 1966 report by Japan would verify Mitchell's numbers.)[27]

The Intelligence Division, never having penetrated Japan's veil of secrecy as Mitchell had, relied on reports of diplomats, who were also on the outside. They knew nothing of Mitchell's private tours to inspect landing sites for an upcoming Round-the-World flight of American planes.

Mitchell, with the force of world publicity, had been able to maneuver the reluctant Japanese into allowing Mitchell to tour airfields that would be used for support and refueling. But they insisted that such visits were to be supervised by Japanese army officers.

Many of those officers doing the supervising were enthralled with Mitchell. They spoke his aviation language and were not at all reluctant to speak with him. Mitchell had, through his fame, elbowed his way past Japan's locked doors by using the upcoming Round-the-World event and the anticipated publicity. Who else could have beaten down the barriers, especially when his orders cautioned to not visit Japan lest relations be strained? In their ignorance, the officers of the Intelligence Division chose to simply proclaim that "General Mitchell made no inspections of air stations in Japan."[28]

His detailed report on seventeen such Japanese air stations and arsenals, and what each was manufacturing, was a direct result of Mitchell's access to these places forbidden to all others. One would think that this detailed report would have piqued the curiosity of a good intelligence officer as to how it originated. But it apparently did not, indicating that the Intelligence Division was anything but intelligent. Their reaction to Mitchell's report about numbers of motors and planes produced each month was to downplay the statistics. Where Mitchell estimated a capacity of the Japanese to produce thirty-eight planes per month, Intelligence, through its flawed sources, simply penned in their capacity at fifteen.[29]

The Operations Division called Mitchell's statements "a misconception of the true role and the proper employment of air units . . . and of the proper employment of the combined arms in warfare, and such an exaggerated idea of the power of aviation."[30]

Most of these men were non-aviators and seemed to take no notice that their accusations about the proper employment of air units were being directed against the officer who, like no other in history, had led a 1,500-plane attack in the climactic battle of the Great War against Germany. That attack had broken the back of the German army.

What was it that these critics in Operations thought Mitchell didn't understand about the proper employment of air units? It was General Pershing himself who had praised Mitchell for the success of "the Air Force under your command." And it was British air chief Hugh Trenchard who heaped praise on Mitchell for "the most terrific exhibition I have ever seen—you have cleaned out the air."[31]

Even the Division of Administration, mostly concerned with personnel, chimed in on the side of outright rejection and phony declarations. It proclaimed that the report "was a recitation of the aspirations of the Air Service." It was not "a description of actualities." It called Mitchell's prediction of a Japanese attack "an interesting description of an attack on Oahu from the air."[32]

In the end, it was Gen. Mason Patrick who abandoned Mitchell for the second time in six months. First, he had sidestepped issuing a review of Mitchell's report with lame excuses and condescending explanations. Then when War Plans and the rest of the General Staff finally came forth with their disparaging reports, it was Patrick who did not support Mitchell, and issued his own vague, negative comments.

Referring to Hawaii as if he didn't understand that it was an integral part of the common defense of the United States, and an area prominently involved in War Plan Orange, Patrick dismissively said, "This should be of value to the department commander. No comments are necessary." To Patrick, the perceived vulnerability of Oahu and Pearl Harbor to Japanese attack was just a supposition. He called it "a suppositious plan of operation" that "would not seem to be possible of execution at the present time."[33]

But Mitchell had never warned that this attack was imminent. His was a warning for the future: "Attack to be made on Ford's Island at 7:30 A.M."[34] It would be an overall assault, to include the Philippines and Guam. He was warning for the future, when Japan ascendency had been fulfilled, not some *present-time* scenario.

He, like few others, saw Japan rising to the stature of a world sea and air power. Yet it was Patrick himself who had said in his annual Air Service report for 1923, "The Air Service is now entirely incapable of meeting its war requirements."[35] So if Patrick felt that his command was so deficient, why was he so cavalier about the defense of Oahu?

Patrick's other comments refuted what he had previously written, and revealed much more about his own character and the stab in the back to Mitchell—and later to his other subordinates. If the two dictums of leadership are "to accomplish the mission and take care of the men," Patrick was an utter failure.

He called Mitchell's claim that Japan was the second-ranking air power in the world "not a correct statement." And when Mitchell warned that the Japanese made excellent aviators, Patrick issued his most ridiculous declaration: "the consensus of opinion is that the Japanese do not make good flyers."[36]

And concerning Mitchell's thorough inspection of the Pacific, especially the details gleaned from his actual presence on Japanese bases and arsenals—forbidden to all others—Patrick said, "The statements herein are at variance with those submitted by the military attaché."[37]

As head of the Air Service, if he truly was relying on the diplomatic service for his intelligence, then why send Mitchell out at all? Why even have an Intelligence Division if the diplomats' observations were sufficient? Mitchell's report had given Patrick every reason to doubt the accuracy of the diplomats. He went on to minimize Japan's ability to wage a modern war. All this was contrary to what he knew was the concern of War Plan Orange and Orange's unwavering belief that the next modern war would be against Japan.

So why did Patrick even send Mitchell on this secret Pacific tour, if his findings were to be refuted simply by proclamations from those who had never been there? The answer is obvious. Despite Patrick's reputation as the only officer who could deal with Mitchell, in reality, he was not. His rank would allow him to bully Mitchell and override him, and demean his work, but it was Mitchell in the limelight, not Patrick. It was Mitchell who was the darling of the press, not Patrick. It was Mitchell who had brought the Navy to its knees by sinking its battleships and forcing the Navy to realize the value of air power. And it was Mitchell who was a national hero. That is what Patrick could not deal with.

Patrick was the exact character that critics of his past and future writings had described. Critics had defined his literary work as "leaden," and leaden he was. As air chief, he had never flown a plane during the war or after, or even been up in one until 1922. Then, at the age of fifty-nine, he received a rating of Junior Airplane Pilot.[38]

Even if his motive had been to send Mitchell away to the Pacific so that he would be out of his hair, Patrick could still have used his copiously detailed report to his own advantage to advance the interests of the Air Service, and even act as if he had been the originator. He could have feathered his own nest.

But he did not, and his actions actually placed him in the company of the "brass hats" that Mitchell so often reviled and railed against. In the end, Patrick was the proverbial wolf in sheep's clothing, and the epitome of a false friend.

In the months to come, Patrick would be a lukewarm witness for Mitchell's defense at his court-martial. He would eventually write a memoir that would perfectly fit his character. Critics described it: "The style is leaden . . . few insights . . . extremely muted . . . shed little light on anything of importance." They also noted his thinly veiled hatred for Mitchell and pointed out that "except for the oft-repeated story of how Patrick confronted Mitchell and won, [Mitchell] is barely mentioned."[39]

This behavior was not the exception to Gen. Mason Patrick's reputation with his subordinates—it was the rule. Air officers high in Patrick's staff were warned that they would jeopardize their careers if they continued to vocally support Mitchell. When three of Mitchell's disciples continued to leak information to friendly congressmen and others dedicated to the aviation mindset, War Secretary Dwight Davis was enraged. And Patrick was more than eager to give up his own men when he was ordered to smoke the culprits out. His sacrificial lamb was to be Maj. Henry H. "Hap" Arnold, an ardent Mitchell supporter and the future commander, and five-star general, of the air forces in WWII.

But Arnold was not intimidated, and was not rolling over for the likes of Mason Patrick. When Patrick presented him with the choice

Hap Arnold, West Point class of 1907. Taught to fly by the Wright Brothers, he was an outspoken Mitchell supporter and future leader of U.S. Air Forces in WWII. (College Park Aviation Museum)

between resignation and a general court-martial, Arnold called his hand and demanded a court-martial. Mason Patrick panicked, and his dominating position collapsed, especially since Arnold's lobbying efforts had actually been to support Patrick's version of a congressional bill.

The specter of a public attack against yet another dedicated Air Service officer like the fiery Mitchell, and the frightening prospect that his own involvement would be revealed, left Mason Patrick outwitted and exposed. But instead of backing off and supporting Arnold, Patrick shamefully tried to save his own face. He transferred Arnold out of the aviation mainstream. Patrick then concocted a press statement concerning the incident and, in it, reached a new low in loyalty and leadership. While never revealing that Arnold had been doing his bidding, Patrick said that Major Arnold had been reprimanded for violating General Order 20: influencing legislation in "an improper manner."[40]

Despite losing on all fronts, and being abandoned by his own commanding general, Billy Mitchell remained undaunted. He shrugged off the intentional ignoring and struck out on his own. He was driven by his quest, and with or without friends, he was intent on bringing to the American people's attention the presence of a dangerous adversary, figuratively camped on their doorstep and capable of deadly action. The military and political leaders seemed to be content with lethargy instead of diligence. And if they chose to be silent, then it was up to Mitchell to sound the alarm, regardless of the consequences.

How to do that was the question. Fate seemed to present him with a sequence of events that would offer him the path to his goal—at a very high price.

Chapter 8

Falling on His Sword

The Army's visits to Niihau "were handled with the utmost secrecy," said Keith Robinson. "The old-timers, even fifty years later, were still terrified to talk about it; they were worried about government retaliation if they ever talked. It was really deep and dark."

During the maneuvers of 1925, Maj. Gerald Brant certainly had every opportunity to contact Aylmer Robinson as he set about preparing his Black air forces to defend Oahu. In his pre-attack reconnaissance, with Mitchell's report tucked in his pocket, he visited all of the islands, including Niihau, to evaluate their tactical significance. Mitchell had written in his report that Kauai and Niihau "offer the most favorable positions for airdromes" for offensive operations against Oahu.[1]

"General Mitchell, in December 1924, gave me a copy of it and told me it would be of a great deal of value to me in formulating my plans for the maneuver,"[2] said Major Brant.

To understand just how deep Mitchell's enemies had buried his report, consider that Brant did not "officially" see a copy of it until eleven months after Mitchell had secretly handed one to him. By that time it would have been useless to him for the maneuvers. They would have been over with for five months. And when Brant did officially receive it, he saw that a derogatory endorsement had been attached to it.

"There was quite a lengthy endorsement by the War Plans Division," he said. "It stated that the recommendations made (in the report) were based on General Mitchell's personal opinions, and therefore no consideration need be given them."[3]

This endorsement had been composed by officers in War Plans and the War Department who had never "made a trip through . . . the Hawaiian Islands thereabouts to determine their potentiality for offensive and defensive purposes."[4]

So where had this report been from December 1924 until November 1925? It was being *studied!*

Shortly after getting his copy from Mitchell, Major Brant tried to get an official copy and learned it had been given to a Colonel Singleton who was in the War Plans Division and was directly concerned with Pacific operations. "I sent around to get it," noted Brant, "and he said he had taken it home for study."[5]

And that is apparently where this *classified* document stayed until, suddenly, on November 7, 1925, the assistant chief of staff, Gen. Fox Conner, handed it to Brant.[6] There was no explanation. It just suddenly appeared.

But because he had his own copy from Mitchell, Brant was able to utilize the full five months of his presence in Hawaii, beginning in February 1925, to recon and plan for the defense of the Hawaiian area. He was the air officer of the Hawaiian Department and the virtual supreme commander of the Black air forces for the maneuvers.[7] Although he was the chief advisor to the commanding general of the department, in his position as air officer, no one was over him.

His appointment to that position was somewhat bizarre, and it raised a few eyebrows. But it offered a glimpse into just how unprepared for war were the Hawaiian defense forces.

Brant had been in Washington assigned to the General Staff, mainly in charge of Supply. Suddenly he was whisked off and sent to Hawaii to be the senior air officer. When asked why he thought this odd transfer had taken place, Brant could only answer, "I think it was because they had no war plans." When he arrived at his post, he confirmed that there were none.[8] So here was the Army, planning for an elaborate war-game exercise concerning the defense of Hawaii from a possible enemy attack—a Japanese attack—and there was no plan!

Brant was also shocked to learn that his Black forces were terribly depleted and the numbers did not reflect what was called for on paper. On paper he was supposed to have two heavy-bombardment squadrons, but "there were not enough planes to equip but one squadron," he said. "There were supposed to be twenty Martin heavy bombers. We only had nine. We were supposed to have thirty-six pursuit planes, and we had twenty-one."[9]

When asked whether this smaller number of planes could replicate the reality of defending against an actual attack on Oahu, which was the stated intention of the maneuvers, Brant shot back, "Absolutely not. We had about half of the equipment and personnel that would have been necessary if this had been actual war."[10]

Brant had his hands full. Perhaps the reason he had been whisked off from Washington to this position was that there was no one who wanted the job.

The command structure was in shambles and was anything but unified. In fact, it was so bungled and convoluted that it invited catastrophe. Orders had to be passed first through one office, and then another, in a seemingly unending maze of *in* and *out* baskets. When it finally reached someone capable of making a decision, if approved, it then faced the gauntlet of a return trip through those same *in* and *out* baskets before arriving where action could be taken.

A perfect example of this ponderous process occurred during the maneuvers. Brant's Black reconnaissance forces had detected the Blue forces preparing a base on Molokai. He proposed an immediate combined air attack with both Army and Navy forces. It was the perfect opportunity to crush the exposed Blue forces.

Up the chain of command his proposal went, and was summarily stopped at the top by the Navy, who for some inexplicable reason refused to cooperate even though the enemy was in sight. The predictable result was: nothing ever got done. The enemy was left unchallenged. In a real war, where such an attack on the enemy force could be a decisive stroke, it would be impossible to deliver such a stroke.

And the targeted enemy force, actually having been discovered and caught on a killing field, would have ample time to simply walk off that field before any shot could be fired. "I think," said Major Brant, "in time of war, it would have been fatal."[11]

There is evidence, some circumstantial, that in his frustration, Brant confided some of his concerns about the vulnerability of Hawaii to Aylmer Robinson as the owner of Niihau. Robinson was also a major landholder on Kauai. Those two islands had been specifically named by Mitchell as the most likely to be used as a Japanese launching point in the event of war.

Since Kauai and other U.S. Hawaiian Islands fell under the War Department for their defense, Brant's chain of command would have taken him to the secretary of war. Anything concerning Mitchell and his report would have run into a dead end there. But this was Niihau, a privately owned island, and it was Aylmer Robinson, not the secretary of war, who was the final authority.

"I found out that a man named Gerry Brant had been involved," said Keith Robinson, nephew to Aylmer. "He was a shadowy, semi-mythical name way back in the Robinson family history. I had never seen any printed reference to his name anywhere."[12]

But Brant was there, shrouded in the same secret veil that surrounded Niihau. He was sometimes referred to in whispers as "Gerry," and it is obvious that he had moved around in the inner sanctum of the Robinson family. "The family had known him and taken a shine to him," said Keith Robinson.[13]

> There is no doubt in my mind that Dad (Bruce Robinson) and Uncle Aylmer knew the contents of that report as it applied to Niihau. My guess is that Major Brant showed up on the doorstep one day and contacted Uncle Aylmer, who would have listened to him very carefully. That's the kind of man he was, and he would have then gone to his father, Aubrey Robinson. These were the men who formed the team of the Mitchell faction to anticipate an attack on Pearl Harbor.[14]

And why would the Robinsons not have listened to Gerald Brant? He presented to them General Mitchell's analysis of the possible fate of Niihau should the Japanese launch an attack with Oahu as their objective. Their island was to be the final steppingstone of a hostile approach from Midway. To Mitchell, either Niihau or Kauai, were perfect for the establishment of enemy offensive airdromes. He had even fleshed out the details of such an attack.

Unless opposed by a strong air force, these islands offer the most favorable positions for airdromes. Niihau has a population of one hundred and forty-eight. [There would be] submarine bombardment and sorties by landing parties. Aircraft would be set up on level pastures near the beach. Working parties would be covered by gun fire from the submarines. The remaining portion of the population would be subdued by air attacks and by garrisons landed for the purpose of protection of the airdromes.[15]

One can certainly picture the consternation of the Robinsons. Their island, inhabited by a few native people, would be defenseless in the face of such an attack. They would be instantly overwhelmed. Even worse was Mitchell's observation that such an attack could be pulled off in total secrecy.

Niihau's tall eastern cliff blocked any view of the rest of the flat island from neighboring Kauai. Sounding an immediate alarm to anyone was impossible. The only means of communications between primitive Niihau and the outside world was through Kauai, and that in itself was the very definition of primitive. A messenger, in a boat, could negotiate the nineteen miles to Kauai. Or failing that, a primitive, prearranged smoke signal could be sent up from the tall eastern cliff. That anyone in Kauai would even see the signal would strictly depend upon the weather.

Brant was the obvious messenger. There was no way that Mitchell could be the one to do the warning. He was *persona non grata* to most everyone but his disciples, and his fame and recognition would have not allowed free movement much less a clandestine visit to Aylmer Robinson. And Brant had every reason to be where he was because of the Hawaiian maneuvers. A visit to Niihau would raise no eyebrows and would have been expected as he reconnoitered all avenues to prepare for his air defense.

It is also a fact that Maj. Gerald Brant, like Mitchell, had been originally in the cavalry; and Aylmer Robinson was a keen horseman. So the oft-repeated story on Niihau in 1925, that Aylmer Robinson had been observed in the company of *an Army officer* riding on horseback across the fields, naturally pointed to Gerald Brant. Aylmer Robinson's sister-in-law specifically identified two presences of Brant.

She confided to her son, Keith Robinson, that "she had seen, in some Society section of a 1930s Honolulu newspaper . . . that the dashing Major Brant had 'returned' to Oahu and was now on the social scene after several years of absence."[16] He was certainly not a stranger to the Robinsons.

After the Hawaii maneuvers of 1925, Major Brant returned to Washington to continue his duties. But in 1930, he was indeed back on the Honolulu scene as the commanding officer of the 18th Composite Wing of the Air Corps.[17]

* * *

Meanwhile, Mitchell's frustrations grew beyond all boundaries. Playing by and within the rules had garnered him nothing. He had conducted worldwide inspections, slipped into confidential zones of potential enemies, written detailed reports, and testified before Congress and before anyone else who would listen. He had even convinced the president that his path was the right one and once had garnered his extreme favor. But it was all to no avail.

He had also played outside the rules, and despite some sensational results, that too had come to naught. He had sidestepped the warnings of his superiors, Mason Patrick and War Secretary John W. Weeks, and pushed his agenda. He had tried to warn the American people through published articles, particularly in the popular *Saturday Evening Post.*

In return he had been shunned and ridiculed as a know-nothing by those who truly knew nothing. After seven years of trying to hammer home his air doctrines, the Air Service was no closer to being an effective force than it had been when he started. The heady days of his decisive air attack at Saint-Mihiel were long gone, and the accolades for his revolutionary air tactics that had broken the German Army's back, were just faint voices in the distant past. In his hatred of Mitchell, Secretary Weeks had even tried to eliminate him from his undeniable position among those who were most influential in the war effort.

He told President Coolidge that he resented Mitchell's criticisms of "those distinguished men who conducted operations on the other side which resulted in . . . the winning of the war."[18] Obviously, in Weeks's mind, Mitchell was not one of those distinguished men.

Politics and inter-service rivalry now seemed to command the defense of the United States and the wellbeing of its people. Mitchell's sinking of battleships, when all said it could not be done, had brought nothing of permanence. Warnings of inept defenses and American vulnerability to a fast-approaching war were summarily dismissed. His was no longer a voice of one crying in the wilderness. His was the voice shouting "Fire" in a crowded theater.

But the theatergoers simply did not want to hear the alarm. To the Navy's high command, its great battleships were threatened with extinction by submarines, airplanes, and economics. The image of *Ostfriesland* sinking beneath the waves was a terrifying omen. To the Army, a separate armed service that threatened its position as king of the battlefield was anathema. To those willfully blind to the great military threat of Japan, Mitchell was a worrisome alarmist.

In the end, all of his actions had run up against a stone wall. It was as if his crusade for United States military modernization and defense had been perfectly described in the words of William Shakespeare: "full of sound and fury, signifying nothing."[19]

In March of 1925, Mitchell's enemies were again on the move. Secretary Weeks took the lead and told President Coolidge that in his opinion, General Mitchell "was unfit for a high administrative position."

Weeks was mindful to choose his words with Coolidge carefully, since the president was sympathetic to economy and aviation. He called Mitchell a "gallant officer with an excellent war record" but then said that the feisty general had "forfeited the good opinion of those who are familiar with the facts and who desire to promote the best interests of national defense."[20] Coolidge agreed with Weeks's assessment and signed off on not promoting Mitchell.

The observant Mitchell could see that although he had won many battles, he had lost the war. Weeks was ready to lower the boom. Although the end of his career was in sight, Mitchell seized the opportunity to get the upper hand on Secretary Weeks one last time. He would preempt the announcement of his firing.

Mitchell dictated a statement to be immediately released whenever Weeks decided to fire him. He offered himself as the martyr. He said that his own reappointment as assistant chief of the Air Service was unimportant. It was national defense that mattered, and he was willing to sacrifice himself to that cause. Couched in his words was the intimation that it was Weeks and those like him who were the real problem.

"As soon as the sound of the cannon had ceased on the western front," Mitchell wrote, "the forces of retrogression began to work in our country."[21] He pledged to keep on fighting from whatever position fate would assign him and made no secret that he was being replaced by political whim.

Among Mitchell's many charges of the incompetence of the military and its leaders, it is obvious that the one that irked Weeks the most was Mitchell's claim that anti-aircraft fire was totally ineffective against attacking airplanes. That charge had been the cornerstone of his proclamations of Army helplessness in the face of a daunting air force. When opponents had challenged him and said that anti-aircraft ground fire could break up an air attack, Mitchell had only scoffed. His own observations on the actual battlefields during the Great War had convinced him otherwise.

So in an attempt to land the knockout blow against Mitchell, and at the same time publically refute Mitchell and his phony claims, Weeks and his General Staff came up with a plan that was sure to do both. They ordered that an actual anti-aircraft-fire demonstration be conducted on March 6, 1925. It would take place at Fort Monroe in Virginia, and at that time the secretary would announce his decision to fire Mitchell.

Savoring the impending demise of his nemesis, the secretary and his staff officers invited all to come and witness the unmasking of Mitchell and the exposure of his "false claims" for exactly what they were. It was Weeks's great opportunity to finally humiliate the loathsome Gen. Billy Mitchell. In the audience were congressmen, reporters, and influential experts. Many were also eager to see Mitchell get his comeuppance, and the fact that it would be Mitchell's own planes that would tow the ten-by-four-foot target sleeves seemed most fitting to his adversaries. Finally people would see with their own eyes the deadly effectiveness of anti-aircraft gunfire against aircraft, and the conclusions would remove all doubt.

The three designated planes took off and, once aloft, reeled out their target sleeves. The towing mission began. It all seemed in slow motion. The three planes droned on, back and forth on a fixed course. They took no evasive action nor varied their speed. At the end of their long towlines, the target sleeves glided along. All below gazed skyward to witness the coastal artillery take aim and pound away at the trailing targets. The sound was deafening, and thirty-nine rounds were fired in a thunderous display of anti-aircraft firepower.

The three aircraft were then ordered to spiral down to a lower altitude so as to offer the targets to a battery of assembled machine guns. The gunners unleashed their hail of bullets in a roar of rapid fire to prove their marksmanship. It was all very impressive and drew oohs and aahs from the onlookers. The fire ceased, and the aircraft crews reeled in their target sleeves and landed for an official inspection.

No one has recorded any of Secretary Weeks's words or expressions, if indeed he had any, but he certainly watched with anticipation as the inspection teams spread out the sleeves to count the many holes. But the inspectors didn't have much counting to do. Not one of the thirty-nine coastal artillery rounds had found their mark, and, of the many thousands of rounds fired by the deployed machine guns, there was but a single bullet hole to mar the otherwise untouched fabric of the targets.

The press had a field day with it all. Reporters raced to file their stories about the humiliating gunnery exercise and the surprising firing of Billy Mitchell by a seemingly outwitted Secretary Weeks. The *Washington Post*'s enlarged headline of March 7 shouted: "Mitchell Ousted . . . Blow to Mitchell Shocks Congress . . . Air Targets Defy Weeks' Gunners."[22]

But despite this humiliation of Weeks and his carefully laid plan to vanquish and embarrass Mitchell, the fact remained that Mitchell was fired. His friends and supporters were downtrodden, and twenty-five of his most loyal officers quickly planned a farewell lunch to see the former general off to his new backwater station in Texas. To a man, these officers were willing to put their own careers on the line. They would request transfers to follow him or, failing that, would resign *en masse*.

When Mitchell got wind of this, he scolded them for entertaining such thoughts. "Sit down, every damned one of you," he demanded. "Not one of you will resign. Not one. And that's an order." But upon deeper reflection, and with an air of resignation, he seemed to realize that he was nearing the end of the road. "Who will carry on when I'm gone?" he was heard to whisper.[23]

And the press was very much in his corner. The *Cleveland Press* opined, "We may wait a hundred years for another such display of courage."[24]

Aviation magazine praised the appointment of his successor, Lt. Col. James E. Fechet. Elevated to the rank of brigadier general, Fechet was much like Mitchell in his devotion to the Air Service. "He is a typical cavalry officer," said *Aviation*. "He is as outspoken in his views as was General Mitchell whom he succeeds, and just as intolerant of red tape and official meddling."[25]

And Mitchell garnered their highest praise. Conceding that it had been "almost a certainty that he was to be sidetracked . . . due to his outspoken criticism of his superiors in the Army and his caustic references to the Navy," the editors noted:

"Long after his demoters are forgotten and the trivialities of the fray . . . are submerged by the weight of the truth, General Mitchell will be remembered and receive the gratitude of history."[26]

* * *

Gratitude was not what Mitchell was looking for. His message needed to be put forward even more forcefully. At a follow-up party hosted by Maj. Hap Arnold, Mitchell was more himself and renewed in spirit. Now "Colonel" Mitchell took the opportunity to make a better farewell speech. He showed no animosity toward his adversaries but had plenty to say about the bureaucracy that had taken over his beloved Army.

Mitchell pointed out that the Army's actions were nothing new. It had always been slow to adapt to changing times. When the world was using kerosene to light their houses, "the Army continued to use candles," Mitchell noted.

"In the Indian campaigns, the savages were better armed than our regular troops," and he added that in the World War, the Germans were outgunned not with weapons brought to the battlefield by the slow-developing United States arms industry but by "the weapons of our associates."[27]

Mitchell's speech revealed that he was hardly through with the fight. Perhaps to put the Navy on alert that they had not heard the last of him, he chose words hauntingly similar to those of their great hero, John Paul Jones, to throw in their face.

"I haven't even begun to fight," he said. "The job is now to jar the bureaucrats out of their swivel chairs."[28]

Jarring the bureaucrats out of their swivel chairs began with a broadside of epic proportions. Mitchell published his book *Winged Defense,* which reinforced all that he had preached during his years of extolling air power. He called the work a "little book . . . thrown together hastily."[29] He had compiled it from evidence he had given during multiple appearances before Congress, from articles he had written for various journals, and from his own experiences both in war and as deputy chief of the Air Service.

Perhaps his seeming downplaying of his work was not to indicate that it was a slipshod assembly of his thoughts but that it had been rushed to press, as if an unseen clock was ticking and time was running out. His message to the reader conveyed that very sense, and his tone was most serious. "We are still backward," warned Mitchell. "We consider it time to make our views known."[30]

And his publisher called the book "a bomb in the lap of American complacency." Its instant popularity proved that. The initial printing in August 1925 quickly sold out, to be followed by a second printing in September and a third in February 1926.

If it had been "thrown together hastily," it missed no opportunity to lampoon all who had stood in opposition to Mitchell's air philosophy. The reader did not even have to get to the first page of text to see that he was taking no prisoners.

Inside the front cover was a compilation of political cartoons casting all the obstructionists to his air-power philosophy as incompetent buffoons. Mitchell had not drawn these cartoons, but they served his arguments just as well as if he had. There was an illustration of Mitchell bursting in and waking the Army brass sleeping in a burning house, only to be told that he was fired for waking the Army up. That could certainly not have been lost on those instrumental in his demotion, especially Mason Patrick, who had been the epitome of a fair-weather friend.

Another cartoon depicted two snoring bureaucrats, labeled *War Department* and *Navy Department,* obliviously asleep as countless aircraft originating from a Rising Sun flew overhead. Yet another showed an Air Service airplane piloted by a Mitchell opponent who had tossed him overboard saying, "We don't care for these high fliers."

Secretary Weeks was especially lampooned as a quack doctor spoon-feeding Uncle Sam the gagging medicine of Mitchell's firing. The medicine bottle was labeled *Noticeable Demotion.* In another frame, the Air Service eagle swooped down menacingly, with extended talons, upon a blissfully unaware collection of Army chickens and Navy ducks.

There was also a flying duck depicted in support of Mitchell. It represented Adm. William Sims, commander of American naval forces in the Great War. In opposition to the vast majority of his fellow Navy officers, he was shown saying, "I will tell the world that a plane can sink a battleship."

It had been Admiral Sims who had supported Mitchell and later said, "The average man suffers very severely from the pain of a new idea. . . . It is my belief that the future will show that the fleet that has 20 airplane carriers, instead of 16 battleships and 4 airplanes, will inevitably knock the other fleet out."[31]

On that inside cover, Mitchell had clearly drawn the battle lines for a final showdown. It is amazing how few understood his tossing down the gauntlet. The 1920s critics displayed the early stages of what the future would call "political correctness." They said that the cartoons were in bad taste since Secretary Weeks was now ill. Mitchell immediately brushed aside those charges as nonsense and reminded the critics that the cartoons "appeared in the public press all over the country a number of months ago."[32]

But since the critics had brought up the subject of Secretary Weeks, Mitchell lost no time exploiting it and pointed out that the secretary had not been immune to Navy influence. He silently suggested that perhaps that influence had tainted his impartiality.

"Secretary Weeks is a graduate of the Naval Academy, and was a Navy officer and has many friends in the Navy, sees them frequently, and this is bound to influence him as it would any other human being. . . . I have the kindest feeling for him individually."[33]

If the book had been "thrown together hastily," Mitchell's passion had not been sacrificed. Its publication had followed on the heels of a scathing article Mitchell had written for *Liberty* magazine in August 1925. It excoriated the meaninglessness of the previous naval disarmament conferences. The title, "Exploding Disarmament Bunk: Why Have Treaties about Battleships When Airplanes Can Destroy Them?" was provocative enough for all to see that the battle had been joined.[34]

Mitchell historian Alfred F. Hurley, however, seemed to miss that point and perhaps is representative of all who also missed it. He begins by slightly misquoting Mitchell's self-assessment of his book by replacing the words "thrown together hastily" with the words "hastily compiled collection." There is a world of difference between the two, and that difference perhaps led Hurley to incorrectly conclude that the work was "a repetitious and disorganized piece of work."[35]

It was hardly that, and if any of it was repetitious, Mitchell intended it to be so. He was intent upon hammering home his long-stated arguments, and repetition was the tool. That August *Liberty* article was a perfect example.

Wasn't that *Liberty* magazine article also repetitious? Mitchell's continuous assault against the value of battleships had been his mantra from the very beginning. And was not the use of the word *bunk* typical of Billy Mitchell's repetitious style? There was no one who had not previously known his stance on battleships.

And his book was anything but *disorganized*. The opening cartoons in *Winged Defense* were a hammer stroke. They immediately identified and castigated the enemy. In the cartoonists' minds, as in Mitchell's, it was the bureaucrats in the Army and Navy and the political players who continued to ignore the proven effectiveness of air power. It was the entrenched establishment that was willing to jeopardize American security. That perception was emphatically conveyed on the inside cover of *Winged Defense*. Who could miss that? If a picture ever painted a thousand words, that was it.

Before reading one word, the reader was well aware of the contentious aviation debate. Mitchell was the undeniable victim, heroically sacrificing himself for the good of the nation and the American people.

Even today's reader would find *Winged Defense* an interesting and exciting read. The World War I reflections are compelling, and the reasoned argument for air power is anything but *repetitious* and *disorganized*. Hurley's assessments are stoutly challenged by the book's popularity, evidenced by the rapidity of the first, second, and third printings. *Winged Defense* was every bit the *bombshell* that the publishers had predicted.

There was another bombshell in the popular work, but it was hidden. Mitchell had, without citation, plagiarized a number of paragraphs from a lecture entitled "Submarines" that had been delivered by Capt. Thomas C. Hart to the General Staff College in 1919.[36] That bomb would explode on another day.

But for now, Hurley's assessment proved that many did not understand that *Winged Defense* offered Mitchell the unique opportunity to present some of his observations contained in his long-buried Pacific inspection report. In his section entitled "Conclusions," he did just that and warned about the defense of Hawaii and the Philippines. This was hardly *repetitious*. It was a *revelation* to most. His Pacific report had never been published. In fact, it was buried so deep, few could even find it. Only Maj. Gerald Brant had secretly gotten a copy of it from Mitchell.

In his exhortations for the American people to understand that enemy air power was a dangerous threat to their safety and wellbeing, Mitchell did not mince his words. "The only defense against aircraft is by hitting the enemy first. The idea of defending the country against air attack by machine guns or anti-aircraft cannon from the ground, is absolutely incapable of being carried out."[37]

If there remained any doubt concerning Mitchell's intentions and anxiousness to publish this book, one needs only to examine his caustic comments when the subject of his writing came up. While at his new duty station in San Antonio, he was asked if this new writing had not violated Secretary Weeks's former instructions to submit all writings to higher authority for approval. Mitchell snapped that he had violated nothing.

"The truth of our deplorable situation is going to be put before the American people come what may. If the War Department wants to start something, so much the better."[38]

Chapter 9

Racing to the Abyss

It had been just over a month since *Aviation* magazine had broken the story that the well-publicized report of the "successful" Hawaiian naval maneuvers was mostly concocted. That report had gone out of its way to glorify the purpose of the battleship while attempting to denigrate Gen. Billy Mitchell.

But the ever-alert Maj. Gerald Brant, ignoring the possible effects on his career, had confronted the hoax. In the article, he had bluntly declared, "Those of us who were serving with the air forces during the maneuvers know that it is far from the truth."[1]

Mitchell had always felt that the Navy had no reservations about risking the lives of aviators if it enhanced their own prestige. In 1921 he had bristled at the Navy's insistence that target ships used for the bombing test would be anchored at the Cape Charles Lightship, 100 miles from Langley Field. That made it a 200-mile roundtrip, placing the bombing aircraft at their extreme range. The ideal location would have been east of Cape Hatteras off the North Carolina coast—only half the distance.[2]

But the Navy would have none of it and insisted, for no reason, that the longer course be used. Mitchell was furious but was so anxious to have the long-denied tests run that he agreed. Fuel capacities would be strained and ensured that Mitchell's aircraft would have only one shot at the target. Mitchell never forgot the cavalier Navy attitude, and during the tests, a fierce storm forced some of his planes down on the long flight back to Langley.[3]

Now the Navy saw fit to showcase its fledgling aviation muscle and planned a flight that would highlight its equipment, aviators, and pioneering spirit. At the end of August 1925, two PN9 seaplanes with twin 500-horsepower engines,[4] and one PB1 prepared to fly from California to Hawaii. The 2,000-mile flight path would be dotted with ten support and rescue ships, spaced every 200 miles. Navy confidence was high.[5] Eight destroyers, an aircraft carrier, and an aircraft tender ship formed the ten-ship picket line. The prevailing winds promised to be an advantage, providing a modest tailwind from the north and east of ten to twenty miles per hour.[6]

But the much-anticipated August 31 start was most disappointing. The PB1 did not even get off the ground, for mechanical reasons. The two PN9 aircraft roared off to the west at 1441. But 300 miles off the California coast, PN9 No. 3 made a forced water landing, with its own mechanical problems. The aircraft was retrieved but was out of the race. With 1,700 miles to go to the Hawaiian destination, PN9 No. 1 was the only survivor to try to salvage the Navy's pride.

The picket ships eagerly reported the progress of the No. 1 plane as it passed over them. At 1300, almost twenty-four hours after the start, PN9 No. 1 passed the eighth ship in the line, the destroyer *Farragut,* which was positioned at the 1,600-mile mark. But eighteen minutes later, with less than 500 miles to go, things went terribly wrong. PN9 No. 1 sent out a series of distress calls.

"Plane very low of gasoline and doubt ability to reach destination . . . Gas is about all gone. . . . Running out of gas; will probably have to land . . . please stand by. We will crack up if we have to land in this rough weather with no motor power."[7]

Obviously out of gasoline, the plane lost all contact with anyone, and no further transmissions were heard. In the vastness of the ocean, the seaplane would be an invisible speck. Airplanes, submarines, and surface ships marshalled their forces to mount rescue operations at first light the following day.

Days passed, but there was no sign of the missing aircraft or crew. The weather had betrayed the fliers. Instead of the predicted favorable conditions, PN9 No. 1 had flown into a storm. *Aviation* magazine printed: "Weather conditions had been against them almost from the start and delayed their progress, causing the extravagant expenditure of fuel as a result of the strong adverse winds. . . . With the disappearance of the PN9 No. 1, the country looses [sic] five of its ablest and most courageous men."[8]

Billy Mitchell took to the airwaves from San Antonio on September 2. He asked everyone to pray for the lost fliers and said, "They are just as much martyrs to the progress of civilization as Columbus would have been had he perished in his voyage to America."[9]

* * *

Three days after the PN9 No. 1 seaplane disappeared into the Pacific Ocean, the Navy launched another flight with the dirigible *Shenandoah* to showcase its aviation acumen. *Shenandoah* was not just another rigid airship; it had become an American idol. Its massive size had spawned an irresistible love affair with all who gazed upon its 682-foot length. It was the longest dirigible in the world,[10] and those enthralled with its intimidating size easily fell under *Shenandoah's* spell. It was every bit as inspiring as *Titanic* had been in 1912.

Its commander, the handsome Lt. Commander Zachary Lansdowne, was the perfect match for this majestic airship. He was a decorated war veteran, having received the Navy Cross and the British Air Force Cross for gallantry in action in the Great War. He took command of *Shenandoah* in February of 1924 and quickly piled up an impressive series of "firsts." He was the first to moor the great ship to the mast of a surface vessel; and on a West Coast tour, he flew 9,317 miles in less than twenty days. Journals of the day touted his flying excellence: "He crossed mountains, deserts, plains and sea from Atlantic to Pacific and from Canada to Mexico . . . far the most extensive operations ever accomplished by an airship."[11]

Seventy-two political leaders had begged the Navy to allow the great ship to fly over their territories on an upcoming flight over the Allegheny mountain range and several Midwestern states.[12] Wherever *Shenandoah* flew, it was a curious sight. Thousands of people gazed skyward, bells ringing and horns blowing. And Pres. Calvin Coolidge was not averse to the political exposure offered to him by the flights of *Shenandoah*. He routinely forwarded all requests for flyovers, from dignitaries and politicians, to the Navy asking if they could be fit into the schedule.[13]

The airship cast off from its mooring at Lakehurst, New Jersey in the late afternoon of September 2, 1925. The weather was clear, with thunderstorms too far to the north to affect this flight. Commander Lansdowne had been somewhat uneasy about flying this route in the late summer, since it was the time when thunderstorms were most frequent, but September usually marked the end of the season.

This flight had been planned, in part, by the Navy's Adm. William A. Moffett to counter some of the publicity that Mitchell had generated in his effort to create an independent Air Service. Moffett was fearful that naval aviation might get sucked under Mitchell's expanding umbrella. His Round-the-World flight had enthralled the nation and the Navy had nothing comparable to showcase. The Hawaii flight just days before had ended in disaster, and now *Shenandoah* could present a positive image. Press releases had been sent out alerting communities about the time that the great ship would pass over them. Lansdowne's orders were to follow that schedule closely and only deviate from it to avoid bad weather.[14]

At 0155, the great ship approached Wheeling, West Virginia, and in spite of the late hour, the locals were up past their bedtimes to greet her. *Shenandoah*'s log reported: "Pass over Wheeling and cross the Ohio river, being greeted with whistles and bells as we cross city and view red flares set off on top high hill. We return the honors by lighting up the ship from stem to stern."[15]

At 0300, Commander Lansdowne was awakened by his weatherman, Joseph Anderson, and told that a dangerous weather situation had developed. Lansdowne immediately went to the control capsule from where, at 3,000 feet, he had a panoramic view of the entire horizon. To the east and northeast, lightning bolts pulsated within ominous clouds. In front of *Shenandoah*, to the west, it was no better. Dark, threatening clouds gathered and swirled, and the headwinds from that direction had virtually stopped the dirigible's forward progress.

Anderson thought they should turn directly to the south, which seemed clear and offered an escape from the surrounding storm.

But Commander Lansdowne balked at doing so and told Anderson, "We've been ordered to fly over a certain course, and I want to keep that course as long as I can."[16]

Lansdowne ordered *Shenandoah* to descend to 2,100 feet. From that position, his forward progress improved; but the ominous weather to his front seemed to intensity with each passing minute. In fact, a series of powerful thunderstorms now linked arms to form a veritable squall-line phalanx, and the thunderheads rose to over 6,000 feet.

At 0350, the airship's log reported: "Storm worst we have encountered to date." At 0455, *Shenandoah* was desperate.

> Log entry: "Members of crew called from gondola pit and sent into runway to aid in keeping ship on even keel. . . . Lightning increasing in intensity. Hope to ride out storm soon. Unable to get radio to function. . . . Order to throw off gasoline tanks given and complied with but does not aid stability. Radio no better, winds increasing in volume, get chance to"—[17]

The writer did not complete the sentence. *Shenandoah* was suddenly ripped into three giant pieces, and the command car, attached to the middle section, was severed from the airship's body and hurled to earth. Commander Lansdowne and the members of his crew, within the capsule, were killed instantly upon impact.

Investigators concluded that the squall line had enveloped the airship and tossed it around like a toy. Vertical updrafts had propelled it upward several thousand feet, and then opposite forces drove it down again. *Shenandoah* was then caught in a "cyclone" that spun it around horizontally like a giant propeller. These forces were too much for the airship's construction, and she broke apart in a violent twisting action.

Lt. Commander Charles Rosendahl, the ship's navigator, was caught in the forward part of *Shenandoah* and later testified:

> Weather conditions were bad. There was lightning and squalls. Although we had all engines going, we could make no ground speed. The storm crept upon us from the northwest. We tried to turn south. Then the line squall hit us. It lifted us up from an altitude of 2,500 feet

to 4,500 feet, where we righted the ship for a few minutes, only to be taken up to an altitude of 7,000 feet.

The vertical air current was so strong that it carried the ship heavenward despite an 18 deg. inclination of the nose. We release helium . . . expecting this to check our ascension. We had dropped overboard all water and I started from the control of the ship to the keel in an effort to throw overboard fuel.

At this moment there was a crash . . . struts breaking, and saw the nose of the ship parting from the control compartment. . . . The nose started across country at about 25 mph, brushing trees and a house or barn. We handled the nose as if it were a free balloon and landed safely at Sharon, twelve miles from the place where the control ship dropped.[18]

That "balloon" flight, to a safe landing, took over an hour with the seven men clinging to anything they could hang on to. The farm that they brushed across belonged to a farmer named Ernest Nichols, whose son, Stanley, remembered seeing the giant nose approaching them.

"I was scared. We were all scared. Very scared," he said after he watched this massive nose section looming before them. It was the equivalent of a floating twenty-story building bearing down upon him. "It was coming right at us, open end first, with long strips of fabric flapping in the wind."[19]

Rosendahl shouted to the gawking farmer to try and help to anchor the massive, floating nose section. Grabbing a loose cable, Nichols's first two attempts failed. A section of fence and an old stump were each uprooted and ripped away when they failed as anchors. He finally secured a makeshift anchor line firmly to a tree. The line strained to pull away but finally held fast. Rosendahl and his men were able to alight, unharmed, after their harrowing ride. Borrowing the farmer's shotgun, Rosendahl blew out the still-inflated helium cells, and the wayward "balloon" collapsed to a final rest.

On September 4, the nation's newspapers were alive with front-page accounts of the *Shenandoah* disaster. Mitchell, in San Antonio, had been alerted by phone calls the previous day but now read the details. The Associated Press reported an alarming story, through the *New York Times,* that a former German dirigible pilot, Anton Heinen, having served as a technical advisor aboard *Shenandoah,* claimed that ten of the eighteen safety valves for the helium cells had been removed. Heinen was outraged. "I would not call it murder," he said, but in his opinion, if the valves had never been removed, "the crash would not have occurred."[20]

The mumblings of discontent against the Navy mounted with each passing hour. In an attempt to put a better face on the catastrophe, Navy Secretary Curtis Wilbur drew an insulting, ill-advised parallel. He called the Navy flight to Hawaii and the *Shenandoah* disaster reasons for American optimism. This proved that no enemy aircraft could make long flights to threaten us.

Historian Douglas Waller contends that Wilbur's stupid remarks were the final straw that broke the back of any restraint that Billy Mitchell might have had. "Mitchell now seethed," he said.[21]

Mitchell spent the rest of the day writing and rewriting explosive comments. He was still editing his remarks in the wee hours of the morning, and it was not until 1130 on September 5 that he finally welcomed four reporters into his office. He handed each a copy of his nine-page, single-spaced, now-typed comments. It was over six thousand words and began:

> I have been asked from all parts of the country to give my opinion about the reasons for the frightful aeronautical accidents and loss of life, equipment and treasure that has occurred during the last few days. This statement therefore is given out publicly, by me, after mature deliberation . . . to find out something about what happened. . . .
>
> My opinion is as follows: These accidents are the direct result of the incompetency, criminal negligence and almost treasonable administration of the national defense by the Navy and War Departments.[22]

Those words—*criminal negligence, incompetency,* and *treasonable*—stood out like beacons in the introduction to his lengthy report. The rest was hardly less volatile. He pummeled the parade of officers who had gone before Congress and testified about air power with "incomplete, miserable or false information about aeronautics."[23]

Real airmen who knew aeronautics were "bluffed and bulldozed so that they dare not tell the truth." Testifying against the Navy and War

Department bureaucracy would jeopardize their careers. Penalties for bucking the system included being "sent to the most-out-of-the-way places . . . and deprived of any chance for advancement unless they subscribe to the dictates of their non-flying bureaucratic superiors."[24]

Mitchell was outraged by the deaths of fliers that he thought were needless but occurred because of the nonstop demand for propaganda to keep aviation in the public eye.

"Instead of building new airplanes," said Mitchell, "our men were given the old crates to fly at those terrific speeds. Of course they came to pieces . . . they were designed for only one race—two years before."[25]

He was especially outraged by the hoax presented at the end of the recent Hawaiian maneuvers. Maj. Gerald Brant had challenged the Navy's conclusions, and now it was Mitchell's turn. "Press representatives and congressional committees galore were handled, fed, and entertained according to the good old Navy's propaganda system," he said. "It was heralded that the Navy had taken the Hawaiian Islands."[26]

Mitchell condemned the Navy for the horrific crash of Shenandoah. (National Archives)

But what would have happened had there actually been a war? Mitchell now laid it on the line. He detailed that if war had existed, as soon as the fleet of surface vessels began to depart from San Francisco, "the Pacific power's [Japan's] submarines would have planted all entrances to the harbor with mines. . . . And if the surface fleet ever got through these, the whole Pacific Ocean would be districted off into squares . . . [and] submarines would be assigned for the purpose for tracking and attacking them."[27]

Those vessels would be subjected to a ferocious attack from a variety of weapons including cannons, gas, and torpedoes. Any ship that managed to survive this second level of attack, and somehow was able to approach within a few hundred miles of Hawaii, "would be sent to the bottom forthwith by aircraft."[28]

To Mitchell, the actual lesson learned from the Hawaiian maneuvers was that "aircraft operating from land bases can destroy any surface fleet coming within their area of operations."[29] Instead of seizing Hawaii, it would have been a climactic disaster.

Nor did Mitchell shrink from lambasting the Navy for the *Shenandoah* disaster. He was especially sarcastic about the reason for the flight.

> I do not know exactly what happened to the poor *Shenandoah*. She was an experimental ship, built in this country. I believe she was about 50 percent overweight. . . . I believe that the number of valves in the gas bags containing helium had been diminished so as to save helium gas which is expensive . . . but which made the ship more dangerous to the crew. The *Shenandoah* was going west on a propaganda mission for the Navy Department to offset the adverse publicity caused by the failures. . . . Note: Propaganda, not service, is the keynote in these undertakings.
>
> What business had the Navy over the mountains, anyway? Their mission is out in the water—not only out in the water, but under the water, out of sight away from the land. That is why we have a navy.
>
> Her survivors are muzzled by the Navy Department pending a whitewash board. Are these things so or are they not? The Navy Department announces that this shows that America cannot be reached by hostile aircraft. What has that to do with it . . . ? What has the loss of a seaplane near Honolulu and an airship over the mountain to do with it?[30]

Mitchell further cautioned against the urge to slow down commercial development of aircraft and airships "due to incompetence in the Navy Department and the criminal negligence in the ordering of this trip. If we took the safety valve of a locomotive off to save water in the desert, and it blew up, killing the engineer and passengers, would we say that railways were no good in deserts and go back to camels?"[31]

Mitchell concluded by declaring that he had ventured out on a political limb with many adversaries eager to cut it off. He was looking for no advancement; his career had been the finest.

"I owe the government everything," he said. The government owes me nothing. . . . I can stand by no longer and see these disgusting performances by the Navy and War Departments, at the expense of the lives of our people and the delusion of the American public."[32]

Aviation magazine's headline announcing his remarks had also contained a revealing subheading: "These Contain Assertions on Which He Expects to be Court Martialed."[33] Mitchell had left no doubt that he fully expected to be disciplined. As he departed for a fishing trip after releasing his comments, he said, "I expect the War Department to arrest me, but doubt they'll get to it before Monday. I'm going fishing today."[34]

Most people agreed that Mitchell's September 5 published comments could cause his downfall. But one editorial was able to accurately speculate why Mitchell had done what he did.

When it is recalled that the Secretary of the Navy, on the day that *Shenandoah* was destroyed, used the occasion to give out propaganda against aircraft, the provocation to [Mitchell] will be apparent. The regular channels . . . had been tried in vain. The Lassiter report remains buried to this day. General Patrick's recommendations have been routed to the pigeon hole of dead hopes. The uses of drastic, even heroic, measures was the only course open to the man who commanded the largest air force ever concentrated in war time. He exploded with wrath and such bursts are usually charged with uncontrollable forces. The country will soon forget any facts that were exaggerated. . . . It will remember that battleships were sunk by aerial bombs when a former Secretary of the Navy said they were unsinkable.[35]

The Lassiter Board had been convened to consider the rebuilding of the Air Service. Its report concluded that this was vital and recommended a ten-year program to expand the service to almost thirty thousand men. But the War Department balked and never pushed Congress to bring the plan to fruition.

In the days following Mitchell's outburst there was even more aviation news. President Coolidge appointed a special board to study the entire aeronautical question; Mitchell would be able to testify. And then, on September 10, there was a seeming miracle. The submarine *R-4,* operating with Submarine Division 9, while plying the waters north of Hawaii transmitted an unexpected message.

"Plane PB9 No. 1 located by *R-4* fifteen miles northwest of Nawiliwili. Personnel safe. Am towing to Nawiliwili."[36]

The "lost" aircraft with the presumed lost crew had suddenly been found. It had survived a rough-water landing without any power and began a long, 400-mile drift to the west before being discovered just east of Kauai.

Meanwhile, Mitchell continued to be the underdog hero. He was, to many, a modern-day biblical David facing the gigantic, bureaucratic Goliath of the Navy and War Department. Some newspapers denigrated his action. The *New York Times* called it "insubordination and folly." The *New York Herald Tribune* further mocked him and his action that "shockingly violates military standards."[37] But those headlines were easily countered by the majority opinion.

Mitchell's arrival at Washington's Union Station on September 25 was more emblematic of the electric mood of the people. Ten thousand onlookers jammed the station while a drum and bugle corps' music split the air.

Mitchell could not resist. Abandoning himself to the moment, he waded into the sea of his chanting admirers and was quickly swallowed from view. The crowd broke into a deafening roar, and Mitchell soon reappeared, tossed above them on the shoulders of a half-dozen joyous supporters. Many were veterans of the war who shouted their undying loyalty to him. Members from two American Legion posts were also there, encouraging him to continue the fight.

And that's exactly what Mitchell intended to do. An editorial in the *Kansas City Star* correctly identified his mindset:

How are you going to punish a man who wants nothing more than to be punished, and is deliberately inviting court-martial? . . . If a military court-martial is ordered, no one will be happier than Mitchell. . . . He may be a prophet without honor only because he came a decade or two decades before his time.[38]

On October 5, 1925, in the middle of the entire Mitchell affair, a prominent aviation journal commented on the results of the official investigation into the *Shenandoah* disaster. It confirmed exactly what Mitchell had charged as reckless behavior by the Navy. "The revelations on ordering *Shenandoah* on trips for the purpose of pleasing crowds at State Fairs, and against Commander Lansdowne's better judgement, have justified the claims made in aviation circles that the real cause for the *Shenandoah* wreck was not to be placed on weakness of design or improper operation, but on the orders of people who knew little about the capabilities of airships."[39]

The investigation revealed a number of letters exchanged between Lansdowne and various high-ranking Navy officers, including the chief of naval operations, protesting the trip and detailing its dangerous aspects. Especially noted was the history of volatile weather through the second week in September.

Lansdowne's caution was rebuffed by Adm. Edward W. Eberle, who, without denying the commander's observation, simply proclaimed, "There is a big percentage of favorable weather with few protracted storms." With that, the flight was ordered for September 2, two weeks before what Lansdowne considered to be safe.

Admiral Moffett chimed in and attempted to minimize Lansdowne's concerns. He told Eberle that after reviewing Lansdowne's concerns— weather, high temperatures, thunderstorms—he had personally concluded that the commander was simply "pointing out" these possible difficulties, as if he wasn't really worried about them.

In a final attempt to downplay Lansdowne and the entire dirigible situation, Moffett noted that the use of the nonexplosive helium was part of the problem and diminished the airship's cruising radius by 50 percent. Ignoring hydrogen's explosive properties, he declared that using hydrogen would have made operating "a very simple matter."[40]

Mitchell missed no opportunity for publicity. While senior military officers scrambled around to attempt damage control, and Coolidge held a press conference that did not address the subject, Mitchell regularly shouted out to all who would listen.

On September 9, he doubled down on his accusations. "What I have said about the conditions in our national defense hurts the bureaucrats in Washington. It ought to hurt them, because it's the truth." When asked about the authenticity of his comments, he shot back, "Whenever I make a statement it is authentic. I am always willing to back up every part of it."[41]

On September 29, Mitchell arrived to testify in Washington at the House Office Building to the shouts of a huge crowd. When he was called to the stand to testify, he asked to be sworn in, but Dwight Morrow, head of the board, said that was not necessary. Mitchell had not confided to anyone what he planned to do during this testimony, but as he began he told the members of the board that "he would *read* his statement without interruption. My statement is in nine parts."[42]

Mitchell began and droned on with little emotion, and the audience soon displayed the same look as churchgoers who were forced to endure a long, mind-numbing sermon. One of the board members finally interrupted and informed Mitchell that they all had copies of his book, *Winged Defense,* and had followed Mitchell's recitation word for word. "We have a copy of your new book right here."[43]

Mitchell shot back, "Senator, I am trying to make a point," and returned to reading. His friends were dismayed. Maj. Hap Arnold, the chief of the Air Service information, could feel the restlessness and boredom of the yawning board. "We of the Air Service practically squirmed, wanting to yell: 'Come on, Billy, put down the damned book! Answer their questions and step down, that'll show them."[44]

* * *

For a man who had routinely charmed and electrified his audiences, Mitchell's cringe-worthy performance before the Morrow Board was a huge disappointment. For whatever it was worth, Mitchell had his say and now geared up for his trial.

Pres. Calvin Coolidge convened Mitchell's court-martial on October

20, 1925, and scheduled it to open the following week, with twelve high-ranking general officers sitting in judgment. Mitchell futilely demanded the court consist of flying officers, not men who knew nothing of aviation. He called the makeup "coercive—like the old trials of heretics."[45]

The trial setting would be in the Emery Building: a red brick, warehouse building on the northwest corner adjacent to the Capitol. Years earlier it had some dignity when it was the home of the Census Bureau, but now it was in a state of deterioration. While it was not quite the dungeon reserved for *heretics,* it was the closest thing to it that the newly appointed secretary of war, Dwight Davis, could find. Waller describes it as "one of the Army's seediest structures."[46]

It more than earned that description, with standing water at various locations that made the whole building musty and dank. Stained and marked walls and scratched tables added to the blighted look, and hastily made signs identified the room to be used for the trial. That room, on the second floor, was best described as a "dilapidated schoolroom." When reporters questioned Davis on the rundown building, the caustic secretary snapped back his true feelings about the whole affair.

To him this building was suitable for "serious War Department business." It was not, in his words, "a vaudeville show nor an advertising scheme."[47]

This *serious War Department business* was the violation of the Ninety-sixth Article of War: a catchall article to snare any violation that the military deemed to be prejudicial to good order and discipline and "to bring discredit upon the military service." Mitchell mocked it, saying, "Officers are tried under it for kicking a horse."

If the War Department had thought that holding the trial in a building akin to a poorly repaired flophouse would deter spectators, they were sorely disappointed. On the morning of October 28, the line outside the Emery Building was stretched down the block. Newspapers estimated 500. The lucky few who managed to get inside crammed into the second-floor courtroom and sat on folding chairs.[48] The little space left over was quickly occupied by standers, defying the Army's order that standers were not allowed for fear that the floor would collapse.[49] The dingy, blighted building, despite all its barnacles, had become the epicenter of the news world.

Sitting in judgment were twelve decorated generals. They were handpicked by the War Department, in the persons of the secretary of war, Dwight Davis—the same man who had picked the ramshackle building—and the Army chief of staff, Gen. John Hines. That instantly placed Mitchell at a disadvantage, since his many accusations were against the War Department. By any standard, neither the secretary nor the Army chief of staff were impartial. Serving as orderlies and bailiffs were fifteen soldiers, some with rifles.

The president of the court was Maj. Gen. Charles Summerall. Five other majors general sat as members: Robert Howze, Fred Sladen, Douglas MacArthur, William Graves, and Benjamin Poore. The brigadiers were: Edward King, Albert Bowley, Frank McCoy, Edwin Winans, George Irwin, and Ewing Booth. None were aviators. The law member of the court was Col. Blanton Winship.

Mitchell's lead attorney was Illinois representative Frank R. Reid, whom Mitchell had befriended while testifying before the Lampert Committee. Reid was most sympathetic to air power and to Mitchell's cause and served as his counsel free of charge.

The 1924 Lampert Committee, chaired by Rep. Julian Lampert, looked into practices in the aviation industry, especially monopolistic practices. Mitchell testified before the committee and used it as a forum to advance his air-power ideas, gripes, and charges against the Navy and War Department, particularly their ignoring of his Pacific strategy report.

The proceedings began with a customary announcing of "the case of the United States versus Colonel William Mitchell." Then the court was asked a few routine questions to determine its *impartiality*. If the defendant was found guilty, "would any member of the court be promoted?" Was any member related to the defendant; did any member have "enmity" against the accused? There was only silence to each of the prosecutor's questions. Satisfied that the silence after each question indicated an honest answer, the prosecution had no challenges.

But Mitchell's team was not as docile and came out swinging. "If the court please," Reid began. He continued by immediately challenging one of the members. His action was so unexpected that the total silence in the courtroom turned to gasps.

He began to read from prepared notes, quoting from a speech made by Gen. Albert Bowley. Bowley had declared that Mitchell's idea of a separate air force to ensure national defense made no sense. "The backbone, of every army, is the infantry," he had said.

To Reid, that smacked of bias. General Bowley could certainly not sit in judgment if his mind was already made up about a separate air force in the nation's defense. He was soon left alone at the table while the rest of the court retired to consider the matter. When they returned, Bowley was dismissed. Was there anything else? wondered the packed house of reporters and spectators.

"Do you object to any other members of the court?" General Summerall now asked. Reid had the presiding officer in his sights. He again rose, slowly from his seat, and looked the general straight in the eye.

"Yes sir. On behalf of the accused, I desire to challenge the right of Major General Charles Summerall to sit as a member of this court-martial on the grounds of his prejudice, hostility, bias, and animosity against the accused."[50]

The audience was thunderstruck. Summerall was dazed, as if he had just been shot. His shocked look turned to fury as he had to sit and listen to Reid present a laundry list of damning quotes, statements, and other evidence verifying Summerall's bias. Reid was also happy to read into the record pertinent portions of Mitchell's long-buried Pacific inspection report. In 1923 Summerall commanded the Hawaiian department, and Mitchell had roundly criticized the state of aerial preparedness. Concerning the existing air force, Mitchell wrote, "As things stand, it would be almost useless."[51] He then proceeded to detail, in seventy-three pages, the steps necessary to bring that Hawaiian air force to a state of combat readiness. He had concluded that the department was unprepared in every aspect.

Summerall tried to save face by accusing Mitchell of "hostile intent" in preparing the report and stating that he "had regarded the report as untrue, unfair, and ignorant."[52]

The remaining ten court members adjourned to deliberate the new challenge. The outraged general was left to seethe in front of the packed house. When the court returned from their deliberations, it was obvious that they had not concurred with Summerall's wounded feelings. The new president, Gen. Robert Lee Howze, Medal of Honor recipient from the Indian Wars, announced: "The challenge is sustained." Summerall was dismissed.[53]

Now the courtroom sat spellbound. Reid had surprised everyone. Did he have any more lightning bolts to hurl? The forty-six-year-old congressman from Illinois again rose from his chair. He had one more shot to fire.

"If the court please, I would like to challenge, peremptorily, without stating any cause, General Sladen."[54] The audience again gasped. Reid needed no reason for the peremptory challenge, and Sladen was dismissed. Now the court was now reduced to nine members, plus a law officer who also voted.

Reid had won the opening round and also an important arithmetic battle. Two-thirds of the court was necessary to convict—now seven votes out of ten—and he had removed three members who were sure to have voted against Mitchell. Reid had no more challenges.

Then came the reading of the formal charges: a more than 6,000-word document that droned on for hours. As the first day came to a close, Reid argued that the Army had no legal grounds to bring charges since they were too vague; and Mitchell had a right to free speech, despite being in uniform. He hadn't slandered anyone. The War Department was an intangible thing, and Mitchell had simply criticized the "system." That was allowed. Even the president had said so.

Reid quoted from Calvin Coolidge's address to the Naval Academy that confirmed officers' rights to "the fullest latitude in expressing their views before their fellow citizens." Had not President Coolidge himself attacked the system of "unnecessary taxation as legal larceny"?[55] That was not deemed to be slander. Mitchell's comments were exactly the same.

Many in the press who had slept through the prosecutor's long reading of the charges filed their reports for the next day's headlines.

The *Washington Star* wrote, "Intoning of Mitchell's Charges Lulls Courtroom in a Doze." Other headlines focused on Reid's successful offensive to remove three of the court's members. The *New York Times* wrote: "MITCHELL PROTEST OUSTS THREE JUDGES AS HIS TRIAL BEGINS."[56]

The Mitchells were pleased with the first day. Billy's sister Harriet, who had sat diligently behind her brother and had witnessed the takedown of the "egotistical" General Summerall, triumphantly said, "He marched off like a little boy kicked out of the clubhouse."[57]

Chapter 10

The Dog Robbers

The problems facing the Mitchell legal team were easily understood. Mitchell had stated that he fully expected to be court-martialed, but that would give him the forum to bring his arguments to the public. For the prosecution, it seemed to be a slam dunk. Using Mitchell's inflammatory public statements would prove the point that his conduct was unbecoming and prejudicial to good order and discipline.

But there was another consideration for the defense. To make Mitchell's point, Reid had to be allowed to call witnesses, and as such, there were two possibilities: to present testimony for mitigation of a sentence or present testimony that would justify his actions.

This was a thorny situation. Reid did not want the court to rule, at the very beginning of the trial, that testimony would be for mitigation only. Such a ruling would most likely cause public interest to wane. As the court opened, just as Reid had successfully challenged some of the court's members, he now successfully argued that the ruling should be put off.

After the lead prosecutor, fifty-seven-year-old Col. Sherman Moreland, had read the charges and introduced Mitchell's published words into evidence as proof of his guilt, he rested the Army's case. It was that simple. Now it was Reid's responsibility to call witnesses to make his case that Mitchell was guilty of nothing more than exercising his free speech.

Reid began by questioning the validity of the whole affair. Who was Mitchell's accuser? "If Colonel Mitchell had been guilty of any offense, it should have been charged by his commanding officer." Mason Patrick had not filed charges, nor had the war secretary.

The record didn't show that the two commanders over Mitchell "thought any crime had been committed," observed Reid. "Where then does this strange power come from?"[1]

After some anxious moments, the court declared that President Coolidge was the commanding officer referring the charges. That conjured up an awkward question. Could the president be called in to testify?[2]

The court's anxiousness was justified when Reid promptly handed them a list of seventy-three witnesses he intended to call, including four cabinet members and the president's secretary. He also demanded a mountain of documents concerning the PN9 Hawaii flights and the *Shenandoah* flight.

He wanted documents on anti-aircraft target practice, naval bombing, and Coolidge's letters forming the Morrow Board. Reid's thought was that the Morrow Board would never have been formed without Mitchell's agitating, therefore proving that his actions were not contrary to good order and discipline but an actual advancement of the nation's defense.[3]

Then Reid moved to dismiss the whole case. The audience gasped. But despite Reid's valid argument that the prosecutor had made no effort to prove that Mitchell's accusations had in any way been detrimental to good order and discipline, his motion to dismiss the case was overruled.

Reid began by explaining to the court the nature of the defense that he intended to present. He repeated each of Mitchell's accusations in rapid-fire succession and the defense's intention to prove them valid. It was a nonstop litany.[4]

Regarding the airship *Shenandoah,* he said: "She was destroyed by pressure of expanding gas . . . breaking cells breaking the structure . . . not a modern airship; . . . overweight; designed for hydrogen . . . ; valves were reduced . . . ; one of six engines removed . . . ; the trip was not necessary . . . ; authorities ordering the flight . . . wholly unacquainted with aviation and incompetent . . . ; dangerous to fly this route . . . ; ordered over protest of commander Lansdowne . . . ; Mrs. Lansdowne [was intimidated] to give false testimony . . . ; not sufficient parachutes on board."[5]

Reid's words came out at lighting speed. When he was through, and the court was able to catch its breath, he called his first witness: Brig. Gen. Amos Fries, the leading Army authority on chemical warfare.

Reid's plan was to challenge and discredit the high-ranking officers who had minimized many of Mitchell's claims and ignored his report. Gen. Hugh Drum was one. He had mocked Mitchell's warnings about the danger of chemical warfare to U.S. cities. He had claimed it was all farfetched, and it would take 5,000 aircraft to deliver thousands of tons of chemicals necessary to cause evacuation. No nation had that kind of air power to carry out such a threat.

But in short order, General Fries shredded Drum's statement, revealing to the amazed court that it would only require twenty aircraft, and twenty tons of chemicals, to force evacuation of any given area.

Next Reid called Maj. Carl "Tooey" Spaatz, a war hero who had shot down two enemy aircraft on one mission. He was now responsible for the Air Service's training and equipment. When asked what percentage of the Air Service's aircraft were fit for service, Spaatz said "slightly over twenty-two percent." If that wasn't damning enough, he reported that the shortage of Air Service officers was even worse. There were only 147 aviators to man the squadrons where there should have been 613. There had been no bombing practice during the last year, and it had been two years since the last major exercise.[6]

The court adjourned for the day. Mitchell waved to all in the courtroom, especially his fans.

The following day, Reid offered the testimony of his third witness, Capt. Robert Olds—an eight year aviator and the deputy commander for war planning.[7] He testified that nonflying officers, such as the chief of staff of the Hawaiian Department, were threatening flyers with disciplinary action. When a pilot had aircraft difficulties the standard procedure was to go into a glide and immediately find the best possible place to land. It was called a forced landing and often resulted in a bumpy touchdown that caused damage to the aircraft.

This chief-of-staff did not like having to pay for the repairs and told pilots this forced-landing procedure had to stop. Even worse, he threatened the pilots with having to pay for the repairs out of their own pockets. This nonflying chief-of-staff wanted the pilots to try to turn the aircraft around and return to the base. It didn't matter that such a move was unsafe.

With those threats hanging over his head, Maj. Sheldon Harley Wheeler took off in his plane from Luke Field on Ford Island and experienced engine trouble. But instead of immediately gliding forward and landing wherever he could, he tried to obey orders and turn back to the field, where he could save the plane by landing on the runway. The result was a fiery crash and Wheeler's incineration.

Reid shifted to a question about national defense. Was there an air force on the West Coast to protect the Pacific flank of the United States? The answer was "No." Had the Air Service recommended to the War Department that there should be?

"The Chief of the Air Service had recommended [that] on several occasions," said Olds. And what happened? Olds gave a one-word answer: "Disapproved."[8]

General Howze, noticing the rapt attention of the packed courtroom, now tried to minimize Olds's damaging testimony with his own question from the court.

"What was the finding of the investigating board in the Wheeler case?" he asked. Olds was ready for it.

"The finding was that he attempted to turn back into the field and had crashed in the attempt."[9]

Now prosecutors and court members began to squirm. Three out of three witnesses had landed major blows that verified Mitchell's charges.

General Howze asked if Olds thought that the General Staff "should always accept *your* recommendations as to the part to be played by the air service in the major defense problems of the United States?"

Olds was not intimidated by this attempt from a senior to talk down to a junior officer. Looking Howze in the eye, he defiantly answered, "Yes."

Now Gen. Ewing Booth joined the fray and tried his hand at tripping up this upstart, young captain. He asked if Olds had ever studied organizing armies for war. When Olds answered that he had, Booth bored in and asked, in what must have been a condescending tone, "How would *you* organize the General Staff?" Organizing a staff was work for senior officers, not for lowly captains.

Olds did not hesitate: "As recommended by General Mitchell."[10] Olds was dismissed and stepped down from the witness seat.

Maj. Hap Arnold was next. He was in charge of the information division of the Air Service. There would be no backing him down either. Gen. Mason Patrick had, on a previous occasion, unsuccessfully tried to scare Arnold to not testify on other air matters; and Arnold brushed it all off. He was not intimidated now.

He opened his testimony by revealing to the court and spectators that in the last six years, 517 airmen had been killed in crashes. He included graphic descriptions of deaths in the outmoded British de Havilland aircraft, where pilots were sandwiched between the engine and fuel tank and were often incinerated upon the crash landing.

He further testified that the British, French, Italian, and Swedish military had adopted a unified air service. This was a direct attack against the Army's General Drum, who had testified before Congress that this was not the case. Arnold's testimony undercut Drum's proclamations as false and deceiving.

When cross-examined, Arnold was pummeled with numerous questions, seemingly to distract from his main testimony. He was asked about publicity, air accidents, why were the de Havillands used, how many people were killed each year in automobiles, did the Japanese have an independent air service, and even a question about Benito Mussolini.

But none of them refuted what he had said about safety and pilots' deaths or the unified air services of other countries. All of that had effectively refuted the false testimony of General Drum.[11]

The newsmen noticed it all. The court seemed to be holed up in a bunker, huddled together for safety against Reid's unrelenting barrages. When the November 10 session ended, they rushed to file their reports; and the next day's headlines confirmed that Mitchell had again won the day.

The *Washington Post* reported that it was not Billy Mitchell but the senior officers of the General Staff who were now under fire. They were on the defensive. Nothing Mitchell had charged had been proven wrong. The *Post's* story began with the headline: "Army High Command on Trial in Mass of Mitchell Data."[12]

The next day, November 11, the generals on the court revealed their anxiety after having read the newspaper headlines. As Howze called the court to order, he had the law officer broach the subject of the purpose of the evidence being presented. Was it being offered for defense of Mitchell's actions or in mitigation and extenuation? Reid again pushed it off.

"We expect to prove as an absolute defense in this case each and every charge in the statement issued by Colonel Mitchell." The law officer pushed harder for a decision, but Reid held his ground and emphatically said, "No."[13]

The first witness of the day was Maj. Gerald Brant. He had testified for only a few moments when the proceedings paused exactly at 11:00 A.M. to commemorate the end of the Great War seven years earlier. It was Armistice Day. Everyone in the court faced to the east and stood silently for two minutes.

When Brant resumed, he testified to the complete hoax of the reported success of the Hawaiian maneuvers in the spring of 1925 and the entire situation of the Black and Blue forces. Toward the end of his testimony, the court broached the subject of Mitchell's long-lost Pacific report and what had been the final endorsement.

Brant answered that the endorsement had stated, "These recommendations were based on General Mitchell's personal opinion, and therefore no consideration should be given them." Later he was asked, "Is the air service receiving maximum development?"

"No," answered Brant.

Reid ventured an explosive question sure to draw an objection. "Is it the expressed policy of the War Department to oppose any legislation which contemplates the development of any one branch of the service without taking into consideration all the other services?"

This was a direct stab at the War Department and went to the heart of Mitchell's accusations. The prosecutor jumped to his feet to object, but he was not quick enough. Brant dropped the bomb. "That is the well-established policy of the War Department." His quick answer brought howls from the prosecution, and a legal harangue ensued to have it stricken from the record. After much back-and-forth, the court ordered it stricken, but everyone had heard it.[14]

Hap Arnold quipped on the aviators' strategy to give quick answers. It had been planned by the testifying airmen. "Before Moreland . . . could even say 'I object!' Spaatz or Herbert Dargue, Bob Olds, Gillmore, Schauffler, Gerald Brant, Horace Hickam, or one of us would have jumped in with the statement the prosecutors didn't want to hear."[15]

* * *

When the court adjourned that day, there was much celebration for Armistice Day. The American Legion was at the Roosevelt Hotel and petitioned the White House to let Mitchell join them. That request was forwarded to the War Department and denied.

The Legion booed the decision and then cheered Mitchell's telegram of regrets. Then the 300 raucous Legionnaires decided to send their own telegram to Mitchell. They cheered him on and compared his ordeal with that of Jesus Christ.

GREETINGS FROM YOUR BUDDIES. AMERICA LOVES A MAN WITH GUTS. 1892 YEARS AGO A PACKED COURT-MARTIAL CONDEMNED A COURAGEOUS SOLDIER FOR TELLING THE TRUTH SO DON'T WORRY. WE ARE WITH YOU AND WE DON'T MEAN MAYBE.[16]

WRNY radio was broadcasting the noisy Legion event. One of the leaders and a signer of the telegram to Mitchell was former combat pilot, and future mayor of New York, Fiorello La Guardia. He announced to all assembled, in a booming voice above the noise:

"Billy Mitchell was not being judged by a jury of his peers. He is being judged by nine *dog robbers* of the General Staff."[17]

Later, when La Guardia was called to court to testify at the trial, the prosecutor, Maj. Allen Gullion, a man known for his sarcastic and demeaning tongue, began by asking, "Did you really say that Mitchell is being tried 'by nine beribboned dog robbers of the general staff'?"

La Guardia shot back. "I did not say beribboned."[18]

By November 12, the trial had been going on for two weeks and the decorum in the cramped courtroom was nothing like it had been at the start, when one could hear a pin drop. The ramrod-straight guards now leaned against the wall or slouched against the windowsills; people read newspapers and noisily turned the pages; the silent audience was no longer silent. Initially they had been shocked at impolite laughter in this chamber of justice, but they were no longer shocked and most often joined in the mirth. One newspaper wrote, "As the days passed, snickers blossomed into guffaws . . . it is expected that stomping will be in order before the trial is over."[19]

The generals themselves were the picture of boredom. Shifting in their seats and suppressing yawns was the usual scene. General King unknowingly kept the audience's attention with his nervous manipulations of a rubber band. When not chewing on it, he bit on one end and stretched it out from his face with his fingers before relaxing it. The anticipation of it snapping and stinging his face kept many from dozing off.[20]

This entire atmosphere was dangerous to Mitchell's defense. People were losing interest, and his friends thought he was taking it all too lightly. Instead of planning the next day's moves with his team, he was usually off with his wife, glad-handing everyone and basking in the attention.

"Sometimes Billy and Betty would have gone riding before the Court opened, coming in gaily and greeting the judging officers before they sat down (after all most of the generals were old friends)," said Maj. Hap Arnold.[21]

But all that ended on Thursday, November 12. A ticking bomb entered the courtroom, at 10:00 A.M., in the person of Margaret Landsdowne, the widow of the *Shenandoah* captain. The audience hushed in anticipation. The generals rose from their seats and welcomed her. She had previously testified before the Navy's investigating board and had confided to her friends, the Mitchells, that a naval officer had even tried to influence the testimony she was to give. It would have been "an insult to his memory," she said.[22]

As she strode to the witness stand to be sworn in, the flashbulbs lit up the room. She was the perfect witness for the defense. Margaret Lansdowne was a beautiful twenty-three-year-old woman, elegantly dressed all in black. A stylish hat was pulled low over her forehead that framed her face and accented her eyes.

Since the *Shenandoah* disaster, her photograph had routinely been seen in all the newspapers. She was the granddaughter of a Navy admiral and was also now the young, grieving, widowed wife of a naval aviator. She had been left behind due to yet another instance of blatant disregard for the life of an aviator, as Mitchell had charged. That disregard had first been presented to the court, in graphic detail, by Captain Olds as he described Major Wheeler's fiery death. While the audience and the court could only cringe at Olds's descriptions, they could, now, see before them the evidence of the shattered life of this young, pathetic woman.

But her potential testimony threatened the War Department and the Navy in more ways than one. While Mitchell had railed over the disregard for the life of aviators, he also had charged, in his inflammatory September 5 remarks, that the Navy would convene "a whitewash board" to investigate the *Shenandoah* affair. Sitting in the witness chair was the woman who could shatter the Navy's believability and verify all of Mitchell's charges.

Attorney Frank Reid began by asking her husband's name. Her halting answer was sure to bring focus directly on her grief and loss. He then bore directly into the subject of the Navy's attempt at witness tampering.

"Was there a communication delivered to you purporting to come from Captain Foley, the judge advocate of the *Shenandoah* court of inquiry?"

There had been a communication, the widow testified, and it had been delivered to her the day before she was to testify at that inquiry.

"Can you state in substance . . . what was in that communication?"

Prosecutor Moreland bolted to his feet and objected. He was the very picture of frustration and went about presenting a tortured explanation as to why Mrs. Lansdowne's testimony was immaterial to this case, since anything that might have happened occurred after the *Shenandoah* inquiry. That had begun one month after Mitchell made his inflammatory charges and could have no relevance at all on these proceedings.

Reid was ready with a hammer stroke.

"May it please the court," he began. "The trial judge evidently does not understand the purpose of this testimony."

In that one sentence, and with the use of the word *"evidently,"* Reid had cast Moreland as yet another person unknowing of his subject, just like those in the long list of Mitchell detractors who also knew nothing about *evidence*.

Reid laid it out. "Colonel Mitchell, in his statement . . . charged that the navy board would proceed to *'whitewash'* the *Shenandoah* accident, and pursuant to that would do certain things. We expect to show that they absolutely did that, by trying to get this witness to give false testimony in regard to the accident."[23]

Moreland read from a thick sheaf of arguments, prepared in anticipation of this very situation. He, at all costs, had to get Mrs. Landsdowne's testimony excluded. For almost half an hour, he flourished forth, but in the end to no avail. General Howze overruled him.

Margaret Lansdowne began in a low voice. It had all begun with an unexpected visit from Capt. Paul Foley just two days prior to her testimony.

"He asked me what I was going to say to the court."

Mrs. Lansdowne told him that she would make her own statement. But Foley did not take no for an answer and pressed the widow.

"He wanted to know what I had on my mind," she said. The aggressive Foley then stepped over all legal boundaries. "Let's rehearse the statement you are going to make to the court." Margaret refused and told him she would say nothing.

Still Foley would not leave. He wanted to know why she was testifying. She bluntly told him that the court had "failed to develop the fact that her husband had been sent on this trip for political purposes."

Foley must have become unnerved since he then told her she had "no right to say that . . . the taxpayers in the Middle West had a perfect right to see their property."

The next day Foley sent her a typed sheet with the testimony he wished her to give. He wished her to say that when she accepted the invitation to testify at the *Shenandoah* inquiry, she had done so because she needed to defend her husband. But now she had changed her mind, and "she thought the court was absolutely capable of handling the situation and was entirely willing to leave it in their hands."

Foley's prepared statement also wanted her to say that her husband thought the airship was a ship of war, and while he did not take it on political flights, this was for military purposes. Therefore, "regardless of the landing facilities and the weather conditions, he was absolutely willing and ready to take the ship."

Reid asked if all this was false, and Margaret repeated, "False . . . It was an insult to his memory to insinuate he would do such a thing."[24]

Reid then had her repeat what she had said to the court of inquiry. Moreland's vehement objections were overruled.

> Margaret said that her husband believed "the flight was made solely for political purposes. . . . My husband was very much opposed to this flight, and protested as vigorously as any officer is allowed to do to his superiors. Everyone knows . . . orders are given to be obeyed and no officer cares to earn the stigma of cowardice or insubordination by refusing outright after his protest has been overruled."

She concluded by saying that her husband truly felt that *Shenandoah* "should not be taken on commercial trips inland simply to give the taxpayers a look at their property."[25]

The prosecution presented an awkward rebuttal and refutation, delving into what she possibly had said or didn't say; but that was going nowhere with the court, or the press. When she was dismissed and stood to depart, the generals rose from their seats as one and bowed in respect to this courageous lady. She had been an outstanding, unassailable witness, and the next days' headlines confirmed the broadside she had delivered against the Navy:

"Mrs. Lansdowne Says Navy Official Asked Her to Give 'Canned Evidence'"; "Foley Urged a Lie, Judges Are Told by Mrs. Lansdowne"; "Foley Begged Her to Twist Truth, Widow Tells Judges."[26]

The newspapers had a field day for the next week. Foley had to step down as judge advocate in the *Shenandoah* inquiry. That inquiry called Margaret Lansdowne to re-testify, and she stuck to her guns and was backed up by her relatives who were present when Foley had made his ill-advised visit. Moreland's next-day attempts to have her testimony struck from the record were denied as was Foley's demand to rebut.

The Army General Staff was reeling, and while most people realized that they saw little hope of Mitchell prevailing in his not-guilty plea to Article 96, he seemed to win every day in court and in the court of public opinion. If he was guilty, then so were those he accused, such as the War Department and the *dog robbers*, as Fiorello La Guardia had called the overstuffed brass.

On November 19, Reid called to the stand the *Ace of Aces*, Eddie Rickenbacker, and Maj. Reed Chambers, who was the second-best Ace in the Great War. Both testified that there was a lot wrong with American aviation. To Rickenbacker, the solution was to "scrap all the wartime equipment and provide up-to-date replacements." Flying without parachutes was "suicide."[27]

He demeaned enemy anti-aircraft fire and said that he knew of no American flyer, other than Lt. Hamilton Coolidge, who had been shot down by anti-aircraft fire; and he thought Hamilton was brought down by an American barrage.[28]

The prosecutor countered by presenting facts and figures to support a better record by anti-aircraft artillery fire. Both Chambers and Rickenbacker labeled the figures as "extraordinary." To the delight of the audience, Rickenbacker added, "I would not be surprised at anything the official records show."[29]

Rickenbacker further testified to the woefully lacking aviation preparedness, by declaring that America was in eighth place in the aviation world. France, England, Italy, Germany, Russia, Japan, and Poland were all ahead.

The prosecution was on its heels. The embarrassing testimony of Margaret Lansdowne had been devastating, and it also served to harden the Army's resolve. They beefed up their team to renew the fight and brought in the sharp-tongued Maj. Allen Gullion—the Army's best lawyer.

On Monday, November 23, he was detailed to cross-examine Mitchell after his testimony. The courtroom was packed. Reid confined his questions mostly to those that would highlight his sterling career, leaving the previous witnesses' testimonies to also make that case on their own.

Then it was Gullion's turn. He began the cross-examination with a flurry of questions that were designed to throw Mitchell off balance—and they did.

Gullion focused his questions on seeming irrelevant minutia. He asked about the nation's wealth and did Mitchell know what it was. How many submarines and minesweepers did Japan have, and how many were in the U.S. Fleet that participated in the Hawaiian maneuvers? How does the fleet protect itself against mines? What are paravanes? How many Japanese submarines would it take for Japan to occupy the defensive "blocks" in the Pacific, which Mitchell had proclaimed they would do in the event of war? It was all a mind-numbing sequence.

Although all these questions had nothing to do with refuting any

Mitchell stands to face the court in his 1925 courtmartial. (National Archives)

charges, they were a ploy meant to elicit a string of "I don't know" answers from Mitchell that might raise the question about what he really knew.

Finally Reid called a halt to the badgering and complained to the court that Gullion "was making an argument instead of asking a question." But Gullion was undaunted by the objection and continued on his same tack for the rest of the day. He asked about other inane subjects, such as Mitchell's qualifications in dirigibles and who did he mean should be ashamed of his uniform?[30]

The press mostly recognized the emptiness of Gullion's statements and cunning questions and did not focus on them. While the Mitchell camp was not happy with his performance that day, they could have taken heart if they had known that the Moreland team was not dancing a victory dance either. Capt. M. G. Cook, one of the naval advisors, opined, "It is not apparent that the accused contradicted himself on any material point."[31]

The next day, Gullion began with the same type of question. Did Mitchell know the flying hours per fatality in 1921? What about 1925? What about the charge that the de Havillands were "old flaming coffins"? Was that not also false?

For all his flourishes and theatrics, Gullion had now stumbled. He read from the investigation report on a crash that had killed Capt. D. W. Bedinger and asked Mitchell if he agreed with its conclusion that the crash was not due to structural defect. Did that not prove the worthiness of the maligned de Havilland?

Reid was quick to his feet and triumphantly demanded that Gullion "read the next paragraph." Major Gullion read, "Combustion was instantaneous upon impact with the ground." He had made Mitchell's point better than Mitchell could have made it for himself.[32]

Perhaps thrown off balance, the embarrassed prosecutor suddenly shifted to another subject. Brandishing a copy of *Winged Defense*, he asked Mitchell if he had written pages 102 to 105. When Mitchell had answered that he had, Gullion asked him to read a few highlighted paragraphs. Reid bolted to his feet. Mitchell was not reading them. If the prosecution wanted them read, he could read them himself.

So Gullion did. It all seemed to be about German submarines

and the last war. What did that have to do with these proceedings? Gullion was now shouting. "I am going to show that the accused cribbed page after page of this book from which he is making money." He referenced some exact wording from Capt. T. C. Hart's lecture of 1919. Mitchell had not cited the work.[33]

The crowd booed and hissed. This was all irrelevant. It was a sideshow. The law officer, Colonel Winship, sustained Reid and left Gullion to proceed to the accompaniment of the growing volume of hisses. "The audience appeared ready to lynch him," wrote Douglas Waller.[34]

Gullion plunged on, almost blindly, as if the inadmissibility of the evidence to embarrass and discredit Mitchell now needed to be substituted with something else. He pursued cross-examining with more irrelevant questions. What was this *air fraternity* to which Mitchell had referred, and what about Mitchell's 1913 opinion to not have a separate Air Service? There were more laughs and derision.

"Sensations, Laughter, Hisses, Feature Mitchell Trial" headlined the *Washington Herald* on November 25, 1925. Mitchell had won another day.

"Billy himself was in strong form at the trial, often putting the prosecution and even the Court on the defense," said Hap Arnold. "It was nothing like the Morrow Board. . . . He was a fighter, the public was on his side, he was righter than hell and he knew it, and whoever wasn't with him a hundred percent was against him."[35]

On December 2, the Morrow Board released its findings. Mitchell was disappointed. The main sentences in the report said it all.

"We do not consider that airpower . . . has yet demonstrated its value for independent operations of such a character as to justify the organization of a separate department. We believe that such independent missions as it is capable of can better be carried out under the high command of the Army and Navy."[36]

On the bright side, the board recommended a separate Air Corps within the command structure of the Army.

The trial rambled on for another twenty-three days. It was filled with noisy confrontation, hostile cross-examination, and even two remarks from generals on the court that could have led to their dismissal.

It also had a very dramatic moment. During cross-examination of Gen. Frank Coe, the Army Chief of Coastal Artillery, Frank Reid scored a devastating blow against the Army's anti-aircraft artillery claims. The defense had presented a string of witnesses to refute the value of anti-aircraft artillery, and the prosecutors presented witnesses to counter the charge.

Now the Army's star witness was on the stand. and General Coe electrified the Army, the court, and the assembled newsmen when he testified, "Ten thousand anti-aircraft guns cannot protect the City of Washington."[37] The newspapers had a field day.

* * *

When Mitchell had finished testifying on his second day, he comforted his wife, Betty, who showed signs of wearing down and was worried over the final outcome. Mitchell's enthusiasm had not waned one bit.

"Suppose they do find me guilty?" he asked her. "Guilty of what? I've committed no crime. Suppose I am dismissed. Well I've always wanted to hunt big game in Africa. Disgrace? What's the disgrace?"[38]

"Everybody realized that a good showing was the best that could come of it," said Maj. Hap Arnold. "Billy was licked, of course, from the beginning. . . . The things for which Mitchell was really being tried, he was guilty of, and except for Billy, everybody knew it, and knew what it meant."[39]

On December 17, the court called for final arguments. Mitchell demanded to make his own. It was brief. "My trial before this court-martial is the culmination of the efforts of the general staff of the Army and the general board of the Navy to deprecate the value of air power . . . which compromises our whole system of national defense. . . . The truth of every statement which I have made has been proved by good and sufficient evidence before this court, not by men who gain their knowledge of aviation by staying on the ground."

He noted that the court had not issued a ruling whether his testimony could constitute an absolute defense, so he was ordering "my counsel to entirely close out part of the proceedings without argument."[40]

Major Gullion then stood and began what he intended to be a sarcastic refutation of the defense's witnesses, but Colonel Moreland interrupted him and said that since the defense chose not to address the court, neither would the prosecution.

Gullion was dismayed. He had prepared a fine closing argument, and he would not be able to give it. But the court overruled Moreland, and Gullion was now free to unleash his pent-up tirade against the defense witnesses.

He began by first patronizing the court, calling them the reincarnation of Gamaliel—the Jewish scholar who had taught St. Paul. He lavished more praise upon them, as if he were addressing a Royal Court, and said that their careers formed "part of the cherished record of our glorious army."[41]

He reminded them not to be distracted, or intimidated, if they heard that a guilty verdict was against the people's will. They, the generals, were the real people—the nine of them.

His closing was an all-out assault against the defenses witnesses. He ridiculed and denigrated them. Admiral Sims was to him an "opinionated, narrow-minded, hobby-riding egomaniac." Lt. Orville Anderson, who had testified concerning *Shenandoah,* was "the pseudo-expert type." Maj. Gerald Brant was "the gay, gallant, lovable type" but was misguided and under Mitchell's "evil influence." Fiorello La Guardia was, to the pompous Gullion, "beyond my powers of description. Thank heaven he is *sui generis.*"[42]

Gullion went on for almost an hour and a half, as if he were auditioning for a part in a melodrama. His voice waxed and waned for maximum effect. He called up images of Moses, George Washington, Alcibiades, Catiline, and Aaron Burr. He ridiculed Mitchell as "self-advertising, wildly imaginative, destructive, never constructive except in wild non-feasible schemes."[43]

When he had finally finished, he called for Mitchell to be dismissed from the service.

When the court returned from its deliberations, the verdict was guilty, on both the charge and all specifications. The court suspended Mitchell from rank, command, and duty, and he was to forfeit all pay and allowances for five years. The court was adjourned.

President Coolidge modified the sentence to forfeiture of only half of his pay, and he was entitled to a small subsistence allowance. Mitchell survived in this state of limbo for six weeks and then tendered his resignation on February 1, 1926.

"From now on I feel I can better serve my country, and the flag I love, by bringing a realization of the true conditions of our national defense straight to the people than by remaining muzzled in the Army."[44]

The Army was finally rid of Billy Mitchell. But perhaps more importantly, Billy Mitchell was rid of the U.S. Army.

Chapter 11

Distant Thunder

On July 2, 1926, after years of contentious debate, Congress finally created the Army Air Corps. That legislation was a direct result of the Morrow Board's recommendations. Everyone knew that the board would have never existed had it not been for Billy Mitchell's constant agitation, but Mitchell was now gone. His disciples were left behind to endure the military and political slings and arrows for having supported him. Mitchell's charges that servicemen were threatened and muzzled, always denied by the War Department, were never more evident than at the end of his trial.

War Secretary Dwight Davis wrote that he was "in a disciplining mood." Vengeance was to be unleashed. Gen. Mason Patrick, always lackluster in his support of subordinates, was ready to participate in the crackdown. "At once the boom was lowered with a bang," said Maj. Hap Arnold, one of Patrick's favorite targets. "After all the trouble with Mitchell . . . there was no way of letting small fry to keep on going."[1]

He and Maj. Herbert Dargue had continued to support Mitchell and write letters on his behalf. They also continued to visit with their many friends on Capitol Hill to provide information about the Air Service, and that activity placed them squarely in Mason Patrick's sights.

"We were both called to the carpet for our 'irregular' correspondence relative to changes in Air Service status," said Arnold. "Dargue got off with a reprimand. I was, as the Press announced, 'exiled!'"[2]

The entire episode leading to Arnold's exile was another, shameful

Mason Patrick episode. War Secretary Davis ordered Patrick to find out who was leaking information to Capitol Hill, and he was all too eager to obey. Patrick knew it was Dargue and Arnold—they'd made no effort to conceal it from him—and he decided that to mollify Davis, he needed to sacrifice at least one of them. He chose Arnold and offered him the choice of resigning or facing a court-martial. Patrick fully expected him to resign.

But Arnold was not one to quit the service under fire. At West Point he had been known to push the envelope of daring and disobedience to the limit. In a class of 110, he proudly "skated along just below the middle of the class—seldom higher than sixty-second . . . nor lower than sixty-sixth."[3]

In 1907, his graduating year, he was a member of the *Black Hand*, a group known for mischief. Its greatest achievement unfolded near the time of commencement. This collection of self-picked collaborators managed to smuggle in a cache of fireworks for a grand finale before graduation.

Arnold described it: "In the exploding glare which rose over the whole Academy, bugles blew, sirens sounded, officers and men tumbled from their beds. The whole reservation was alive! In the center of it all, atop the Barracks, I touched off the *piece de resistance*. '*1907*' my pinwheels spelled out: '*Never Again*.'"[4]

So it was not surprising that this officer, always up for a challenge, would return the next day with his answer for Gen. Mason Patrick. "I'll take the court." A shocked Patrick immediately caved in on his court-martial threat and instead "exiled" Arnold to the Army's backwater station at Fort Riley, Kansas. But as a parting shot, he released a derogatory statement to the press.

"Two officers had been involved," Patrick said. "Both of them will be reprimanded, and one of them, no longer wanted in my office, will be sent to another station."[5] To complete his vindictive actions, Patrick attached a letter of reprimand to Arnold's file. In his mind, he had finished Arnold's career. Arnold never forgave him for his pettiness.[6]

Mitchell, meanwhile, shrugged off the conviction and lost no time in flexing his new muscle. He put his pen to work to continue presenting his longstanding arguments. He had hardly resigned when *Collier's* sought after, and published, his newest provocative essay: "When the Air Raiders Come."[7] It was meant to shock the citizens out of their indifference to national defense.

Now unencumbered by Army demands to review and censor his every word, Mitchell was free to broach the heretofore un-broachable subject: attacking the enemy's vital centers to break his back and win the war. The *Collier's* article was especially enhanced to attract readers. The layout editors overlaid the text of Mitchell's essay on a graphic of airplanes flattening the New York skyline.

A half-dozen other magazine publishers also approached Mitchell and were anxious for his thoughts. He was only too happy to write. Now, instead of his work being buried in the Army's "Flying Trash Pile," it was available for all to see; and millions of subscribers did just that. For the next two years, Mitchell's name was very much up in journalistic lights.

Flying under the radar, there was one officer who had not been targeted for *exile* during Davis's witch hunt, even though he had been the most vocal of Mitchell's supporters. Maj. Gerald Brant had boldly "testified" on Mitchell's behalf on at least three occasions: at the court-martial trial, as a contributor to *Aviation* magazine denouncing the phony Hawaii maneuver results, and in front of the President's Aviation Board—the Morrow Board. He had never been intimidated by thinly veiled threats from the War Department.

When the court-martial ended, Brant returned to his regular duties in the War Department on the General Staff in Washington. By 1927 he was the commanding officer at Crissy Field, California, and soon after promoted to the rank of lieutenant colonel.

In November 1930, his path took him back to familiar territory— Hawaii. It was there, in 1925, as commander of the Black forces in the Hawaiian maneuvers, that he first gained attention. He had adamantly refuted the Navy's *glowing* results of those maneuvers and had gone public to blow the lid off of War Department and Navy "proclamations." Brant had scoffed at such conclusions and refuted the entire idea that Oahu had been captured.

Now, in 1930, he was back and assigned to Fort Shafter as air officer

Gerald Brant, a Mitchell disciple and secret emissary. (National Archives)

of the Hawaii Department; he became the first commander of the newly formed 18th Composite Wing. It would be part of the defense of the Hawaiian Islands. Brant was the perfect choice. He was no stranger to Hawaii. The 1925 maneuvers had made him a familiar sight. He was also well known to the Robinson family on both Niihau and Kauai. An obscure article on the Society page of a 1930 Honolulu newspaper had said that "the dashing Major Brant was now back on the social scene after several years' absence."[8]

* * *

On Christmas Day 1926, just a year after the end of the Mitchell court-martial, Emperor Taisho of Japan died and was succeeded by his son Hirohito who ushered in the *Showa* era (Enlightenment and Peace). Hirohito had been the crown prince and in effect been the emperor for several years. His father had been unable to rule—handicapped both physically and mentally.[9]

Hirohito was a great admirer of Great Britain and their constitutional monarchy, and he was determined to govern in that model. His good intentions began with great promise, but a 1927 financial crisis was soon followed by the Great Depression. That depression left his idea of democracy in a shambles, and the population suffered from need and want. The military turned its eyes to aggression to solve the problem. Those problems affected every family. Farmers were destitute, only 20 percent of graduates could find jobs, those out of work roamed the streets, and police cracked down on organized dissenters.

Historian Edwin Hoyt wrote:

> As the country wallowed in depression, the soldiers and sailors learned of the plight of their families and grew ever angrier. Among the military men, the civilian government of Japan was thoroughly discredited. . . . The solution to Japan's woes, said the generals . . . was to take over Manchuria. This fabulous grain bowl, with its water power and coal and iron ores, was the colony that would solve all Japan's economic woes and provide the base for expansion into Mongolia and China.[10]

A secret Japanese government plan, initiated by Prime Minister

Tanaka Giichi, proposed that any problems threatening either Manchuria or Mongolia would trigger a Japanese military response. When an incident happened, it would be the excuse for the Japanese to invade and take control of all of Manchuria. When asked by a skeptical general if that position was what the prime minister really wanted, Tanaka was adamant that it was.

The general then said, "It is bound to precipitate war between Japan and the United States. Are you prepared to risk war . . . even a World War?"

Tanaka answered, "I am determined to cope with whatever consequences this policy may bring."[11] The United States had emphatically told Japan on many occasions that it regarded Manchuria as belonging to China.

When no "incident" occurred for the Japanese to exploit, two Japanese colonels took matters into their own hands and planned one. It became known as the Mukden or Manchurian Incident, and it was sophomoric both in plan and execution.

On September 18, 1931, Japanese soldiers detonated a weak explosive charge—so as not to damage the tracks—on the rail line near Mukden. The plan was to make a loud noise, and when the nearby Chinese garrison responded to investigate, the Japanese would blame them for the whole affair. They now had their excuse to invade.[12]

The following day, the Japanese Army attacked and routed the Chinese defenders and set up their puppet state of Manchukuo. The international community was not fooled, and when China referred the matter to the League of Nations, the members demanded that Japan withdraw from Manchuria. The United States declared it would never recognize any leader of that puppet regime.

But Japan refused to withdraw. Instead, after a year of expansion and militaristic violence, including harsh oppression and political assassinations, Japan withdrew—from the League of Nations.[13]

The world had a front-row seat for the troubles unfolding in the Far East. Moviegoers could watch, in Friday nights' theaters, the fierceness of Japan's militarism and the devastation left in the wake of attacks. Pathé News clips brought the horror of the battlefield to Americans.

In 1932, as the Japanese aggression unfolded, Billy Mitchell was still writing articles for magazines. His long-predicted Japanese military designs were now coming to fruition in China and Manchuria.

On June 25, 1932, *Liberty* magazine published his latest essay, "Will Japan Try to Conquer the United States?"[14] The editors identified him as *General* William Mitchell, shrugging off his final rank of colonel.

"The United States is faced not only with the possibility of war with Japan in the comparatively near future but the extreme likelihood of it sooner or later," he wrote. "While we have been chasing butterflies of international debt, or the will-o'-the-wisp of disarmament . . . Japan has been strengthening her position all the time."[15]

Nor did Mitchell miss the opportunity to once again expound on his belief in vital centers and total war. In this 1932 *Liberty* article, he identified the vital centers.

> Everyone composing the nation is brought into its service when war occurs. The women, children, and old people cultivate the fields, and men work in factories to produce war-making equipment.
>
> If a hostile air force caused the evacuation of New York, Philadelphia, Pittsburgh, Detroit, and Chicago, it would be very difficult for the United States to carry on a war or its ordinary manner of living. During the last war, the scattered air raids of Germany over England caused all the lights to be turned out at dusk. Whenever aircraft were heard, people were huddled up in cellars and caves, or they completely left the cities and spent nights out in the fields—suffering hardships. Think of what this condition will be in future war when enormous projectiles, high explosives, and gas will be employed![16]

This warning was almost Mitchell's last. His writings and warnings faded and were finally silenced four years later. On February 19, 1936, Billy Mitchell died in New York. He was fifty-six years old.

* * *

The impact of the China-Japan confrontations reached the tiny island of Niihau and the Robinson family. "The Manchurian Incident that began in 1931 got the family awfully upset," said Keith Robinson. "It made a big impression on both my father and mother. They realized that there was a pretty savage force loose that was highly aggressive and malevolent. They had an instinctive sense of these things."[17]

Obviously Lt. Col. Gerald Brant had also been moved by the ever-increasing belligerence of Japan. He visited Aylmer Robinson. If Japan was the threat that Mitchell had long predicted, then that threat would come directly at Robinson and his island from the northwest. It would come from the direction of Midway, as Mitchell had detailed in his inspection report. It would deeply involve Niihau as a forward operating base for an attack on Oahu. As commander of the 18th Composite Wing, Brant would have the direct responsibility of stopping such an attack.

He had an advantage that few other military men had. He had the report from Mitchell and the details about the strategic significance of the various islands. In the 1925 maneuvers, he had commanded the defending Black forces using Mitchell's report.

If Niihau was to become the advanced operating base for an invading Japanese force, how could a defense be installed that would thwart such a move? It would be an impossible task to meet the attack head on with such a small defending force as he had in the Hawaiian Department.

He met with Aylmer Robinson, and it was most likely Robinson who decided on a drastic step. He certainly had to have been in agreement with the thoughts of Colonel Brant, but he decided to make Niihau a place where no airplane could possibly land. Robinson would transform every flat portion on the island into a gridiron of trenches. In 1948, Aylmer Robinson would make only a brief statement about the plan.

"At Army request," he wrote, "Niihau Ranch had previously furrowed all areas where it was thought planes might land."[18]

His nephew, Keith Robinson, said:

I found out when I was twelve that furrows had been plowed, crisscrossing the entire island. They had been plowed before WWII. The family had been warned from the 1930s by a man named Gerry Brant, and that set off the plowing of furrows. The plowing began with draft animals.[19]

The furrows were in response to Mitchell's warnings that the island would fall easy prey to attacking Japanese, who would land by submarine, overwhelm the few islanders, and set up an airfield. Then a successful attack on Oahu and all the other islands would have the island chain fall into Japanese hands and form an impregnable defensive line. Ships from the United States coming to the rescue would be attacked and defeated long before they could reach the islands. Furrows on Niihau would deny the island, as an air bastion, to the enemy. Keith Robinson continued:

> Two-thirds of Niihau was checker-boarded with furrows that were plowed eighteen to twenty-two inches deep, one hundred feet apart, that were intersected at ninety-degree angles. They were even on land that was only partly level; even on a slope of up to twenty degrees. There were fifty square miles of furrows on that island.
>
> This plowing began lackadaisically, with a team of draft animals. . . . These were big strong animals, but even so they had their limitations on the amount of furrows they could plow in one day.
>
> I calculated that there was 2,500 to 5,000 miles of furrows put on Niihau. It wasn't making very fast headway.[20]

* * *

By 1937, the world had changed dramatically. The troubling news clips shown to moviegoers in 1933 were tame in comparison to 1937 horrors. The Rape of Nanking and Shanghai now unfolded before American moviegoers' eyes. A burning city with an abandoned young, crying baby sitting among the flaming rubble shocked American sensibilities.

Other photos of Chinese bodies, piled up on a riverbank, and rampaging Japanese troops bayoneting and beheading were brought, despite censorship, to the public's attention. And those atrocities were just the tip of the iceberg as later photos, enthusiastically taken by the marauding soldiers themselves, revealed rampaging barbarians running about with dead Chinese infants skewered on their bayonets.

Then on December 12, 1937, the American gunboat *Panay*, while at anchor in the Yangtze River, was suddenly attacked and sunk by

Japanese aircraft. Five Americans were killed and others wounded. The Japanese claimed they did not see the American flag painted on the ship, and apologized and paid an indemnity.[21]

There were also three American flags flying from the ship at the time of the attack. But many thought that this was just another indication of an out-of-control, radical Japanese Army. It was a repeat of the Mukden sham that had been initiated by two other radical officers.

"The *Panay* incident made a big impression on the family," said Keith Robinson. "'We'd better hustle with the furrowing.' It really shook them up, and they went out and bought a Cletrac caterpillar to speed up the furrowing."

Historian Syd Jones wrote, "Joseph Keoua Kele drove the machine while Oliva Kamala, Kauileilehua Keamoai, and Kamakaukiuli Kawahalau cleared the brush and rolled away the boulders in front of it. The Cletrac-drawn plow advanced [steadily] across Niihau's red dirt."[22]

From 1938 to 1941, this furrowing on Niihau continued. The plow's blade cut through the hard red earth. If the land was anywhere

The Cletrac caterpillar that furrowed the thousands of miles on Niihau (Author's Collection)

deemed to be even somewhat flat, it fell victim to the plow and was furrowed. The project that had been ongoing for seven years was finally completed in the summer of 1941. Local movement around the island by vehicle became an unpleasant endeavor.

"If you tried to drive a car or truck anywhere, it was abominable," said Keith Robinson. "You had to keep it in low gear every time you came to a furrow. You had to creep through them. Either the two front wheels went down, or they would go down separately and the frame would get racked."[23]

But few of the 200 islanders had to worry about driving around. Transportation on Niihau was mostly on horseback. The residents lived in the tiny village of Puuwai on the western coast and were the closest thing to a community from another time. They were mostly pure Polynesians, and the Robinsons had devoted their lives to preserving their culture, effectively sheltering them from all outside influence.

Aylmer Robinson was both their protector and employer. The islanders were in no way prisoners on Niihau. They were free to come and go as they wished, but most chose to not venture off the island. They were born, lived, and died there, perfectly content with their peaceful existence. Schooling usually lasted to the fourth grade, and English was taught, but soon after the child left school, he reverted back to his native Hawaiian tongue.

Their main occupation was with cattle, and they were in the truest sense of the word "cowboys." There was other livestock—sheep and thousands of turkeys roaming free—and they all demanded attention. Pigs were feral, and there was a thriving cottage industry in bees and honey. Sunday was a day of rest, relaxation, and self-generated entertainment. Music from guitars and ukuleles provided a soft Sunday scene after church. Everyone lived in small frame houses, some widely separated, and the small church was the center of community activity.[24]

＊ ＊ ＊

The unfettered aggression of the Japanese Army, and the seeming autonomy of its command, led the Imperial Japanese Navy to want a similar command structure. In a series of daring political moves, the admirals managed to wrest command over the navy from the Navy Ministry and vested it in the Navy General Staff. A Japanese prince hailed the revision as "a great reform for the rebirth of our imperial navy."[25]

While there was much celebration among the aggressive younger officers in the navy, many senior, older officers had grave misgivings. But they soon found themselves on the outside looking in—suddenly retired or placed on reserve lists. One of those with doubts was Rear Adm. Yamamoto Isoroku, who remarked while attending the London naval conferences, "Perhaps there is no way left to rebuild the navy until it has wrought its own ruin by such an outrage."[26]

This purge of the senior officers in the navy silenced the voices of moderation and opened the door for the more radical middle-echelon officers to influence policymaking. These junior officers followed a practice that called for "consensus of views," and they pressed for adoption of their views by their superiors. One of them was an urgency to go to war with the United States.[27]

They thought it was inevitable because of a rock-ribbed conviction that the United States lusted after economic control of East Asia, especially in China. They pointed to the recent Washington and London naval conferences as part of the grand plan to keep the Japanese Navy inferior to those of the U.S. and Great Britain. To them, it was all part of an insidious plan of undaunted expansion of "materialistic Westward civilization."[28] Was not the present U.S. possession of Guam and the Philippines proof of that dangerous expansion?

But there were still a few naval minds that refused to rush headlong into the inevitability of war with the United States. Admiral Yamamoto said, "Anyone who has seen the auto factories in Detroit and the oil fields in Texas, knows that Japan lacks the national power for a naval war with America."[29]

Yamamoto had been an attaché in Washington at a time when Billy Mitchell was regularly expounding the virtues of air power and was greatly influenced by Mitchell's ideas. His interest in aviation led him to pursue a career path that, in 1935, found him in charge of the Naval Aviation Headquarters. Repeating Mitchell's charges about naval power, Yamamoto preached that battleship engagements were a thing of the past. Money spent to build battleships was wasteful since they could so easily be defeated by air power. By 1936 Yamamoto readily stated that "he who controls the air controls the sea."[30]

Equally important was the impression that Mitchell's thinking had made on the likes of Commander Minoru Genda—an excellent Japanese naval aviator. In 1936, he was called upon to submit a paper outlining his thoughts on how to arm the Japanese Navy in preparation for a possible encounter with the Americans.

This was a touchy subject in an age when most navies thought in terms of battleships. That included the vast majority of the Japanese Navy, who proudly reflected upon their decisive victories with battleships in 1895 and 1905. The Washington and London naval conferences had been all about limiting capital ships, and that meant battleships.

Genda said: "The main strength of a decisive battle should be air arms. While its auxiliary should be built mostly by submarines, cruisers and destroyers will be employed as screens of carrier groups, while battleships will be put out of commission and tied up."[31]

His thoughts, like Mitchell's, were roundly criticized. "Not only was my idea attacked," said Genda, "but even my mental soundness was doubted. Virtually I had no support, and I had to fight back alone."[32]

Like Mitchell, Genda was persistent and vocal. When he saw the plans laid out for the construction of the super battleships *Yamato* and *Musashi,* he could no longer hold his tongue.

"We are building something that is useless," he scoffed. "These ships could not stand an attack from the air. . . . These ships will be just another one of the three [useless] defenses built by man, and the world will laugh. These are: The pyramids; The Great Wall of China; and *Yamato* and *Musashi.*"[33]

Billy Mitchell had recently died. He'd gone to his grave mostly ignored by his own military leaders. But he had made a great impression on other leaders, men such as Yamamoto Isoroku and Minoru Genda. Both knew that air power, not battleships, was the weapon of the next war.

The Japanese military mindset was deeply entrenched. Yamamoto had an uphill battle. To those naval leaders who still railed against the

5:5:3 ratio for capital ships among the U.S., Great Britain, and Japan and how that disadvantaged Japan, Yamamoto could only scoff. He called it "ratio neurosis." To him, the ratio actually worked to Japan's favor. It stopped the two Western powers from outdistancing Japan.

In Yamamoto's mind, it was all obvious. If Japan dominated the air in the Western Pacific, why would anyone think the United States leaders would be "so stupid or reckless" to venture into those waters when its ships could be so easily destroyed by aircraft?[34] But his logic was mostly shunned.

In April 1940, Japan made a significant military decision. A conference of naval section chiefs declared that now was "the finest chance to occupy the Dutch East Indies."[35] Japan was on a road with no return. In July 1940 the army demanded an end to political government. Gen. Hideki Tojo became prime minister, and totalitarian control of Japan was now vested in the military. Then on September 27, Japan entered into an alliance with Germany and Italy (the Tripartite Pact) and seemed hypnotized by Germany's mounting military victories.

Exactly when Yamamoto embraced the idea for the Hawaiian operation is unclear. Mitchell's forethoughts on Hawaii, and the likelihood that Japan would attack, were clearly spelled out in his 1924 report. But Yamamoto never embraced that conclusion and had steadfastly dismissed such a thought. He was a staunch advocate of air power, but venturing out on the end of a limb, to cross thousands of miles of ocean with a severely extended supply line, offered little allure.

But the Japanese fixation with the idea of a single climactic battle, or what was called a "main fleet encounter," was an entrenched tactic. The first-strike, surprise-attack philosophy had brought Japan to naval prominence.[36] Those strikes against China and Russia had ended wars almost before they had even started. Quick strike, quick victory was the motto.

The obvious flaw with the idea of a main fleet encounter was: what if America did not choose to play the game? What if the United States refused to take the bait and chose to not make the cross-ocean sortie to engage the Japanese Navy in a main fleet encounter? Japan was not going to cross the ocean to meet the U.S. Fleet in such a battle, so what if the Americans just sat tight, and waited, until their industrial might would raise a fleet so powerful that it could overwhelm any Japanese fleet—no matter where the battle was fought? What if war with the United States turned out to be a long, drawn-out war of grinding attrition for which Japan was ill suited?

Those troubling thoughts had obviously crossed some minds in the naval high command, but like an annoying fly, they were always brushed off. They were simply future bridges to be crossed. The naval planners dismissively wrote, "Such expedient measures as the occasion may demand shall be taken."[37]

This flawed naval dogma was best described by Hori Teikichi as "creeping formalism." The Japanese Navy became "a smug little society . . . anyone who tried to embark on a new and different course was promptly branded a heretic, ignorant of tactics."[38]

Yamamoto had undoubtedly recognized the real possibilities of the alternatives to the dogma of the "main fleet encounter." But he had also ruled out the radicals' clamor for a first-strike attack at Pearl Harbor and the "bring on America" mindset.

So what changed Yamamoto's mind? It seems to have occurred at a debriefing following a Japanese naval maneuver, much like the American debriefings after the 1925 Hawaiian maneuvers. It was there that he first commented about a possible Hawaiian attack.

In September 1939, Yamamoto had become commander-in-chief of the Combined Fleet and, one month later, ordered a naval maneuver called Operation 123. Yamamoto positioned himself on his flagship, the battleship *Nagato,* and set sail. The objective was for the air forces to first find and then attack his battleship. To make the exercise even more challenging, Yamamoto ordered the operation to be conducted at night.

The attacking air force consisted of twenty-seven torpedo planes commanded by Lt. Commander Fuchida Mitsuo. Even though *Nagato* sailed shrouded in the dark, Fuchida's planes found her and launched the attack. The twenty-seven torpedo planes swooped down on the battleship, and *Nagato* flooded the dark with powerful searchlights to illuminate Fuchida's attack. The giant ship twisted and turned in evasive maneuvers while putting up a tremendous volley of anti-aircraft fire.

But *Nagato* could not escape, and with Yamamoto watching from the combat bridge, Fuchida's planes bore in and dropped their torpedoes. Amazingly there were no misses. Each torpedo dropped scored a hit. Yamamoto signaled, "Operation 123 splendid."[39]

One year later, in 1940, he ordered similar war games. When the maneuvers concluded, the top officers from all ships boarded their gigs to meet on the fantail of *Nagato*. The broad stern of the battleship served as the debriefing hall, and a large awning was spread to protect against the elements. Yamamoto told his officers that honest appraisals were guaranteed and ordered that rank had no influence on opinions. This was exactly the opposite of the phony "success" proclamations of the U.S. Navy after the 1925 exercises—stoutly refuted as propaganda by Maj. Gerald Brant.

There were the predictable arguments. Anti-aircraft gunnery officers claimed that they had shot down the attacking planes. Aviators countered that no such downings had occurred. But one thing was irrefutable: the torpedoes had all found their marks.

Real torpedoes had been used in the exercise. They were only modified in that they were lacking their explosives. They had been adjusted for depth so as to not collide with the ships' hulls and to pass under the battleship; but there was no denying that their paths had been true, and they had all been on target. Yamamoto was again more than impressed. He remarked to Navy Chief of Staff Shigeru Fukudome: "It makes me wonder if they couldn't get Pearl Harbor?"[40]

By the end of September 1941, Commander Minoru Genda, tasked with developing the plans for the attack, had detailed models constructed of both the island of Oahu and Pearl Harbor. He placed them on the aircraft carrier *Akagi,* designated to be Vice Adm. Chuichi Nagumo's flagship.[41] On November 3, the Imperial Staff authorized the attack, and X-Day was scheduled for December 8—Japan time.[42]

* * *

At 0800 on November 26, the thirty-five ships of the great Japanese task force sailed out from the remote northern anchorage at Hitokappu Bay. All transmitters on all radios were sealed, fuses removed, and all personnel were ordered away from any machine.[43] The fleet would only *listen*. It would never transmit.

Lt. Commander Sadao Chigusa, on the destroyer *Akigumo,* said, "We were in a raging snow storm when we . . . at last left Hitokappu Bay for Hawaii to attack Pearl Harbor. The sally of our great fleet was really a majestic sight. It was no wonder since it was composed of the first-line ships of the Imperial Navy, all especially selected for this crucial mission."[44]

For the next six days, the huge fleet plowed through the lonely seas. On December 2, after crossing the International Date Line, the silent fleet received Yamamoto's cryptic message to attack Pearl Harbor: *"Niitaka-yama nobore 1208."* This translates as: "Climb Mount Niitaka December 8" (December 7—Hawaii date).[45]

The great armada continued on its 4,000-mile trek, sometimes in heavy seas and shrouded in fog. That trek took it far to the north of Midway and all regular shipping channels, and it moved in absolute silence. On December 7, 230 miles north of Oahu, the six aircraft carriers separated from the great fleet and moved to the south. Then, turning into the wind, they launched their planes for the attack. The carriers were *Akagi, Kaga, Soryu, Hiryu, Shokaku,* and *Zuikaku.*

At 0600, just thirty minutes before sunrise, 183 aircraft took off from their carriers to form the first strike wave. The seas were exceedingly rough: carrier decks pitched from seven to sixteen degrees. The natural winds, and the ships steaming full speed into them, created a gale force that easily lifted the planes into the air. In fifteen minutes, the first strike force had rendezvoused and headed south. As soon as the last planes were airborne, ships' elevators began lifting the aircraft of the second wave from the hangar decks to the flight deck.

At 0740, the first-wave attackers approached the northern shore of Oahu. On signal, groups broke off right and left to approach their predesignated targets. The first bombs fell on Ford Island at 0755. In 1923, Billy Mitchell had predicted that the Ford Island attack would commence at 0730.

It was an absolute melee of diving and swerving aircraft seemingly everywhere. The forty torpedo planes were the workhorses and were devastating to every type of ship they targeted. In short order, eight battleships, three cruisers, and three destroyers were destroyed or severely damaged. Pearl Harbor became a swirling, exploding inferno. The forty-three Japanese Zeroes swarmed everywhere.

Battleship *Arizona* exploded in a spectacular fireball and black cloud of smoke. A bomb, made from a converted 16-inch naval shell, penetrated its deck and exploded in a forward magazine.

Within fifteen minutes, Pearl Harbor was ablaze. The first wave had wrought the worst destruction ever suffered by the U.S. Navy. But within five minutes of realizing that this was a genuine attack and not a drill, U.S. Navy ships began putting up anti-aircraft fire. The cumulative total of guns the Navy might bring to bear against the attacking planes was 353 long-range guns and 427 short-range weapons.[46]

At 0854, the second wave began to arrive, with 170 aircraft, and continued the island-wide attack on all military installations. The increased American fire took its toll, as 20 of the total 29 Japanese

Fiery explosions at Pearl Harbor (National Archives)

aircraft lost were from the second wave. At 0945, the last planes from that second wave departed, leaving behind a Hawaiian panorama of burning and sunken ships, destroyed aircraft, and dead Americans. No target was left untouched. The airfields at Hickam, Wheeler, Ewa, Kaneohe Bay, Barbers Point, and Bellows were left riddled and flaming.

On board *Akagi,* Commander Genda paced and listened intently for reports from the air armada. "I don't remember the exact time, but perhaps about half past [eight], or near that time, I received a wireless message, 'TORA' which meant, 'I succeeded in surprise attack.'"[47]

The last planes to depart from the Pearl Harbor attack were the Zero fighters. Flying with the second wave had been the nine fighters from the carrier *Hiryu.* They had combined with twenty-seven other Zeroes from other carriers, to provide high cover for the bombers and torpedo planes against any American fighters that might rise to engage them. If no American opposition materialized, the Zeroes were to attack airfields.[48] They were specifically ordered to strafe grounded airplanes at Hickam Field, Ford Island, Wheeler Field and Kaneohe Bay, including the tiny airstrip at Bellows Field.[49]

One of those nine *Hiryu* Zeroes was piloted by Naval Airman First Class Shigenori Nishikaichi. He quickly saw that no American aircraft were up to threaten the force and began strafing airfields as ordered. The only threat was anti-aircraft ground fire that was more intense than had been directed at the first wave. The Americans were now fully awake.

As he pulled out of his last attack against the small gunnery-training airfield at Bellows, and began climbing for his flight back to the rendezvous point, he felt that something was not right. The controls responded smoothly and there was no glitch in the sound of the engines. His fuel gauge did not show an abnormal consumption, but a distinctive odor of gasoline filled his cockpit. He leveled off and slid the cockpit canopy back a few inches to vent the fumes.

A quick inspection of the surface of his wings revealed a steady liquid mist escaping out of the top of the wing fuel tank—actually being sucked out at a rapid rate due to the lower air pressure on the

Naval Airman First Class Shigenori Nishikaichi (Pacific Aviation Museum)

top of the wing. Fate had previously smiled broadly on the Japanese attack force, and no American aircraft had gotten up to challenge Nishikaichi and his squadron of fighters. They had been able to go about their business of strafing airfields in a very one-sided contest. But fate now appeared to have allowed some randomly fired bullets, from the small band of outgunned defenders on Bellows Field, to find their mark. Maybe there were other holes he couldn't see.

Actually there were: four more holes, in various parts of the fuselage and in the empty, centerline external fuel tank. But none was leaking precious fuel. He still had almost two-thirds of his fuel, more than enough for the 200-mile return flight to the carriers.[50]

The rendezvous point was only 20 miles to the northwest of Kaena Point on the western extremity of Oahu. The gathering aircraft were to meet and circle at a very low altitude—3,500 feet—for thirty minutes. When the fighters rejoined the group, the whole force would track out on a northerly heading for the remaining flight to the waiting carriers.[51] That course would also take them near to the island of Niihau, 124 miles to the northwest of Oahu. The Zeroes would act as a rear guard during the return flight.

That path toward Niihau was important. Mitchell had predicted a significant role for the island in his 1924 report. He had envisioned it as an advanced air base from which the Japanese could launch attacks against Oahu. But 1941 was far removed from 1924, and aircraft carriers now made it possible for a formidable air force to approach an enemy target without a land base.

Mitchell's prediction presumed an air attack from a permanently occupied island to subdue the fleet and air forces at Oahu. The 1941 Japanese plan did not embrace that bold occupation plan. The 1941 attack was to be a raid: hit and run. There would be no permanent occupancy to interfere with future American movement and maneuver in Hawaiian waters. While occupation of enemy territory was very much a part of the Japanese plan in the Western Pacific, it was not here. In reality, once the attack was over, no enemy would be encamped on America's doorstep.

But Niihau was still earmarked for a role in the Pearl Harbor attack, not as an offensive airdrome but as a final refuge for wounded warriors. The pilots had been briefed that should they experience airplane malfunctions, they were to try to make an emergency landing on the reportedly uninhabited island.

"We were told," said Haruo Yoshino, "that if we had trouble, to land on the southern shoreline so the rescue sub could . . . come in. There was a submarine, waiting off the coast of Niihau, waiting to pick up any aviators whose planes were damaged."[52]

And, indeed, many of the thirty Japanese submarines with the task force had been charged to stay on the scene for possible rescue operations. Admiral Nagumo himself had ordered it.[53]

So, Naval Airman First Class Shigenori Nishikaichi, with fuel vaporizing out of the top of his right wing, reduced speed to conserve fuel and departed from the battle area. If he ever even flew to the rendezvous area, he found no one there. No one knows the path of his flight from Bellows, but it seems that he wandered about for up to two hours. Somewhere along the way, he came to realize that he was now on his own and low on fuel. He replotted his course to Niihau.

Chapter 12

Infamy and Treachery

All but four of the small Niihau population were Hawaiian. Thirty-eight-year-old Yoshio Harada had been born in Kauai of Japanese immigrants. His wife, Irene, thirty-six, had also been born on Kauai of Japanese parents. Both, by virtue of their birth, were American citizens and were further identified in their Japanese background as *Nisei*—or second-generation Americans born of immigrant Japanese parents.

They had ended up on Niihau by virtue of an employment opportunity. In 1938, Aylmer Robinson was looking for a housekeeper for his seventy-eight-year-old Scottish superintendent and paymaster, John Rennie, and also for someone to tend to the 1,615 hives of bees that flourished on Niihau. A deal was arranged with the Haradas, and in January 1939, the couple moved to Niihau and also opened up a general store.[1]

The fourth non-Hawaiian on Niihau was Ishimatsu Shintani. He had left Japan as a nineteen-year-old and arrived in Hawaii in 1900, and ended up on Niihau as an employee of the Robinsons. He was a general handyman and proficient in tending the bee farm. He married a local girl and had three children. On December 7, 1941, he was sixty.

When Rennie died in September 1941, Robinson moved to appoint Yoshio Harada as paymaster.

Sunday church services on Niihau were at the village of Puuwai in the late morning, and it was close to noon when Nishikaichi's Zero approached Niihau. The parishioners were still milling around the church after services. They had witnessed an earlier, strange event. Although he didn't know it, Nishikaichi was not the first to fly a Japanese Zero over the islanders.

Hawila "Howard" Kaleohano had been standing outside of his home, also around noon, when he saw two planes fly over. "One looked like it was in trouble," he said. "The other one was flying all around it. Then the first plane goes down in the ocean. The other one flies around some more and then goes away."[2]

The Haradas had also seen the two previous Zeroes. Irene was giving Yoshio a haircut when they flew over, one sputtering with visible smoke. Harada simply exclaimed that one of them was in trouble, but they did not investigate further and sat down to lunch.[3]

As Nishikaichi approached the island, he searched for a place to land. As he flew, first along the west coast of the island and then down the east coast, all he could see were the strangely furrowed fields. The islanders watched the circling Zero for over half an hour before it seemed to prepare to land. A circling aircraft was not a common sight over the island.

"He searched for over half an hour to find a place that wasn't furrowed," said Keith Robinson. "He thought he finally found this nice thick smooth-looking area covered with mao weeds. They were very dense and he couldn't see the boulders underneath."[4]

The final decision to land there was made for Nishikaichi when his engine simply ran out of fuel. He prepared for a glide landing with no power. He put down full flaps to give his aircraft maximum lift and lowered his wheels as he approached the inviting green carpet. His prop was no longer turning as he approached the slight upslope of the boulders covered by the carpet of mao weeds.

He probably saw the danger of the boulders at the very last moment, because he pulled the nose up, just clearing the weed-covered slope. His landing gear snagged a wire fence, uprooting the posts. The Zero was wrenched to the right and brought to a sudden, shattering halt among some strewn lava rocks. The wheels folded back, and the impact also dislodged the empty center-line fuel tank. The two prop blades that had come into contact with the earth were bent under, but the third blade still pointed straight to the sky, undamaged— further proof that the engine was not turning.

Nishikaichi's silent approach and shattering landing came as a complete surprise to Hawila Kaleohano, who had earlier seen the two aircraft fly by. At the time Nishikaichi came to ground, he was looking away, distracted by the nervous antics of his agitated horse.

Recovering from the initial shock and surprise of an airplane crashing almost on top of him, the twenty-nine-year-old Hawila bolted the few steps necessary to leap up on the Zero's wing. As the dust settled, he saw the stunned pilot, who after seeing Hawila, fumbled for his pistol; but the young Hawaiian was too quick for him. He snatched it out of his hands and grabbed Nishikaichi around the shoulders and dragged him from the cockpit. As he did, a pocket on the pilot's flight suit snagged on the plane and was ripped off, revealing a map and papers. Hawila grabbed those too and began escorting Nishikaichi toward his house.[5] Along the way, Nishikaichi asked Hawila, in his rather good English, if he was Japanese.[6] Hawila informed him that he was Hawaiian.

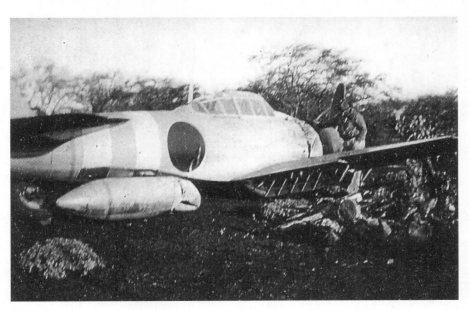

The crashed Zero on Niihau December 7, 1941 (Syd Jones Collection)

Hawila Kaleohano, the first to the crashed Zero, disarmed Nishikaichi.
(Pacific Aviation Museum)

Knowing nothing of the Pearl Harbor attack, Hawila and his wife, Mabel, suddenly became good Samaritans and prepared food and coffee for the pilot; after fish, pancakes, and coffee, the two men smoked cigarettes. Nishikaichi must have felt more at ease after the friendly treatment and hospitality because he broached the subject of his confiscated papers and asked for their return. Hawila said no. There was still the subject of an explanation as to how Nishikaichi came to crash land on this island in a Japanese fighter—and what about the other fighters that had flown by earlier?

Like moths drawn to the flame, it wasn't long before the curious Niihauans circled around the crash site and Hawila Kaleohano's house. When they entered the home to see the Japanese pilot, they saw him trying to write on his notebook paper for Hawila, but all communications were at a standstill.[7]

Hawila sent someone running for the Japanese beekeeper, Shintani, who, other than the Haradas, was the only Japanese speaker on the island. He arrived and spoke very briefly with the pilot before departing, showing signs of distress. Whatever was said between them, he kept from the gathered Hawaiians.

With Shintani having departed, the next logical translators were the Haradas. They arrived and Yoshio and the pilot immediately engaged in a rapid discussion. Nishikaichi must have thought that time was not on his side and his best course was to reveal everything to another Japanese who might possibly help him. Perhaps Harada could help recover his papers and weapon and, more importantly, get him back to the plane to attempt radio communication with his rescue submarine. The Haradas now knew about the Pearl Harbor attack, but after the conversation ended, both chose to remain silent and not inform their fellow islanders.[8]

Since it was approaching evening on Sunday, and that was a day set aside for relaxing music and eating, the entire group moved from Hawila's house to Joseph Kele's house, a short distance away, for a luau with their new guest. As the evening wore on, there were whispered questions as to just who was this visitor from the sky.

Nishikaichi spent the night at Kele's house, under guard, and the next morning freely roamed around the village. On Tuesday,

December 9, he was taken, under the guard of Harada and Shintani, by tractor, to the northernmost part of the island, to the boat-launch area at Kii. They proceeded the eight miles along the western road from Puuwai to the north end of the island and then cut across the narrow neck to the eastern side.

Aylmer Robinson had a sampan at Kii, along with a whaleboat secured in a boathouse. They intended to launch either craft and take the aviator to the authorities in Kauai. But it was not possible since the sea conditions were bad, and waves crashed on the shore. A second trek was made the following day, the tenth, but was no better.[9]

Harada obviously grew tired of being Nishikaichi's guard on those

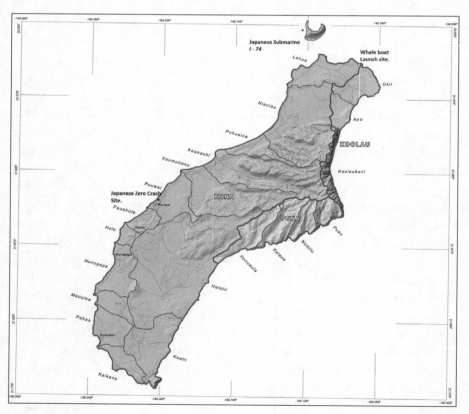

(Map by author)

treks and asked for relief. Both he and Shintani were relieved of that duty, but later in the day Harada sent for Shintani to come and discuss some matters. He didn't reveal what those matters were, but Shintani refused to come. Nishikaichi was held under guard in Harada's house.

The following day, Shintani went about his bee business and was seen having lunch with other Hawaiians. But at the end of the day he worked his way to Hawila's house. He knocked on the door, but the sleeping Hawila did not hear him. The knock turned into a rapid pounding, and when Hawila finally answered, a nervous Shintani entered and asked the Hawaiian if he had the aviator's papers. Hawila nodded that he did and produced the map of Oahu. But Shintani wasn't interested in the map. He wanted the other papers.

This unexpected performance by the normally meek beekeeper made it obvious that the matter of Nishikaichi's papers had been an important subject for discussion on those two days of trekking back and forth to Kii.

When Hawila produced the other papers, Shintani became very agitated and blurted out that he had to have them and that it was a matter of life and death to him.[10] Hawila refused, and Shintani became even more agitated. "Won't you give them to me so that I can burn them?" he desperately asked. But Hawila again refused and rebuked him. He told him it was against the law, and they could both get into bad trouble.

Shintani was now utterly at his wit's end. Reaching into his pocket, he pulled out $200—a virtual king's ransom for any Niihauan. Again Hawila refused, and Shintani ran dejectedly from the house still shouting his dire warning about life and death.[11]

This intrigue was only the beginning of a sinister, concocted plot. Sometime Friday afternoon, Harada and Nishikaichi conspired to free the pilot from his guard. Feigning a need to use the outhouse, the Japanese aviator exited Harada's house and walked across the yard with the guard following closely behind. Harada also exited but detoured to the honey warehouse, where he seized the only weapon on the island—Robinson's shotgun. He leveled it at the surprised guard and then locked him in an adjacent warehouse.[12]

Not seeing Shintani after he had gone to see Hawila, Harada and Nishikaichi now broke into his house looking for the missing papers;

and then broke into Hawila's house, where they found the pilot's pistol. But at neither break-in did they locate the papers.

Perhaps they assumed that Shintani had them on his person, and they tracked him to the middle of Puuwai, where he had joined other Hawaiians. Harada and Nishikaichi were now fully aroused and raced in to grab him. A chase ensued, but the small Japanese beekeeper was too quick for them and ran away. In their rage, the two attackers took several islanders as their prisoners and tied the others up.

Next they spotted a Niihau wagon approaching the village from a house just on the other side of the hill, and they targeted it for their own transportation. Driving the wagon was Mrs. Neheu, a mother of four, coming into town from her nearby home for supplies. She had her children with her, including an infant. An older girl, Loisa, was not in the small wagon but actually riding on the horse pulling the wagon. Harada shouted for her to stop, but Mrs. Neheu saw the danger and did not. Brandishing their weapons, Harada and Nishikaichi ran after her as she quickened the horse down the hill. They caught the horse by the bridle and brought it to a stop. Harada ordered everyone off the wagon, threatening their lives, and pointed his pistol at the terrified mother.[13]

The older girl, Loisa, was told to remain mounted on the horse and the two Japanese clambered aboard, training their guns on her. The terrified girl was ordered to gallop the horse and wagon off toward Hawila Kaleohano's house. As they approached, they first stopped at the crash site. A teenaged boy, Kalihilihi Niau, was guarding the Zero, and the two Japanese took him hostage at gunpoint. Then they went to Hawila's house, stopped at the gate, and prodded Niau in front of them with the shotgun in his back.

Hawila was in the outhouse at the time, a short distance from the main house, and remained concealed. Having left the cart at the gate, the two Japanese shouted out for him. Loisa realized her unique opportunity and somehow unhitched the horse and galloped away with Niau. Hawila continued to watch from the outhouse as the two Japanese walked around calling for him. It was almost 6:00 P.M., and darkness was descending. The villagers, who had witnessed Mrs. Neheu's ordeal, scattered. Frustrated at not finding Hawila, Harada and Nishikaichi retraced their steps to Puuwai village, leaving Mrs. Neheu's now-horseless wagon at the gate.

At one end of the village they captured a second boy, whom they ordered to call out for all the villagers to come out into the street. The boy balked, but the weapon jammed in his back forced him to shout out. One man, frantically trying to evacuate his own family, thought the boy was calling out for help and went running to his aid. He fell into the hands of the two terrorists, who took him prisoner and immediately tied his hands. With the boy, he was marched down the street, as Harada shouted for the all villagers to show themselves.

They stopped at Joseph Kele's house: the very house where the villagers had shown such hospitality to Nishikaichi when they hosted the Japanese aviator at a friendly luau on the day he had crashed. Now this same aviator was a gun-wielding fanatical enemy who, with Harada, threatened to kill everyone in sight. Yoshio Harada had gone from a Dr. Jekyll to a Mr. Hyde to collaborate with Nishikaichi in a Japanese blood pact. He would wage war against his own countrymen.

And where was Irene Harada, also American born, during all of this? She knew about the plan and was complicit with it. To her, Japanese blood trumped all. She would later say, "Mr. Nishikaichi desperately wanted to recover that map. Because Harada was a Japanese too, he decided to help. . . . Although he was a Hawaiian Nisei, he still had a Japanese spirit."[14]

She also wrote, "I am an American citizen, born in the United States. However under our skin, the blood that flows is Japanese. Therefore, I do not think that my husband did anything wrong."[15]

Her *innocent* husband was now on a terror rampage. With their two hostages, he and the aviator retrieved the wagon parked at Hawila's gate and revisited the Zero. The captives noticed that Harada and Nishikaichi must have earlier removed a large amount of ammunition from the guns and stacked it on the wing. Harada prodded the boy to help carry some of it to the wagon.

They then removed one of the machine guns and placed it, too, on the wagon. While the transfer of gun and ammunition was taking place, Nishikaichi got into the cockpit and tried his radio. He put the earphones on and transmitted multiple times in Japanese. But no one heard an answer.[16]

Yoshio Harada betrayed his country to fight with the Japanese pilot.
(Pacific Aviation Museum)

In the plans for the attack, in addition to naming Niihau as an emergency landing site, submarines had been assigned to rescue patrols along the aircrafts' routes of approach and withdrawal. As such, on December 7, the IJN submarine *I-74* (later designated *I-174*) was stationed south of Niihau. *I-74* had arrived in the Oahu area on December 4 and was assigned to Submarine Squadron 3 for lifeguard duty.[17]

While Nishikaichi tried to transmit, perhaps to the submarine, Harada continued his terror tactics. He must have thought that his possession of a weapon and his bullying would automatically force his victims into total submission. Turning to the captive man, he ordered him off, still with his hands bound, and instructed him to go tell his wife, Irene, that he wouldn't be back that night. The man, predictably, ignored the order and raced to the beach where his family was hiding. His wife quickly untied his hands.

As soon as he was free, he sought out the six-foot-tall Benehakaka "Benny" Kanahele, a giant of a man by Niihau standards. His strength was legendary. The islanders often witnessed him, at age fifty-one, sling a fully grown sheep across his shoulders or, even more impressive, carry two honey containers to load on the sampan. Each weighed 130 pounds.[18]

Benny listened as his friend told him that they had to recapture the ammunition for the machine gun. To terrify him, Harada had boasted that he had enough ammunition "to kill off every man, woman, and child on the island."[19] Harada and Nishikaichi had gone off with the machine gun, mounted on the cart, and, while they were gone, there was a golden opportunity to sneak back to the abandoned Zero and snatch the rest of the ammunition.

Moving in the dark, the two men crept back, first up the beach and then toward the crashed Zero. The wagon and machine gun were indeed gone, but the extra ammunition was still stacked on the wing. Moving quickly, they grabbed it all and raced back to the beach, where they hid it.

Hawila Kaleohano had, meanwhile, escaped from his hiding place in the outhouse. So too had the guard locked in the warehouse, by jumping from the second floor. Together, they raced through the village, shouting the warning that Harada had joined forces with the Japanese pilot and was threatening everyone. After a quick meeting, Hawila was soon on horseback, galloping for the high mountain peak at Paniau. Stuffed in his pocket were Nishikaichi's papers.

The mountain, thrusting 1,281 feet in the air, was directly west of Kauai. The high peak essentially blocked Kauai's view of any other activity on Niihau.[20] When Hawila arrived, other islanders were already there, attempting to signal Kauai. They had kerosene lamps with reflectors and flashed signal after signal to Kauai, nineteen miles away. Hawila then rode north to Kii, where he and five other men decided to row the whaleboat to the neighboring island for help.[21] The sea was still not calm.

At half-past midnight on December 13, the whaleboat set off in turbulent seas. The men would not reach their destination until fifteen hours later, at 3:30 in the afternoon.[22]

Some islanders had not been able to run and were rounded up by the two terrorists, who through the night had continued to search for the missing papers. Around 3:00 A. M., they ransacked Hawila's house and then burned it to the ground, hoping that the inferno would destroy the "hidden" papers. They then went to the Zero and sought to incinerate it too, perhaps with the thought of not letting it fall into American hands.[23]

One writer suggested that Nishikaichi doused the Zero with fuel, but that would have been impossible since the fuel tanks were bone dry. However, there were plentiful fuel sources in the area.

"Dead, dried kiawe wood burns with great heat," said Keith Robinson. The villagers collected it and piled it near their houses for cooking. It would have been a simple thing to pack the wood into the Zero cockpit and ignite it.

Harada and Nishikaichi then rolled the wagon with the machine gun into the village and let loose with bursts of automatic fire through the trees. Their intention was to so frighten the Niihauans that they would produce the missing papers or at least give up Hawila. Brush and foliage cascaded down on the assembled hostages, who took off yelling and screaming.

"It was exactly counterproductive of what they wanted," said Keith

The skeleton of the burned and gutted Zero. (Pacific Aviation Museum)

Robinson, "having them in submission, saying, 'Oh sir, we'll get what you want. We'll get your papers back.' Instead, they split like a fish in front of the shark.

"Milimilinihi described the chaos in colorful pigeon English. *'Dem Kanakas been deeg!'* Translated it meant, 'The Hawaiians took off running in a cloud of dust.'"[24]

All, that is, except for the elderly Mrs. Hulu-o-Ulani. She had stoically observed the two Japanese and their smoking machine gun. The elderly woman was sitting in her rocking chair, reading her Bible, when they now threatened her life. But the two Japanese were further frustrated when Mrs. Hulu-o-Ulani calmly told them, "Only God has the power of life and death," and went back to reading.[25]

As the sun came up on Saturday, December 13, the Niihauan whaleboat was being rowed, agonizingly slow, toward Kauai. The rough waters made for a very difficult crossing. At Puuwai, the terrorists rounded up the remaining islanders who had been hiding along the beach. They found Benny Kanahele's family in a cave. They now ordered Benny, his wife, Ella, and some others into the bush to find Hawila, threatening to shoot the women.

Benny led them into the bush, calling out for Hawila; but it wasn't long before Nishikaichi suspected that he was being led to nowhere. Screaming to Harada to tell Benny and his wife that he would shoot them both if they did not find Hawila, he stopped the search party near a lava-stone wall.

Standing next to Ella, the big Hawaiian suddenly saw a brief opportunity and grabbed for Nishikaichi's pistol. But as he swiped for it, he missed, and the Japanese pilot pulled it back. Ella was immediately on him, grabbing his arm, but Harada wrestled the woman away, and Nishikaichi shot Benny—the bullet hit him in the ribs. The wounded Hawaiian was like a man possessed and, despite his wound, rushed the Japanese pilot, who leveled his weapon and shot Benny a second time. This one hit Benny in the hip. A third shot hit him in the groin.[26]

Benny Kanahele would later tell an interpreter, "That's when I got mad."[27]

Undaunted, he grabbed the pilot bodily, raised him into the air, and smashed him, headfirst, into the lava wall. The crushing blow most likely killed Nishikaichi, but as his body slumped to the ground, Ella jumped on him and, with a big lava stone, pounded on his head.[28]

The panicked Harada, seeing that he was alone, turned the shotgun on himself and discharged both barrels into his abdomen.[29] The terror was over.

When the whaleboat reached Kauai on Saturday December 13, Hawila immediately reported to a worried Aylmer Robinson. He detailed the treachery unfolding on Niihau, and the Army dispatched a force to go to Niihau at once. One can only imagine the panic in the Army command, envisioning invasion as they tried to recover from the December 7 attack.

Radioman 1/c George C. Larsen, with the United States Coast Guard, had been recently transferred to the Coast Guard cutter *Kukui*, an ancient ship built in 1909. The 185-foot vessel was a buoy tender and, in the aftermath of Pearl Harbor, was tasked with extinguishing all the automatic lights that came on in the dark, flashing navigational warnings.

Larsen recalled, "During our trip to the Island of Kauai and surrounding area we put out a light atop a 750-foot rock north of Niihau by shooting tracers at the gas bottle house because it was too rough to land at the only landing spot. It turned dark. As we started back we got a message . . . that there was a Japanese submarine lurking on the east side of Kauai."

When the cutter returned to port in Kauai, they were ordered out on a special mission. "The Army requested us to help them recapture Niihau Island, as a Japanese fighter pilot had crashed on the Island and had taken control of the natives with the help of two Japanese workers. So we went over to Niihau Island arriving a little after dusk with a squad of Army raiders and four of the ship's crew ready to jump ashore for the rescue, they were all armed to the teeth and ready to go."[30]

When the force landed on Niihau, they discovered that the crisis

Ella and Benny Kanahele at the hospital after the attack. (Pacific Aviation Museum)

was over and both terrorists were now dead. They returned to Kauai with the two Japanese, Irene Harada and Shintani, as prisoners. They also brought the wounded Benny Kanahele and his wife, Ella. Benny refused help and insisted on walking off the boat under his own power. Larsen called him "one tough native."

* * *

On December 16, 1941, a second military expedition was mounted from Kauai. This mission, led by Aylmer Robinson, was to visit the Zero crash site, photograph it, and retrieve parts and samples from the aircraft. It mounted out from Kauai, in the dark, on two sampans. To provide air cover for the little flotilla, a Navy PBY seaplane flew in lazy circles overhead. The expedition approached the northern tip of Niihau and entered the small channel between Niihau and its offshore satellite, the island of Lehua.

Lehua was not really an island. It was a strange, almost out-of-place appendage to Niihau. It was the remaining half-rim of a long-dormant volcano. The concave half of this broken cone formed a crescent and faced to the east The outer, convex portion faced to the west.

The little convoy was just exiting the channel between Niihau and Lehua, ready to make its run down the western side of Niihau toward the village of Puuwai. Suddenly the PBY maneuvered toward the western face of Lehua and went into an attack dive.

"The waters immediately adjacent to the sheer west wall of Lehua Island are probably the best place in all Hawaii to hide a surfaced submarine," said Keith Robinson.

In fact, just a few yards offshore, the water depth plunged to 700 feet. "A gray submarine would be extremely difficult to see against the brownish-gray background of Lehua Island's sheer western sea cliffs."[31]

Nor would the PBY have seen it until it was directly overhead. On its east-to-west flight path, the towering western wall of Lehua would have blocked all view. The submarine, tucked against that sheer wall, would have made radar detection virtually impossible. It would have surfaced after dark to spend the night recharging its batteries; but on the surface, sweeping radar might have easily spotted the sub. Tucked tightly against the western wall, partially submerged, she became part of the image of the great rock and virtually invisible.

The PBY attack was short. It ran in, dropped a bomb, and almost immediately went into a nosedive and crashed in the shallow waters about four hundred yards off Niihau's northern shore. The sampans beached at once, and in the next hours, the islanders attempted a rescue of the survivors. The pilot and copilot, who could have given details of the encounter, died in the crash.

Naval authorities later said that the PBY crashed because of a wind shear, but islander eyewitnesses, from three separate locations on Niihau, and at least one witness on the sampans, testified to the presence of the Japanese submarine. In the panic following the December 7 devastation, the "wind-shear" report might have been a reasonable substitute for further panic. The Japanese seemed to be still around. Were they ready to invade?

In 1978, the Reverend Paul Denise (Dee-nice), who had been the

Lehua, with Niihau in the background. The Japanese submarine was hidden against the right-side cliffs. (Christopher P. Becker Collection)

official photographer on the December 16 Army expedition, visited Niihau to preach in the church where he had preached before Pearl Harbor. After church, Keith Robinson approached him. Denise had taken over five hundred photos of the Zero, the terrain, and the expedition.

In an ensuing casual conversation, Denise said, "There was a lifeguard submarine off Niihau. We ran into it on the way over. The PBY escorting us discovered it, attacked it, and then crashed."[32]

When Robinson showed astonishment at that information, Denise realized that Robinson had not been told of the submarine, and, even after thirty-three years, perhaps he had said too much. The old code of Niihau silence kicked in and ended any further conversation.[33]

Robinson, however, sought out some of the older islanders for details. For all the mystery that surrounded the Niihau connection both prior to and after Pearl Harbor, this was the most mysterious. The submarine connection had never been mentioned in his family during the thirty-three years since the war ended. He turned to the islanders and confronted one who had been a little younger at the time of the attack.

He was William Apelahama, Sr. When Robinson asked why Apelahama had never told him, the man became nervous. He finally confirmed the story in halting sentences and concluded by saying, "We were told never to talk about that."[34]

It is inconceivable that so many eyewitnesses to the submarine attack could have gotten the story wrong. It is most conceivable that an incorrect reason for the PBY's crash had been inserted in the report, when one examines the mood and terror of the American people in those dark days immediately after the attack on Pearl Harbor. A later attack by two Japanese bombers on Mount Tantalus near Pearl Harbor in March 1942, attempting to delay repair operations and strike the fuel storage areas missed on December 7, was passed off by authorities as Army and Navy ammunition detonations.

It is also more than conceivable that the Niihau people, already sheltered from the twentieth century, should be told to never say anything about what happened lest they experience some harsh consequences for violating national security. This was top secret.

Thirty years after breaking the German enigma code, the British codebreakers were still sworn to silence about what they had done. They had signed the "Official Secrets Act," valid for thirty years, with draconian penalties if violated. Those codebreakers said nothing for those thirty years, and they were a lot more sophisticated than the Niihauans. Why would these gentle islanders, facing security sanctions, not remain tightlipped, especially when ordered to do so by the Army through their island lord, Aylmer Robinson?

The threat of invasion was in the air. The members of the December 16 Army expedition to Niihau had ventured out, armed to the teeth. This was not just a casual investigating team. The official photographer, the Reverend Paul Denise, a clergyman by trade, was carrying, not a sidearm, but a Browning Automatic Rifle. After the submarine attack, the two sampans beached themselves on the northern shore of Niihau, just across the channel from the Lehua Rock.

Certainly they wanted to help the survivors, but while some islanders rushed to help the PBY survivors, Reverend Denise, Aylmer Robinson, and the rest of the party took off on horseback to cover the remaining seven miles to Puuwai. If there was no submarine, why not take one of the sampans and leave the other to assist in the rescue and care for the PBY injured? Not taking the sampan to the Puuwai dock meant that whatever they might choose to remove to return to Kauai would be limited and would have to be transported on horseback to the anchored sampans.

But it is easy to understand those actions if there was a submarine. Getting off of the sampans was the prudent thing to do. Aylmer Robinson well knew Billy Mitchell's attack scenario, which included Niihau in an invasion plan, and the Japanese had indeed attacked Oahu just as he had outlined in 1924. Brant had restated Mitchell's belief in the 1930s. Mitchell had written, "Physical action taken by Japan . . . will be followed by the seizure of one of the Hawaiian Islands, probably the island of Niihau, and an air and submarine base established there."[35]

What was there not to understand? Several Japanese planes had flown over Niihau, one had crash-landed, and now a submarine had shown itself.

All arguments to the contrary regarding the presence of a Japanese submarine were rendered moot when later documents revealed the lifeguarding missions of the submarine force. An official Japanese document revealed that the submarine *I-74* had been assigned lifeguard duty on December 7, in the vicinity of Niihau, and departed those waters on December 17, 1941—the day after the reported PBY attack.[36]

Were there far-reaching consequences of the Niihau Zero incident? On January 26, 1942, Capt. Irving Mayfield, the Fourteenth Naval District's intelligence officer, produced an intelligence report. The subject was: JAPANESE RESIDENTS FOR THE T. H. [Territory of Hawaii], LOYALTY OF.[37]

Mayfield's report narrated the details of the Niihau incident and concluded with a paragraph entitled, "Deductions": "The fact that two Niihau Japanese, who had previously shown no anti-American tendencies, went to the aid of a pilot when Japanese domination of the island seemed possible, indicates likelihood that Japanese residents, previously believed loyal to the United States, may aid Japan if further Japanese attacks appear successful."[38]

On February 19, 1942, Pres. Franklin Roosevelt signed Executive Order 9066, directing Secretary of War Henry Stimson "to proscribe military areas in such places . . . from which any or all persons may be excluded."[39] On March 21, Congress ratified it.

Two days later, a letter arrived, by special messenger, at the White House. It was addressed to Maj. Gen. Edwin M. Watson, secretary to the president, and was marked "Personal and Confidential."

The author of this personal letter was J. Edgar Hoover, director of the Federal Bureau of Investigation, and he had written a detailed report to Roosevelt concerning the Niihau incident. "I thought the President and you might be interested in the incident of a Japanese being forced down in his plane on December 7, 1941, on the outlying Island of Niihau . . . where with the aid of two Japanese, one a citizen and one an alien, gained possession of firearms and terrorized the natives . . . until overcome and killed on December 13, 1941, by a Hawaiian native he had shot and wounded. A memorandum covering the details of this incident is transmitted herewith."

The Niihau incident was over, and as time and war pressed on, its drama faded from view, as 25,655 enemy aliens were interned away from sensitive military areas. Of these, 11,299 were Japanese. The rest were from the other Axis countries, including 10,905 Germans and 3,278 Italians. Surprisingly, 5,620 *Nisei,* Americans like the Haradas, born of Japanese parents, renounced their citizenship.[40]

A songwriter, R. Alex Anderson, penned a popular ballad called "They Couldn't Take Niihau Nohow." Hawila Kaleohano received the Medal of Freedom and the government paid him $800 to compensate for the loss of his incinerated house. Benny Kanahele was awarded the Purple Heart and the Medal of Merit.

Billy Mitchell's war against Japan had begun on December 7, 1941, with his predicted attacks on Oahu and the Philippines. It would last for 1,364 days.

Epilogue

Billy Mitchell never lived to see the devastation of Pearl Harbor and the Philippines. Nor did he see the superiority of aircraft over surface ships proven during a war. His disciples lived to lead the air forces in the offensives that Mitchell had pressed for. Many of his antagonists did live to see his proclamations come to fruition.

Gen. Mason Patrick survived to see Japan bomb Pearl Harbor; Secretary of War Dwight Davis survived to see the 1,000-plane bombing raids that crushed both Japan and Germany, and even the dropping of the atomic bomb. Also living during the war was Gen. Black Jack Pershing.

Gen. Charles Summerall also lived on. He hated Mitchell for declaring, in his 1924 inspection report, that Summerall's command in Oahu was unprepared. Mitchell had written, "There is no real organization of the air forces for war in the Hawaiian Department." For all of the offended general's huffing and puffing, it was obvious that seventeen years later, nothing had changed. Adding insult to injury, Summerall further detested Mitchell for having successfully challenged him off his court-martial trial.

A cursory research did not reveal any of these men expressing regret for having been so wrong or uttering an apology to the deceased air pioneer. None acknowledged that Mitchell had been spot on in his warnings of the beginning and the unfolding of WWII against Japan.

Mitchell was honored far more than any of these former critics could have expected. Memorializing Mitchell was left to Lee Atwood, vice president of North American aircraft builders who named their B-25 bomber after the general, and the Army Air Corps readily agreed. It was indeed an honor since no bomber, before or since, has been named after a person. It was further fitting that this bomber carried the bombs for the first offensive to targets in Tokyo in April 1942 during the daring Doolittle Raid.

But why has Mitchell's military acumen been so steadfastly misunderstood and avoided by historians during the years following his death and the end of WWII? A number of biographies have been written, including *The Billy Mitchell Affair,* by Burke Davis in 1967; *A Question of Loyalty,* by Douglas Waller in 2004; and a 1975 revision of his 1964 work, *Billy Mitchell: Crusader for Air Power*, by Alfred F. Hurley.

All three focus on Mitchell's dogged determination to advance air power as an equal service to the Army and Navy, and his dramatic 1921 bombing tests. But not one delves into the ignored 1924 report on Mitchell's Pacific inspection. And it is that report that best reveals the heart and soul of Mitchell's thinking. As historians, they seemed to have mimicked the exact actions of the 1924 Army brass, who snubbed him and his report and consigned it to the "Flying Trash Pile." Some historians today seem to have been consigned to a "Literary Trash Pile."

In fairness to the Waller work, its advertised thrust was "to capture in detail the drama of the court."[1] And it did that spectacularly well— until it went off course in an attempt to minimize Mitchell's amazing prediction of the attack on Pearl Harbor.

Waller wrote, "Of course the time of the attack was *easy* to predict. Military forces usually begin them early in the morning."[2]

Considering the four European invasions—Sicily, Italy, Normandy, and Holland—only Normandy would have qualified for Waller's *easy-to-predict* claim. The invasions of Sicily and Italy began in the dark, at 3:00 A.M.; Holland began at 2:00 P.M.

If this prediction was so easy, Waller failed to list the people who, in the past, have made similar ones—seventeen years before the event. Mitchell had also predicted that air power had the ability to be decisive and end a war on its own. Waller found fault with that and wrote, "Air power did not win the war alone as he [Mitchell] believed it would." But Waller was parsing words: Mitchell actually had said it "could."

When he presented this idea in 1924, Mitchell's critics howled and laughed; but twenty-one years after the laughter had subsided, in 1945, an American occupation Army walked ashore on the Japanese homeland, unopposed. Air power not only "could" end but had ended the war. There was not one casualty lost in Operation Downfall, an invasion of Japan that didn't happen and which had expected upward of one million American casualties.

Burke Davis's excellent work was handicapped by not including any aspect of Mitchell's Pacific report. In the end, the author noted, "A potentially valuable document, a complete diary of the inspection tour, once included in the Mitchell Papers, is now missing."[3] Obviously he never found it.

Alfred Hurley proclaimed his own book to be "the first documented, critical, and hopefully, balanced study of Mitchell and his work."[4] But although he referenced Mitchell's Pacific report, he mostly ignored it and then drew a conclusion that seemed to run off the rails. He declared that "[Mitchell] was not an original thinker."[5]

But Hurley's conclusion did not explain why he thought that Mitchell's Pacific report was not *original* thought. And his very own words betrayed his conclusion. He had earlier written, in the same work, "Mitchell's own manual on bombardment in 1923 . . . was the basis for a conception of bombardment *far ahead of the times*"[6] (emphasis added).

And a brief examination of some of the ideas in Mitchell's "Flying Trash Pile" would have revealed an avalanche of original thought.

Historians and military enthusiasts agree that the war with Japan was the most predictable of any war ever fought. But that begs the question that if it was so predictable, why did these same military thinkers miss Japanese intentions so badly? War Plan Orange was the offensive dogma of the time and the very model for war with Japan during the four decades prior to December 7, 1941. But while Plan Orange bristled with details for offensive action once the war began, it never anticipated starting the war *after* the Pacific Fleet had been *sunk*.

Consider for a moment, when evaluating Mitchell's forecasting of events and the mindset that seeks to minimize its uniqueness: he had not just predicted an eventual war with Japan, and how it would begin and how it would unfold, but he predicted the actual attack on Oahu and the exact time. Any claim that others might have done the same, or that "the time . . . was easy to predict" as Waller absurdly suggested, should be denounced, especially when compared to the following event.

On November 27, 1941, Adm. Husband Kimmel, commander of the Pacific Fleet, asked his War Plans officer, Capt. Charles H. McMorris, "what the chances of a surprise raid on Oahu were?"[7]

The room was full of the top brass in Hawaii. McMorris said emphatically, "None!" No one disagreed; Gen. Walter Short, commanding the Army in Hawaii, took no issue with McMorris's evaluation.[8] This was just days before the attack. With warning messages flying around fast and furious about a possible crisis with Japan, why was it not "easy" for McMorris to predict?

From the original confrontations with Japan by Commodore Perry and his Black Fleet in the 1850s, all recognized that his actions initiated a battle for control of the Pacific Ocean area. In 1911, Gen. Homer Lea first identified Japan and the United States as two irresistible forces moving to a point of inevitable collision. Lea saw it as a threat to the American homeland and specifically to the West Coast.

So what set Mitchell apart from all other earlier strategists and tacticians? Simply this: recognizing an inevitable war, and anticipating how it would begin and later unfold, are two entirely different things.

In his Pacific report, Mitchell revealed these details largely due to his unique ability to get inside the mind of the Japanese military planners and figure out what they might do. Many commanders have sought to do that, and in 1923, Mitchell saw the path that Japan would have to take if it were to have any chance, in an armed conflict, with the United States. In fact, his thinking was so advanced that the Japanese did not think of it until 1941.

In 1923, Mitchell saw the vulnerability of Hawaii in the way it was being defended. The defenses were arranged to stop a seaborne invasion of Oahu. Mitchell never thought that to be even a remote possibility. Understanding air power as no one else had, Mitchell asked himself what he would do if he were Japan.

His detailed inspection armed him with information necessary to anticipate a Japanese plan. When he formed his conclusions and presented them to his superiors, to men such as Gen. Mason Patrick, he was jeered. His valuable report was dismissed and buried. It was labeled as his "personal opinion." Some even questioned his sanity.

But absolutely no one envisioned a Japanese air attack. No one, other than Mitchell, ever presented an idea that an air attack would come at all, much less that it would come from the north, tracking and retreating, over the island chain. While the air attack did not originate from a captured Hawaiian island, as Mitchell would have launched it, it came on the exact path that he had predicted.

Somehow this amazing reasoning has eluded historians. But if Mitchell missed on the idea of launching the attack from an island, as Waller criticizes, it was not because it was a bad tactic. It was because the Japanese decided to launch a raid instead of a decisive stroke. Mitchell was not laying out how to conduct a raid on Oahu; he was identifying the path of attack for decisive victory or conquest.

What about the March 3-4, 1942, "second" attack on Pearl Harbor, an event buried from the public for years? Two Japanese seaplane bombers attempted to strike some of the missed targets from December 7.

The Japanese called it *Operation K*. Two massive *Emily* bombers, each capable of carrying four, 500-pound bombs, would fly the "exact" route that Mitchell had warned would be the approach for the Japanese to attack on Oahu. After a 1,600-mile flight from the Marshall Islands to French Frigate Shoals, the two seaplane bombers landed. This remote atoll, part of the U.S. Hawaiian territory, was strangely unattended, even in the aftermath of the December 7 attack. It was strategically located 550 miles northwest of Oahu and 800 miles southeast of Midway. Amazingly, it was unguarded by the Navy.

On March 3, 1942, two Japanese submarines, *I-15* and *I-19*, were waiting in the lagoon for the bombers to complete their thirteen-hour flight and rendezvous for refueling. By 9:00 P.M. they were on their way to bomb Oahu. Just past midnight on March 4, they passed between Kauai and Niihau on a course to avoid detection.[9]

As they searched for Pearl Harbor, and particularly the large 1010 Dock just across from Ford Island, cloud cover obscured their targets; and the two bombers blindly dropped their bombs. Four fell harmlessly in the ocean, and the other four landed on Tantalus Ridge near Honolulu. But this unguarded path had been detailed by Mitchell and described as a route of secure communications and supply for the Japanese all the way back to Midway.

* * *

Other critics have faulted Mitchell for dismissing aircraft carriers as a decisive weapon that would carry the air offensive against the enemy. But Mitchell did not say that, nor did he dismiss aircraft carriers as nonessential. What he said was, "the air offensive must be assumed and maintained until a successful conclusion of the war is obtained."[10]

Aircraft carriers could not, and did not, do that. They could not launch air forces sufficient in number to operate successfully against landbased aircraft. They could not launch sufficient numbers "to cope with air forces setting from shore bases," Mitchell said.[11] He was absolutely correct. How long would aircraft carriers have lasted if deployed against Germany's landbased *Luftwaffe?* And in the last fanatical attack by Japanese *kamikazes,* as Japan ran out of pilots, forty-seven ships were sunk and many more damaged by these suicidal bombs.[12]

It was not carrier aircraft that carried the sustained, devastating air offensives against Germany and Japan. It was massive landbased airfields that were able to launch the thousands of planes to "assume and maintain" that offensive. Carriers were effective in moving the force necessary to capture the required islands for future aircraft operations.

Consider the battle history of aircraft carriers. Arguably there were only three, and they were all against each other. The first at Coral Sea was a virtual stalemate—each side lost a carrier. The second at

Midway was climactic regarding the shift of naval power, and the offensive, from one side to the other; and the third, in the Philippine Sea, was the "Turkey Shoot." By then Japan's powers had waned and their pilot pool had been virtually exhausted.

But in each, Mitchell's assessment concerning carrier vulnerability was proven. He had written, "There is no sufficient means of defense against aircraft from the vessels themselves."[13] While Midway was a great American victory, the extreme vulnerability of carriers was fully exposed. The cumulative losses from Coral Sea and Midway, in aircraft carriers, were horrific. Japan lost two-thirds of its carrier fleet, and the U.S. lost half.

Add in a fourth battle, albeit the one-sided carrier attack at Pearl Harbor, and Mitchell's carrier assessment remained valid. "There is nothing whatever to fear from so called naval airplane carriers, because . . . they cannot place sufficient aircraft in the air at one time to insure a concentrated operation."[14] While it was shocking and sensational, Pearl Harbor was not a concentrated operation; it was a raid—hit and run.

That did not mean that carriers and their aircraft could not conduct such a spectacular raid, but the Japanese were not able to sustain their attack with carriers and were forced to withdraw— much to their later lament. The raid had left the American fleet, although badly damaged, still in place at Pearl Harbor. Instead of being driven back to the West Coast, its drydocks and fuel supplies were untouched; and the Americans immediately began a rebuilding program, unchallenged by a second Japanese strike or even the threat of a Japanese presence.

On the other hand, Mitchell described exactly what was necessary to achieve such a concentration. "A hostile air force will seize land airdromes from which to launch its attacks against its intended victims."[15]

And wasn't that exactly what Admiral Yamamoto was attempting to do at Midway in June 1942? After missing his golden opportunity at Pearl Harbor, with the American fleet now being repaired and rebuilt there, his landing forces were ready to invade and occupy Midway.

From Midway, Yamamoto would then be able to unleash a sustained air operation against the United States at Hawaii—to drive the fleet back to California and keep it there. If successful, his defensive line would then extend from the Aleutian Islands, through Hawaii, to Fiji. He was not relying on carriers to do that. He would occupy the already existing American airdrome at Midway. His plans were thwarted when he was surprised and successfully attacked by the American carrier force that he failed to detect.

Imagine if, on December 7, 1941, Japan would have made their surprise attack at Pearl Harbor by first clandestinely seizing Niihau. That was hardly a stretch of the imagination. After the first strike, they would not have had to withdraw. With supply and communication lines secured all the way back to Midway, and even to Tokyo, the Japanese could have continued sustained air operation. Just as the Japanese carrier attack force had successfully sailed undetected across the "vacant sea" of the Northern Pacific, a similar force, or part of the existing force, could have followed the path to seize Niihau. Mitchell certainly thought so and wrote the details on how to do it.

Most biographical works have either ignored Mitchell's predictions of how this air war would unfold once it began or ventured to say that Mitchell got it all wrong. But incomplete research has made these misconceptions possible.

Mitchell had advanced an air offensive of total war. Because of Army policy, "total war" was mostly discussed quietly and internally among Army officers. But after his court-martial and dismissal from service, Mitchell presented the concepts of "total war" and "vital centers" more freely. If ever this theory was even mentioned by others in the service, it was rejected or silenced. After the air war against Germany, the idea of attacking vital centers became acceptable. The question now became how to get into a position to unleash this offensive against Japan—how to take it from theory to reality.

Mitchell had dismissed any thought of an advance toward Japan along a southern line. He thought it had little hope of success, especially if it went through the Philippines because "Japanese air power completely dominated it."[16]

The other axis of approach, which he favored, was along a northern line from Alaska. That would mean constructing airdromes along the coastlines and leapfrogging toward Asia to bring sustained air operations into range.[17]

Mitchell had said, "An advance against Japan by the northern line would completely turn [outflank] the position of the Bonin Islands [Iwo Jima]."[18]

But Mitchell added one caveat to his 1924 assessment of the southern-line approach. It concerned the island of Guam, and he was greatly impressed with it as an advanced military base. "It can hold any size air force," he said. And it offered a plus for a possible approach from the south. "If we ever use a southern line of operations against Japan," he said, "Guam is a point of tremendous importance."[19]

In 1942, the WWII planners, especially Gen. Hap Arnold, now leading the U.S. Air Forces, rejected Mitchell's northern approach from the Aleutian Islands for reasons of supply, construction, and weather. He approved an advance through China as the best route toward Japan to conduct long-range air operations. But that choice proved to be a big mistake. Scattered airports and the ability of the Japanese to interdict operations led to a reevaluation.

The planners took a second look, not at a southern route, but at a Central Pacific route. Were any islands there that could be used as "suitable bases from which to operate 1,000, B-29 Superfortresses?" asked Arnold. "Guam, Saipan, and Tinian came closer to filling the bill than any other."[20]

And filling the bill meant unleashing a sustained air attack similar to the offensive of the Allied Air Forces Europe. Without respite, it had hammered and bombed Germany into submission. On a far grander scale, it had replicated Mitchell's 1918 massed air attack that had crushed the German air forces.

Now, with Germany defeated, the Americans were on the last enemy's doorstep, but bringing those devastating blows down upon Japan was impossible. She was still out of range. Without suitable bases from which to launch the only plane able to do the job, the air offensive was simply a plan on paper. Saipan, Tinian, and Guam changed all that.

"It was the B-29s, and the B-29s only that could put tons and tons of bombs on Japan," said Arnold. "The fleet couldn't do it; the Naval Air couldn't do it; the Army couldn't do it. The B-29s could."[21]

In 1932, Billy Mitchell had said that to conduct such an air campaign, a bomber would have to be designed, and built, to fly at 35,000 feet and have a range of 5,000 miles. It would be based at Midway.[22]

Mitchell's ability to think that far into the future, to wage a future war with future weapons, was extraordinary. It was all in his mind and the very essence of original thought.

While the bomber necessary for Mitchell's air campaign was only in his head in 1932, in 1944 the B-29 Superfortress was just the weapon for the job. It was present on the ground, and it was only looking for a home to get started. Beginning in late 1944, it began its round-the-clock, sustained operations—not from Midway but from the Mariana Islands.

Hap Arnold well understood his mission, which had been approved in 1943 at the Cairo and Teheran conferences. He stated it simply: "We had received confirmation of our present plans for bombing the

B29s roll on Tinian runways for attacks on Japan. (National Archives)

interior of Germany to a pulp, and for bringing the B-29's into action against Japan as soon as we could get them there."[23]

"One hundred B-29s left Saipan on November 14, 1944," said Hap Arnold. "Tokyo was hit for the first time since Doolittle's raid in 1942. . . . That number was to be built up until it reached a total of about 1,000 planes."[24] Mitchell's "vital centers" attacks had begun.

To deliver the most devastating blows, the big B-29s were to be crammed with the maximum load of bombs. Carrying those weights required great flying skills. There was little patience for pilots who were squeamish about flying on the edge.

Maj. Gen. Curtis LeMay, whom Arnold had placed in command of all the B-29s in the Pacific, said to his commanders, "Pilots who are weak must be either replaced or trained to a point where they can obtain the maximum from their airplane . . . every bomb that is carried on each B-29 will contribute to the overall air effort against Japan."[25]

As an Air Division commander in Europe, he had confronted a high incident "abort mission'" rate among B-24 pilots with a stern warning. Aborting a mission, for varied reasons, was the easy way out for such squeamish pilots to not fly into the teeth of the enemy. LeMay would have none of that.

"I will be in the lead plane on every mission. Any plane that takes off will go over the target, or the crew will be court-martialed."[26]

LeMay now promised Hap Arnold that he could destroy the Japanese industrial facilities and warmaking capabilities. It would require destroying the facilities in thirty to sixty cities, and to do that, LeMay designed bomb loads to include incendiary bombs.

Pres. Franklin Roosevelt died on April 12, 1945, and Pres. Harry Truman was sworn into office. In late June, Gen. Hap Arnold received a cablegram from the Chief of Staff of the Army, Gen. George Marshall. Arnold was to leave the Marianas at once and return to Washington for a meeting with the president and the Joint Chiefs of Staff. There was a burning new question to discuss—"Can we win the war by bombing?"[27]

Gen. Billy Mitchell had addressed that question in 1925 and had written that air power could overcome any anti-aircraft defenses.

"Once supremacy of the air has been established, airplanes can fly over a hostile country at will."[28] The time for that flyover was now at hand.

Arnold immediately drew up the particulars. These included: occupying Kyushu (the southern island of Japan) and installing forty groups of heavy bombers, giving priority to B-29 attacks, planning for the complete destruction of Japan proper, and removing all administrative restrictions to the bombing effort.[29]

The maximum bombing effort against the warmaking ability of Japan now unfolded. In advance of the massive pummeling of "vital centers," the United States dropped leaflets to the Japanese living in the targeted cities. Each resembled a postcard with the photograph of five B-29s dropping an absolute rain of bombs from their cavernous bellies. Printed in Japanese was this dire warning:

"Unfortunately, bombs have no eyes. So, in accordance with America's humanitarian policies, the American Air Force, which does not wish to injure innocent people, now gives you warning to evacuate the cities named and save your lives."[30]

A leaflet dropped to warn Japanese to evacuate and flee the cities named. (National Archives)

In the first four months of 1945, the Army Air Forces had already dropped half a million tons of bombs on Japan; and it contemplated dropping another half-million tons. But on July 16, 1945, in a remote section of the New Mexico desert, the U.S. detonated an atomic bomb. Ten days after the successful test, the Allied leaders meeting in Potsdam issued the Potsdam Declaration, demanding that Japan surrender unconditionally or face certain destruction. At that same time, General Arnold wrote to the Joint Chiefs of Staff:

"While the presently-planned scale of air bombardment is expected to create conditions favorable to invasion of the Japanese homeland on November 1st (1945), it is believed that an acceleration and augmentation of the strategic air program culminating in a land campaign, will bring about the defeat of Japan with a minimum loss of American lives."[31]

The Japanese refused the Potsdam demands, and President Truman ordered the atomic bombing of Japan as soon as possible after August 2. On August 6, 1945, the B-29 *Enola Gay* dropped the first atomic bomb, a uranium bomb, on Hiroshima. Three days later, on August 9, a second B-29, *Bock's Car*, dropped a plutonium bomb on the city of Nagasaki.

There was no Operation Downfall, no November 1 invasion of Kyushu. There was no second invasion of the main island of Honshu, planned for March 1946. The predicted one million casualties never occurred. The air war had ended it.

* * *

One year later, on August 8, 1946, a grateful nation finally told Billy Mitchell, "Thank you." Congress honored him by enacting Private Law 884:

AN ACT Authorizing the President of the United States to award posthumously in the name of Congress a Medal of Honor to William Mitchell.

Be it enacted by the Senate and House of Representatives of the United States of America in Congress assembled, That the President of the United States is requested to cause a gold medal to be struck, with suitable emblems, devices and inscriptions, to be presented to the late William Mitchell, formerly a Colonel, United States Army, in recognition of his outstanding pioneer service and foresight in the field of American military aviation.

SEC. 2. When the medal provided for in section I of this Act shall have been struck, the President shall transmit the same to William Mitchell, Junior, son of the said William Mitchell, to be presented to him in the name of the people of the United States.

SEC. 3. A sufficient sum of money to carry this Act into effect is hereby authorized to be appropriated, out of money in the Treasury not otherwise appropriated.[32]

Notes

Introduction

1. B. H. Liddell Hart, *Strategy: The Indirect Approach* (London: Faber and Faber, 1954), 291.

2. Ibid., 292.

3. Mark R. Peattie, *Nanyo: The Rise and Fall of the Japanese in Micronesia, 1885-1945* (Honolulu: University of Hawaii Press, 1988), 43.

4. Ibid., 234.

5. Ibid., 244-45.

6. "With lips the gods had condemned to disbelief." Virgil, *The Aeneid* 2.342.

Chapter 1

1. Matthew Calbraith Perry and Lambert Lilly, *Narrative of the Expedition of an American Squadron to the China Seas and Japan: Performed in the Years 1852, 1853, and 1854, Under the Command of Commodore M. C. Perry, United States Navy* (New York: D. Appleton, 1856), 5.

2. Ibid., 6-7.

3. Louis Delplace, "Japanese Martyrs," in vol. 9 of *The Catholic Encyclopedia* (New York: Robert Appleton, 1910); http://www.newadvent.org/cathen/09744a.htm, accessed August 6, 2015; "Hidden Christians of Japan," https://en.wikipedia.org/wiki/Hidden_Christians_of_Japan.

4. David John Lu, ed., *Japan: A Documentary History* (Armonk, NY: M. E. Sharpe, 1997); http://wps.pearsoncustom.com/wps/media/objects/2426/2484749/chap_assets/documents/doc17_2.html.

5. Perry and Lilly, 4.

6. Ibid., 38-39.

7. Ibid., 40.

8. Ibid.

9. Ibid., 23.

10. Ibid., 41.

11. Ibid.

12. Ibid.

13. Ibid., 16.

14. Ibid., 60.

15. Ibid., 60-61.

16. "Our Navy in Asiatic Waters," *Harper's New Monthly Magazine* 97, no. 581 (October 1898): 741-42.

17. Imprisoned American Seamen, Senate Executive Document, United States Congress, Senate, 31st Congress, 1st Session, vol. 10, no. 84 (Washington, DC: GPO, 1850), 8-28.

18. Perry and Lilly, 61.

19. Imprisoned American Seamen, 18-20.

20. Perry and Lilly, 61.

21. Ibid., 97.

22. Pres. Millard Fillmore's letter to the emperor of Japan (presented by Commodore Perry on July 14, 1853), http://ocw.mit.edu/ans7870/21f/21f.027/black_ships_and_samurai/presletter.html.

23. Perry and Lilly, 98.

24. Ibid., 261-66.

25. Ibid., 267.

26. Ibid., 269.

27. Ibid., 270.

28. Ibid., 273.

29. Ibid., 276.

30. Ibid., 288-89.

31. Ibid., 302.

32. Ibid.

33. Ibid., 303.

34. Ibid., 315.

35. Ibid., 318.

36. Ibid., 380.

37. Ibid., 383.

38. Ibid., 393-94.

39. Ibid.

40. Ibid., 407.

41. Ibid., 420.

42. Ibid., 441.

Chapter 2

1. Homer Lea, *The Valor of Ignorance* (New York: Harper and Brothers, 1909), 36-37.

2. "Coast at Mercy of Any Hostile Force Says Noted War Expert," *San Diego Union,* December 17, 1910.

3. Lea, xiii.

4. Ibid., 56.

5. Ibid., 57.

6. "Writer Who Fears Japan," *New York Sun,* July 7, 1911.

7. Lawrence M. Kaplan, *Homer Lea: American Soldier of Fortune* (Lexington: University Press of Kentucky, 2010), 20.

8. Ibid., 19-20.

9. Ibid., 9.

10. Ibid., 32-33.

11. Ibid., 33.

12. The revolution movement was named *Pao-Huang Hui*.

13. Kaplan, 4.

14. Simon Rees, "Homer Lea: Author of *Valor of Ignorance*," *Military History Magazine* (October 2004).

15. Kaplan, 5.

16. Rees.

17. The Homer Lea Research Center, http://www.homerlea.org/.

18. Lea, xi.

19. Ibid., xxii.

20. *San Diego Union,* December 17, 1910.

21. The Homer Lea Research Center.

22. "Writer Who Fears Japan."

23. Lea, 200.

24. Hector C. Bywater, *Sea Power in the Pacific: A Study of the American-Japanese Naval Problem* (London: Constable, 1921), 35.

25. William Braisted, *The United States Navy in the Pacific 1897-1909* (Austin: University of Texas Press, 1958), 191.

26. Ibid., 192.

27. Ibid., 193.

28. Ibid., 195-96.

29. Ibid., 198.

30. Theodore Roosevelt, *Theodore Roosevelt: An Autobiography* (New York: Macmillan, 1913), 593-93.

31. Braisted, 223-32.

32. Lea, 319.

33. Bywater, 38.

34. Ibid., 77.

35. "Writer Who Fears Japan."

Chapter 3

1. William Mitchell, *Winged Defense: The Development and Possibilities of Modern Air Power—Economic and Military* (New York: G. B. Putnam's Sons, 1925), iii.

2. Burke Davis, *The Billy Mitchell Affair* (New York: Random House, 1967), 31.

3. Alfred F. Hurley, *Billy Mitchell: Crusader for Air Power* (Bloomington: Indiana University Press, 1964), 23.

4. Mitchell, iv.

5. Maurer Maurer, ed., *The Final Report and Tactical History,* vol. 1 of *The U.S. Air Service in World War I* (Washington, DC: Office of Air Force History Headquarters United States Air Force, 1978), 51.

6. H. A. Toulmin, *Air Service American Expeditionary Force 1919* (New York: D. Van Norstrand, 1927), 360.

7. Quoted in Davis, 37.

8. Davis, 30-31.

9. Quoted in Davis, 32.

10. Ibid.

11.Davis, 34.

12. Ibid., 33.

13. Quoted in Davis, 33.

14. Davis, 35.

15. Ibid., 40.

16. Quoted in Davis, 40.

17. Mason Patrick, *The United States in the Air* (New York: Doubleday, Doran, 1928), 27.

18. William Mitchell, "The Air Service at St. Mihiel," *World's Work* 38 (August 1919): 365.

19. Ibid.

20. Ibid., 364-65.

21. Thomas H. Greer, *The Development of Air Doctrine in the Army Air Arm 1917-1941* (Washington, DC: Office of Air Force History Headquarters United States Air Force, 1985), 10.

22. Col. E. S. Gorrell, "Early History of the Strategical Section, Air Service," *Air Service History* ser. B, VI (1919), 371-87.

23. Greer, 14.

24. "The Mitchell Trial," *Aviation* (November 23, 1925): 748.

25. http://www.strategypage.com/cic/docs/cic417a.asp.

26. Quoted in Greer, 17.

27. Quoted in "Colonel Billy Mitchell and His Aerial Armada" (May 28, 2016), http://www.homeofheroes.com/wings/part1/5_mitchell.html.

28. Ibid.

29. Davis, 44.

30. Ibid.

31. Ibid., 48.

32. Quoted in "Colonel Billy Mitchell and His Aerial Armada."

33. Davis, 49.

34. Some say as low as 200. Hurley, 41.

35. Ibid.

36. Ibid., 52.

37. Ibid.

38. Ibid., 53.

39. Ibid., 46.

40. Ibid., 57.

41. Isaac Don Levine, *Mitchell: Pioneer of Air Power* (New York: Duell, Sloan, and Pearce, 1943), 183; Davis, 58. Davis misidentifies Adm. William Benson as Adm. "Charles" Benson.

42. Davis, 61-62.

43. Ibid., 66.

44. George Gay, interview by Ronald J. Drez, April 13, 1991; George Gay, *Sole Survivor* (Naples, FL: Midway, 1979), 28.

45. Davis, 62.

46. Quoted in Davis, 68.

47. Naval History and Heritage Command, "Dictionary of American Naval Fighting Ships," http://www.history.navy.mil/research/histories/ship-histories/danfs, accessed February 2, 2016.

48. Levine, 208-11; Hurley, 61.

49. Ibid.

50. Quoted in Davis, 71.

51. Davis, 72.

52. Ibid., 75-76.

Chapter 4

1. Hurley, 62.

2. Davis, 80.

3. Ibid.

4. Ibid., 83.

5. Ibid., 92.

6. Hurley, 65.

7. Ibid.

8. Davis, 78.

9. Ibid., 83.

10. Quoted in Davis, 84.

11. Mitchell, *Winged Defense*, 45.

12. Davis, 85.

13. Mitchell, *Winged Defense,* 40.

14. Ibid.

15. Ibid., 41.

16. Ibid., 57.

17. Davis, 96.
18. Mitchell, *Winged Defense,* 62.
19. Ibid., 65.
20. Ibid., 53.
21. Ibid., 72.
22. Davis, 103.
23. Ibid., 83-84.
24. Mitchell, *Winged Defense,* 141-42.
25. Davis, 105-6.
26. Ibid., 106.
27. Mitchell, *Winged Defense,* 72.
28. Ibid.
29. Ibid.
30. Davis, 108.
31. Ibid., 109-12.
32. Quoted in Davis, 113.
33. Ibid., 114.
34. Greer, 34.
35. Mitchell, *Winged Defense.* 126-27.
36. Davis, 115.
37. Quoted in Davis, 115.
38. Mitchell, *Winged Defense*, 73.
39. Ibid., 110.
40. Ibid., 99.
41. Ibid.
42. Ibid., 110.
43. William Braisted, *The United States Navy in the Pacific 1909-1922* (Annapolis: Naval Institute Press, 1971), 503.
44. Ibid., 503-4.
45. H. H. Arnold, *Global Mission* (New York: Harper and Brothers, 1949), 105.
46. Mitchell, *Winged Defense,* 145.
47. Ibid., 80.

Chapter 5
1. Hurley, 13; "Colonel Billy Mitchell and His Aerial Armada."

2. "Colonel Billy Mitchell and His Aerial Armada."

3. Edwin Hoyt, *Japan's War: The Great Pacific Conflict* (New York: McGraw Hill, 1986), 45.

4. Ibid.

5. Hurley, 86.

6. William Mitchell, *Report of Inspection of United States Possessions in the Pacific and Java, Singapore, India, Siam, China & Japan by Brigadier General Wm. Mitchell Assistant Chief of Air Service, October 24, 1923* (Washington, DC: Thomas Dewitt Milling Collection, National Air and Space Museum Archives), 280.

7. Ibid., 279.

8. Ibid.

9. Ibid., 283.

10. Ibid., 279.

11. Ibid.

12. Ibid., 291.

13. Sun Tzu, *The Art of War*, trans. Samuel B. Griffith (New York: Oxford University Press, 1971), 84.

14. Stephen Mercado, "Intelligence in Recent Public Literature," *Studies in Intelligence* 52, no. 4 (December 2008): 24, https://www.cia.gov/library/center-for-the-study-of-intelligence/csi-publications/csi-studies/studies/vol-52-no-4/pdfs/Review-Nisei%20Linguists.pdf.

15. Mitchell, *Report,* 286.

16. Ibid., 292.

17. Ibid., 284.

18. Ibid.

19. Ibid., 285-86.

20. Ibid., 288.

21. Ibid., 278.

22. Ibid., 291.

23. Ibid., 12.

24. Ibid., 20-21.

25. Quoted in Davis, 87.

26. Mitchell, *Report,* 31.

27. Ibid., 11.

28. Ibid., 10.

29. Ibid., 48-49.

30. Ibid., 52.

31. Ibid., 52-58.

32. Ibid., 57-58.

33. Ibid., 56.

34. Ibid., 153.

Chapter 6

1. Gavan Daws and Timothy Head, "Niihau: A Shoal of Time," *American Heritage Magazine* 14, no. 6 (October 1963), https://web. archive.org/web/20080828002753/http://www.americanheritage. com/articles/magazine/ah/1963/6/1963_6_48.shtml.

2. Ibid.

3. Hugh Laracy, *Watriama and Co.: Further Pacific Islands Portraits* (Canberra: Australian University Press, 2013), 42-43.

4. Ibid., 36.

5. Ibid., 38.

6. Ibid., 38-39.

7. Ibid., 45.

8. Ibid.

9. Quoted inLaracy, 45-46.

10. Daws and Head.

11. Syd Jones, *Before and Beyond the Niihau Zero: The Unlikely Drama of Hawaii's Forbidden Island Prior to, During and After the Pearl Harbor Attack* (Merritt Island, FL: Signum Ops, 2014), 6.

12. Daws and Head.

13. Keith Robinson, interview by Ronald J. Drez, March 18-20, 2011. Hereafter *Robinson interview*.

14. Daws and Head.

15. Ibid.

16. Robinson interview.

17. "Lisianski Island," http://www.janeresture.com/lisianski/index. htm.

18. Mitchell, *Report,* 77.

19. Ibid., 79.

20. Ibid., 77-78. Mitchell mistakenly called Tern Island, "Seven

Sand Island." During WWII the United States built an airfield exactly there.

21. Ibid., 76.

22. Ibid., 84, 87.

23. Robinson interview.

24. Mitchell, *Report,* 1.

25. Ibid., 118.

26. Ibid., 119.

27. See charts 11 and 14, prepared December 12, 1923, and chart 15, prepared December 6, 1923, in Mitchell, *Report.*

28. Ibid., 79.

29. Ibid., 49.

30. Ibid., 51.

31. Ibid., 50-51.

32. Ibid., 286.

33. William Shakespeare, *Macbeth,* Act 5, Scene 5.

34. Braisted, *United States Navy in the Pacific 1909-1922,* 681.

35. Ibid., 683.

36. Edward S. Miller, *War Plan Orange: The U.S. Strategy to Defeat Japan, 1897-1945* (Annapolis: Naval Institute Press, 1991), 3.

37. Ibid., 4.

38. Ibid., 123.

39. Mitchell, *Report,* 147.

40. Miller, 125.

41. Ibid., 126-29.

42. Braisted, *United States Navy in the Pacific 1909-1922,* 512.

43. Ibid.

44. Ibid., 286.

45. "Rainbow 5," Hearings Before the Joint Committee on the Investigation of the Pearl Harbor Attack, United States Congress, 79th Congress, 1st Session (Washington, DC: GPO, 1946), 957.

46. Ibid., 958.

Chapter 7

1. Mitchell, *Report,* 279.

2. Clifton Daniel, ed., *Chronicles of the 20th Century* (Mount Kisco, NY: Chronicle, 1982), 298-314.

3. http://www.u-s-history.com/pages/h1398.html.

4. Dorothy Borg and Shumpei Okamoto, eds., *Pearl Harbor as History: Japanese-American Relations 1931-1941* (New York: Columbia University Press, 1973), 533.

5. Isaac Marcosson, "The Changing East," *Saturday Evening Post* (October 7, 1922): 36.

6. Ibid.

7. Ibid.

8. Speech by Ellison DuRant Smith, April 9, 1924, *Congressional Record,* 68th Congress, 1st Session, vol. 65 (Washington, DC: GPO, 1924), 5961-62.

9. Ibid.

10. Ibid.

11. Borg and Okamoto, 533.

12. Ibid., 534.

13. Ibid., 534-35.

14. Mitchell, *Report,* 278.

15. Borg and Okamoto, 537.

16. "The Senate's Declaration of War," *Japan Times and Mail,* April 19, 1924.

17. Stephen Turnbull, *Samurai: The World of the Warrior* (Oxford: Osprey, 2003), 73.

18. Davis, 182.

19. Ibid., 183.

20. Ibid.

21. Ibid., 357.

22. Ibid., 183.

23. Ibid.

24. Mitchell, *Report,* 30.

25. Ibid., 25-26.

26. Davis, 184.

27. Ibid., 186n.

28. Ibid., 186.

29. Ibid., 188.

30. Ibid., 185.

31. Ibid., 42-44.

32. Ibid., 189.

33. Ibid., 190.

34. Mitchell, *Report,* 56.

35. "An Indictment and a Warning," *Aviation* (January 28, 1924): 86.

36. Davis, 190.

37. Ibid., 191.

38. James P. Tate, *The Army and Its Air Corps: Army Policy Toward Aviation 1919-1941* (Maxwell AFB, AL: Air University Press, 1998), 18.

39. http://arlingtoncemetery.net/mpatrick.htm. Patrick's autobiography is *The United States in the Air* (Garden City, NY: Doubleday, Doran, 1928).

40. Thomas M. Coffey, *Hap: The Story of the U.S. Air Force and the Man Who Built It, General Henry H. "Hap" Arnold* (New York: Viking, 1982), 122-24.

Chapter 8

1. Mitchell, *Report,* 79.

2. Alexander H. Gault, official reporter, "Colonel William Mitchell Air Service: Trial by General Court Martial" (Washington, DC: November 11, 1925), 598. Hereafter *Trial transcript.*

3. Ibid., 584-85.

4. Ibid., 590.

5. Ibid., 599.

6. Ibid., 598.

7. Ibid., 571.

8. Ibid., 591.

9. Ibid., 572.

10. Ibid., 573.

11. Ibid., 576.

12. Robinson interview.

13. Ibid.

14. Ibid.

15. Mitchell, *Report,* 79.

16. Robinson interview.

17. http://www.af.mil/AboutUs/Biographies/Display/tabid/225/Article/108024/major-general-gerald-clark-brant.aspx.

18. Davis, 205.
19. Shakespeare, *Macbeth*.
20. Davis, 205-6.
21. Ibid., 206.
22. Ibid., 207.
23. Ibid.
24. Ibid., 208.
25. "A New Flying General," *Aviation* (March 16, 1925): 289.
26. Ibid.
27. Davis, 207-8.
28. Ibid., 210.
29. Mitchell, *Winged Defense,* viii.
30. Ibid.
31. C. V. Glines, "William 'Billy' Mitchell: An Airpower Visionary," *Aviation History* (September 1997).
32. Davis, 213.
33. Ibid.
34. Ibid., 212.
35. Hurley, 100. Historian Douglas Waller used the words "slapped together hurriedly." Douglas Waller, *A Question of Loyalty: Gen. Billy Mitchell and the Court-Martial That Gripped the Nation* (New York: HarperCollins, 2004), 250.
36. Waller, 402n.
37. Mitchell, *Winged Defense,* 213.
38. Quoted in Davis, 212.

Chapter 9

1. Gerald C. Brant, "What Really Happened in Hawaiian Maneuvers," *Aviation* (July 20, 1925): 66.
2. Davis, 93.
3. Ibid., 103.
4. "Statistics of All the Aero Engines of Packard," http://www.enginehistory.org/Packard/StatsAllPackardAero.pdf, accessed June 27, 2016.
5. "Navy Ready for Hawaiian Flight," *Aviation* (August 17, 1925): 174-75.

6. "PN9 No. 1 Lost on West Coast-Hawaiian Flight," *Aviation* (September 14, 1925): 315.

7. Ibid., 316.

8. Ibid., 317. Hurley notes that it was justifiable to question attempting the flight due to the "prevailing westerly winds." But that statement ignores the Weather Service's forecast of expected winds from the north and east.

9. Davis, 214.

10. The German ZR3 was larger in all other aspects and had more lift, using hydrogen gas instead of helium.

11. "A 'Twister' Wrecks the Shenandoah," *Aviation* (September 14, 1925): 312.

12. Waller, 11.

13. Ibid., 28.

14. Ibid., 14.

15. "A 'Twister' Wrecks the Shenandoah," 313.

16. Trial transcript, 2347-49.

17. "A 'Twister' Wrecks the Shenandoah," 313.

18. Ibid., 314.

19. "Dirigible Disaster," *Cleveland Plain Dealer,* September 1925, http://mike.whybark.com/archives/93, accessed June 28, 2016.

20. "Heinen Lays Crash to Valve Removal," *New York Times,* September 4, 1925.

21. Waller, 19.

22. "Col. Mitchell's Statement on Govt. Aviation," *Aviation* (September 14, 1925): 318.

23. Ibid., 318-20.

24. Ibid.

25. Ibid.

26. Ibid.

27. Ibid.

28. Ibid.

29. Ibid.

30. Ibid.

31. Ibid.

32. Ibid.

33. Ibid.

34. Davis, 221-22.

35. "Publisher's News Letter," *Aviation* (September 21, 1925): 371.

36. "PN9 No. 1 Found Off Hawaiian Islands," *Aviation* (September 21, 1925): 350-51.

37. Quoted in Davis, 225.

38. Ibid.

39. "The Shenandoah Investigation," *Aviation* (October 5, 1925): 451.

40. Ibid., 451-52.

41. Davis, 223.

42. Ibid., 229.

43. Ibid.

44. Arnold, 119-20.

45. Davis, 235.

46. Waller, 36.

47. Ibid., 37.

48. *Washington Star,* October 28, 1925; *Washington Daily News,* October 29, 1925; *New York Times,* October 29, 1925.

49. Davis, 236.

50. Trial transcript, 1-7.

51. Mitchell, *Report,* 60.

52. Trial transcript, 1-7.

53. Ibid.

54. Ibid.

55. "The Mitchell Trial," 744.

56. *Washington Star,* October 29, 1925; *New York Times,* October 29, 1925.

57. Waller, 60.

Chapter 10

1. "The Mitchell Trial," *Aviation,* November 25, 1925, 744.

2. Ibid.

3. Ibid.

4. Trial transcript, 190-350.

5. "The Mitchell Trial," November 25, 746.

6. Ibid., 352-60.

7. Some authors have incorrectly spelled his name *Oldys.*

8. Trial transcript, 374-81.

9. Ibid.

10. Ibid.

11. Ibid., 464-95.

12. *Washington Post,* November 11, 1925.

13. Trial transcript, 557-60.

14. Ibid., 585-88.

15. Arnold, 120-21.

16. Quoted in Davis, 263.

17. Waller, 193-94.

18. Trial transcript, 1639-45.

19. Davis, 267.

20. Ibid., 268.

21. Arnold, 120.

22. Davis, 269.

23. Trial transcript, 659-81.

24. Ibid.

25. Ibid.

26. *Washington Star,* November 12, 1925; *New York Times,* November 13, 1925; *Washington Herald,* November 13, 1925.

27. "The Mitchell Trial," *Aviation,* November 30, 1925, 771.

28. Ibid., 772.

29. Ibid.

30. Waller, 240-46.

31. Ibid., 247.

32. "The Mitchell Trial," *Aviation,* December 7, 1925, 803.

33. Waller, 249-52.

34. Ibid.

35. Arnold, 121.

36. "President's Air Board Reports," *Aviation,* December, 14, 1925, 834.

37. Trial transcript, 3438-53.

38. Davis, 293.

39. Arnold, 120.

40. Trial transcript, 3690-781.

41. Ibid.

42. Ibid. The term *sui generis* literally means "of his own kind." Gullion used it here to derogatorily describe La Guardia: "Thank heaven he is 'like no one else.'"

43. Ibid.

44. Quoted in Davis, 333.

Chapter 11

1. Arnold, 122.

2. Ibid.

3. Ibid., 7.

4. Ibid.

5. Coffey, 126.

6. Waller, 329.

7. William Mitchell, "When the Air Raiders Come," *Collier's* (May 1, 1926): 8-9.

8. Robinson interview.

9. Hoyt, 59.

10. Ibid., 60.

11. Ibid., 60-61.

12. Edward Behr, *The Last Emperor* (New York: Bantam Books, 1987), 180.

13. Hoyt, 115-17.

14. William Mitchell, "Will Japan Try to Conquer the United States?" *Liberty* 9, no. 26 (June 25, 1932): 6-11.

15. Ibid.

16. Ibid.

17. Robinson interview.

18. Aylmer Robinson's letter to G. Allen (July 23, 1948), quoted in Jones, 132.

19. Robinson interview.

20. Ibid.

21. Harlon J. Swanson, "The *Panay* Incident: Prelude to Pearl Harbor" (United States Naval Institute Proceedings, December 1967).

22. Jones, 16.

23. Robinson interview.

24. Ibid.

25. Asada Sadao, "The Japanese Navy and the United States," in Borg and Okamoto, 231.

26. Ibid., 232.

27. Ibid., 233.

28. Ibid., 234.

29. Ibid., 237.

30. Ibid.

31. Minoru Genda, "How the Japanese Task Force Idea Materialized," in Donald M. Goldstein and Katherine V. Dillon, eds., *The Pearl Harbor Papers: Inside the Japanese Plans* (Dulles: Brassey's, 1993), 6.

32. Ibid., 7.

33. Goldstein and Dillon, 19-20.

34. Borg and Okamoto, 237.

35. Ibid., 250.

36. Ibid., 236. Also described as "The Great All-Out Battle," in Goldstein and Dillon, 1.

37. Borg and Okamoto, 236.

38. Hiroyuki Agawa, *The Reluctant Admiral: Yamamoto and the Imperial Navy* (Tokyo: Kodansha International, 1969), 196-97.

39. Ibid., 176.

40. Ibid., 200.

41. Goldstein and Dillon, 27.

42. Ibid., 147.

43. Ibid., 151, 278.

44. Ibid., 183-84.

45. Agawa, 244.

46. Stetson Conn, Rose C. Engelman, and Byron Fairchild, *Guarding the United States and Its Outposts* (Washington, DC: Center of Military History, United States Army, 2000), 187-88.

47. Goldstein and Dillon, 43.

48. Ibid.

49. Naval Analysis Division, *The Campaigns of the Pacific War*:

United States Strategic Bombing Survey (Pacific) (Washington, DC: GPO, 1946), 23.

50. Jones, 1-2.

51. Goldstein and Dillon, 104.

52. Dan King, *The Last Zero Fighter: Firsthand Accounts from WWII Japanese Naval Pilots* (Rockwall, TX: Pacific Press, 2012), chapter 3.

53. Goldstein and Dillon, 161.

Chapter 12

1. Allan Beekman, *The Niihau Incident* (Honolulu: Heritage Press of the Pacific, 1982), 42-49.

2. Jones, 27.

3. Beekman, 53.

4. Robinson interview.

5. Jones, 33.

6. Beekman, 39; "Crash of Enemy Plane on Niihau," Hearings Before the Joint Committee on the Investigation of the Pearl Harbor Attack, United States Congress (1941), 1448-53. Hereafter *Pearl Harbor Attack Hearings*.

7. Beekman, 40.

8. Jones, 37-38.

9. Pearl Harbor Attack Hearings, 1449.

10. Ibid., 1451.

11. Ibid.

12. Ibid.

13. Ibid., 1452.

14. Jones, 80-81.

15. Ibid., 78-79.

16. Pearl Harbor Attack Hearings, 1452.

17. http://www.combinedfleet.com/I-174.htm, accessed August 8, 2016.

18. Robinson interview.

19. Pearl Harbor Attack Hearings, 1452.

20. Beekman, 63.

21. Pearl Harbor Attack Hearings, 1450.

22. Ibid.

23. Ibid.

24. Robinson interview.

25. Ibid.

26. Blake Clark, *Remember Pearl Harbor* (New York: Modern Age Books, 1942), 103.

27. Ibid., 104.

28. Ibid., 106.

29. Pearl Harbor Attack Hearings, 1450.

30. George C. Larsen, "Pearl Harbor: A Memoir of Service," http://www.uscg.mil/history/weboralhistory/georgeclarsen_ww2_memoir.asp.

31. Quoted in Jones, 154-57.

32. Keith Robinson to Craig Barnum, March 22, 2004.

33. Robinson interview.

34. Robinson to Barnum.

35. Mitchell, *Report,* 286.

36. http://www.combinedfleet.com/I-174.htm.

37. U.S. Naval Intelligence Source File No. 14 ND, ONI File No. 1798.

38. Ibid.

39. Michelle Malkin, *In Defense of Internment* (Washington, D.C.: Regnery, 2004), 83-84.

40. Ibid., 53-54.

Epilogue

1. Waller, overleaf.

2. Ibid., 358.

3. Davis, 354.

4. Hurley, viii.

5. Ibid., 148.

6. Ibid., 81.

7. Conn et al., 180-81.

8. Ibid.

9. John J. Stephan, "The Night They Bombed Tantalus," *Honolulu* (1980); Zenji Orita with Joseph D. Harrington, *I-Boat Captain* (Canoga Park, CA: Major Books, 1976), 56-57.

10. Mitchell, *Report,* 30.

11. Ibid., 23.

12. http://www.wgordon.web.wesleyan.edu/kamikaze/background/ships-sunk/, accessed August 15, 2016.

13. Mitchell, *Report,* 23.

14. Ibid., 47.

15. Ibid.

16. Ibid., 24.

17. Ibid.

18. Ibid., 38.

19. Ibid., 142.

20. Arnold, 477.

21. Ibid., 536.

22. "Are We Ready for War with Japan," *Liberty* (January 1932).

23. Arnold, 476.

24. Ibid., 540.

25. Coffey, 354.

26. Quoted in Errol Morris, *The Fog of War: Eleven Lessons from the Life of Robert S. McNamara* (2003), documentary film.

27. Arnold, 566.

28. Mitchell, *Winged Defense,* 9.

29. Arnold, 567.

30. Josette Williams, "The Information War in the Pacific, 1945," *Studies in Intelligence* 46, no. 3 (2002), https://www.cia.gov/library/center-for-the-study-of-intelligence/csi-publications/csi-studies/studies/vol46no3/article07.html.

31. Arnold, 596.

32. There is some debate as to whether William Mitchell was in fact awarded the Medal of Honor or the Congressional Gold Medal. http://www.history.army.mil/moh/asaoc.html#mitchelNote, accessed August 15, 2016.

Index